MARY MACKILLOP

Inspiration For Today

EDITED BY

PAULINE WICKS RSJ

Celebrating

the

Tenth Anniversary

of the

Beatification of Mary MacKillop

Published by
The Trustees of the Sisters of St Joseph of the Sacred Heart,
New South Wales Province.
5 Alexandra Avenue, Croydon NSW 2132.

First published 2005
Reprinted 2007

Cover Design and Artwork
Mary in Front of Old Inn, Pamela Griffith.
Mary with Children, Pamela Griffith.

Prepress and Print Production
Lindwall and Ward Printing Pty Ltd
8 Sloane Street, Marrickville NSW 2204.

Letters of Mary MacKillop
Archives of the Sisters of St Joseph of the Sacred Heart
9 Mount Street, North Sydney NSW 2060.
Used with permission.

ISBN 0 9579002 4 4

1. MacKillop, Mary 1842-1909.
2. Sisters of St Joseph of the Sacred heart - Biography.
3. Nuns - Australia - Biography.
4. Blessed - Australia - Biography.

Wicks, Pauline, 1941- .

271.97602

Contents

Foreword

This tenth anniversary of the Beatification of Mary MacKillop provides an opportunity to look again at her life, this time from different points of view, to go beyond the historical details of her life and meet the person. To those who have known her, she has always been an inspiration, but in the ten years that have passed since the proclamation of her Blessedness by Pope John Paul 11, more and more people look to her, want to know her better and place their trust in her as an intercessor.

The details of Mary's life and what she did are readily available. This series of articles aims to lead people to recognise the common human experience of Mary MacKillop. They offer an invitation to reflect on their own lives and, in the light Mary's living of the Gospel, inspire each to live with concern and compassion for others.

What captivated Mary's mind and heart, what led her to do what she did? What was "the fire burning in her heart"? In this collection we meet a very human and ordinary Mary. Yes, she was the "excommunicated one"; yes, she did disagree with Church authorities. But we will meet a Mary who kept lollies in her pocket for the children, a woman always sensitive to the less fortunate, a woman who loved animals, a woman who allowed creation to speak to her of God. We meet Joanna Barr Smith, Julian Tenison Woods and others with whom Mary maintained intimate friendships which crossed religious and societal boundaries.

Mary was free from all illusions about her own self importance. Grounded in reality, she readily accepted the truth about herself and others. She readily forgave others and always spoke kindly about them, even about those who had hurt her deeply. This humility brought a freedom to Mary, a freedom to love and serve others, especially the poorest of the poor, for Mary's Scottish heritage had taught her that each person had innate value. Although Mary was "wrapped in God", she was a practical mystic, one whose mysticism led naturally to meeting the needs of Australia, in particular through her great contribution to education and the service of the poor.

Like all of us, Mary's journey in life was an unknown one. No matter how each of us shares in the tradition of Mary MacKillop, our journey can be inspired by her virtues; we too can learn that "we are but travellers here" (Mary MacKillop to Flora MacKillop, August 14th 1866), and be encouraged to "Go on" and walk in her spirit. She remains with us – interceding, praying, leading and pointing a direction.

As we move into the third millennium the ambiguity and unknown character of our future needs to be placed in the hands of a "good God". Mary offers us a way to live the Christian paradox - that of life coming through death. Like the grain of wheat that must fall on the ground to die and so "yield a rich harvest", Mary lived the Eucharistic memorial, constantly dying and rising with Christ, as she united her will with that of her "good God". Mary's trust that "God would take care of all" allowed her to transcend the many hardships and uncertainties of her life. These hardships at times almost physically broke her. Others, she said, crushed her to the heart. Mary did discover the treasure, the treasure of God's Providence. This is a Providence that did provide for Mary and is the same Providence that will provide for our world today.

The Sydney artist, Pamela Griffith, has provided us with a profound image of Mary as she waits... reflects.... and is ready.... ready to go on. Pamela has freely given of her artistic talents in the creation of this cover and the other art works found in this book. For Pamela, too, it is obvious that Mary MacKillop is an inspiration!

Thanks are due to those who first came up the idea of producing a series of articles on Mary MacKillop to commemorate the tenth anniversary of the Beatification. For those many people wanting to know our Australian "Saint" better we are happy to present this volume to you. Thanks are also due to the staff of the Mary MacKillop Archives in North Sydney who have graciously helped many contributors throughout the process of their writing. To the many others who helped in this project your assistance was much appreciated.

In the Tradition with Mary MacKillop

Virginia Bourke rsj

The Painting

Just inside the entrance to the Province Centre of the NSW Josephites in Croydon hangs my favourite image of Mary MacKillop, the one painted in 1994 by Mary Brady, a Dominican Sister. Though it holds that kindly expression found in most photos and paintings of her, it is not the face of Mary MacKillop which I find most striking. It is, instead, the artist's recognition that her life gave great impetus to a faith tradition embracing different kinds of people. It is this matter of inclusiveness in the Josephite tradition which I have chosen to reflect upon in this article.

The Tradition

In the picture of which I write, from behind and in front of Mary's right arm there flows a steadily growing stream of brown-habited Sisters interspersed with colourfully dressed men, women and children. Some stride confidently and purposefully; a few journey as if in conversation; a Sister moves out to recover a straying child; an occasional person walks slightly apart from the main band, but headed in the same direction. Below Mary's left arm stands a simple wooden structure - the church of a former era - suggestive not only of Penola, the founding-place of the Josephites of Australia and New Zealand, but of all those other places where, across 140 years, the people and the Sisters have shared life and faith. I love the sense conveyed in this painting that the "charism" Josephite Sisters try to live is not held exclusively by us, but is a gift shared with many other people, equally indebted to the Spirit, the source of all charisms.

Mary's Right Hand People

In 2001 I participated in the making of a video in preparation for the NSW Province Chapter of the Central Josephites.[1] In the background was hung the picture of Mary of which I write. Concluding the film, I commented on the painting's significance, expressing too my regret that, in this otherwise inclusive image of the tradition following Mary MacKillop, there were no black-habited Sisters. Reviewing the video later, I could observe myself teaching. There, in my bright yellow blouse, not only did Mary seem to be looking over my left shoulder, but I seemed to have joined the band of those moving forward as part of her right arm. Though challenging, the image was welcome.

Within the Tradition

For me, both as a "Black" (Federation) Josephite, and as one of the descendants of a family who knew Mary and passed down a revered memory of her, it is quite important to believe that my own life lies within the tradition in which Mary MacKillop lived and made meaning in Christian faith.

Mother Mary at Kincumber

I ought mention now that my family never spoke of her as "Mary MacKillop". She was "Mother Mary of the Cross", pronounced to rhyme with "salt", in the Irish fashion inherited by my grandfather, Michael Bourke. As a lad in 1887, Michael and his brother, Jack, had been given the job of meeting the steamer bringing Mary from Sydney to the Central Coast of NSW for the first time. From Blackwall, near Woy Woy, they rowed her in an open boat around the Brisbane Water to Kincumber. With the accommodation in St Joseph's Providence, Cumberland Street Sydney proving inadequate for the Sisters' many needs, Mary had journeyed north to consider the invitation of Cardinal Moran to establish an Orphanage for boys on the Eastern shores of the Brisbane Water. In the spot where one of the district's earlier priests, Father Woolfrey, had hopes for establishing a Cistercian Monastery, the local parishioners committed themselves to supporting Mother Mary's Orphanage. Under the guidance of Dean Sheridan, Messers O. Norman, P. Byrnes, W. Melville, W. Woodward, P. Murray, F. Humphreys, and my great-grandfather, John Bourke, drew up plans for welcoming and supporting the Sisters.[2] I am unsure whether any of their wives attended the meeting or simply provided the supper, but it would be hard not to argue for some mutuality of interest and benefit arising from the coming among them of other women bent on caring for children and doing better than surviving in that pioneering, albeit beautiful environment.

"The Originals" and the Oarsmen

At the end of the long voyage from his native Limerick, the John Bourke who had been party to these plans, when aged 19, had survived the storm which struck the clipper, *Catherine Adamson*, off Sydney Heads in October, 1857. For his assistance to the crew that night, he was given a silver fob watch by the captain and this watch is still held in my family. With his wife Brigid, John went on to use his knowledge of the ways of the sea to establish a boating service just across the narrow stretch of water from the Church at Kincumber. All their sons, and I like to think their daughters, had a hand in conveying mail and market produce, as well as passengers, around the Brisbane Water settlements. And so it was that through their gift of "oarsmanship" they met Mother Mary, Sister Philippa, and the revered Sister Anne Joseph and the others that followed. In their own way, I believe my ancestors saw themselves as participants in the mission of those Sisters whom they called "The Originals".

Gatherings at "Holy Cross" Church

One night, for example, the boys met Mary and rowed her to Kincumber so she could fulfil an orphan boy's dying wish to see her again. He lies now not far from my great-grandparents, my grandparents and my kindly great-auntie Maggie who ran a little shop for the Sisters, opposite the Church. There they all lie awaiting that form of the Providence of God we call "the Resurrection", close to the graves of pioneering Sisters and other families, in the cemetery beside the old stone church of the "Holy Cross", where they and the Sisters of St Joseph gathered each Sunday, and where in my turn, I was baptised.

Leaving Home

My grandparents, Michael and Hannah, later established citrus orchards on the Saratoga peninsular opposite Kincumber. When I was little, there was still a grove of mandarin trees close to our home on the hilltop overlooking the wide expanse of water. Whenever I had a mind to "leave home" or simply avoid my brothers, I would run to the mandarins till I thought better of it. Later, at the age of 17, in the custom of the Church of the day, I really did leave home, this time to join the "Black" Sisters of St Joseph of Lochinvar in the Maitland diocese, where I had boarded for Secondary school.

Youthful Perspectives

At the time, my father made the wry comment that I was joining those "Renegades" he had heard about in boyhood. But I simply thought the Brown Sisters of my Primary school in Gosford and the Black Sisters of my Secondary days at Lochinvar were the same: same style of habit, veil and guimp, same rosary beads and cross and, perhaps most obviously of all, the same large, bright blue design of the braided monogram spelling the combined A+M for "Ave Maria" across their breasts.[3] They seemed to me too to be the same kind of down-to-earth hard workers, funny characters and mavericks among them, women who without fuss put their collective shoulder to the wheel, and all the other potential of their young lives aside, to make a difference in the world "for God".

I recognise that these, my particular experiences of the Josephite story, are not everyone's. I also respect that people hold quite different views from mine on these matters, and indeed that others are more learned in the historical events of the times concerned. Furthermore, I am aware I am transmitting some mythology here, but I believe that mythology can carry some of the deepest truths, the ones that are otherwise hard to articulate. For me, therefore, as a youngster operating simply out of the data of my own experience, the colour difference between the Josephites seemed superficial and inconsequential. Now, though I do not consciously discount the realities of difference, I still catch myself operating largely out of that early perspective.

Differences

Since childhood, I certainly have learned more of the painful history lying behind the differences in colour and the awkward divisions of loyalty occasionally evident between those who see themselves following one of the Josephite co-founders, Mother Mary of the Cross or Father Julian Tenison Woods, rather than both of them. I have learned to appreciate too the less-than-perfect Church context which helped foster awkwardness in those times. I have also come to realise that it is possible to identify certain cultural differences between the Josephite groups, probably determined more by socio-geographical factors than by anything else. Yet I am convinced that these differences apply as much among the five now-Federated Congregations as they do between the Sisters of the original Congregation and the Sisters of the Federation. Most of the latter are now pontifical rather than diocesan Congregations, and all would prize their own uniqueness and independence, just as the original Congregation has always prized all that is meant for it by "central government."

Providence

So it is that from family heritage, from four decades of life in my own Lochinvar Congregation, significant contact with other Federation Congregations, and frequent work amongst members of different Provinces of the centrally governed Sisterhood, it is important to me to believe that my life lies in the tradition of the founding experience that includes both co-founders. As I see it, something unique of the Spirit's charism, something Providential in God's plan happened for the Church in this part of the world in that founding at Penola in 1866, through the instrumentality of Julian Tenison Woods and Mary of the Cross working together. I believe that this, much more than any subsequent event, provides the vision for all Josephite Congregations. My own conviction is that Divine Providence has continued to work through the varying ways that founding charism has been lived across six different Josephite Congregations and amongst their co-workers and benefactors ever since. Had the original Josephite Congregation remained the only one, a number of country dioceses in Australia and New Zealand, and indeed the dioceses of Vanimo and Aitape in New Guinea, may never have shared in the particular flavour of Christian tradition expressed through the Josephite charism in this part of the world.

Mary's Beatification

Ten years ago, the leaders of all the Josephite Congregations sat together around the sanctuary for the beatification of Mother Mary of the Cross. That this could happen testifies both to the generous vision of the leadership of the Brown Congregation at the time and to the abiding conviction of the five Black Congregations that they did hold legitimate places there. This year, in marking together the milestone of the tenth anniversary of that beatification, the net of inclusion has been cast further. For over the decade there has been real commitment in a number of the Congregations to acknowledge that their associates and many of their co-workers and benefactors also live a commitment to that mission set in motion in Penola by Mary MacKillop and Julian Tenison Woods.

A "Catholic" Tradition

Such hospitality to diversity, such loosening of a former tightness of categories amongst Church people gives prophetic witness to the rest of the community. Christian history shows that we have often failed across the centuries to keep our nerve in maintaining a belief in that inclusivity of differences which spells out what is really entailed in being 'Catholic'. Our failure has meant that the history of Christian differences is a history too often characterised by uncritical exclusivism, provincialism and triumphalism, and even outright discrimination and demonising of "the other".

"The Charism Alive in Many Hearts"

For its attempts to promote the very opposite of such a mentality of narrowness in our day, I find myself inspired by the booklet of the Acts of the 24th General Chapter of the Brown Sisters of St Joseph of the Sacred Heart held in 2001. In working with members of that Congregation I have come to love this document. As an onlooker, I find its guidance for the contemporary life of the Central Josephite Congregation impressive in its articulation of the Sisters' deliberate option for inclusivity. From its opening chapter on Charism, the ideal is set, "The Chapter calls us to be bold in honouring and nurturing the charism alive in many hearts."[4]

It challenges Sisters to "open (their) hearts to all"[5] and "(make) room for all".[6] It sets itself against the paralysing effects of "fear, conformity, lack of truthfulness, (and) arrogance".[7] It promotes instead an expansiveness of mind and heart which can both recognise and welcome the charism in others, perhaps as I did spontaneously myself, when young, "Whilst charism is indefinable, when we encounter that spark of it in another we recognise it with joy."[8]

It is this wisdom which provides the context for the first recorded decision of this Chapter, "To continue to strengthen the relationship with the Federation Josephites and other Josephite Congregations throughout the world." [9]

This decision is deeper than just establishing inter-Congregational links, I think. It is a decision supported by the Chapter's further commitment to reclaim the vision of its founding through a renewal in appreciation of traditional symbols, including that of the Monogram, with its accompanying spirituality of the Cross, and the Holy (extended) Family of Jesus, Joseph and John the Baptist![10] That the vision is meant to be realised personally and practically is made evident in the Chapter's challenge to its women to engage in a searching form of conversion which can "look again at the 'landscapes of our hearts and minds.'"[11]

Unlearning

In 2005, such a call to openness entails hard work. Josephites of all hues not only have learning to do, but some unlearning, with respect to their own past and that of others on parallel journeys. Furthermore, there may be surprises waiting to be uncovered, as I learnt myself recently in the following way.

Last year I was invited by the Central Josephites to give a presentation to Sisters gathered from across the six Provinces of that Congregation for a spirituality seminar designed as follow-up to their 24th General Chapter of which I have been writing. Because, from my youth, I had considered the prominent wearing of the blue Monogram by both Brown and Black Sisters as significant in my assessment of their similarity, I decided to reflect on this symbol in my presentation. It was therefore necessary for me to consider again the Penola founding of 1866 and the different steps in the story by which the Original Congregation came to be followed by five other separate diocesan-based Josephite Congregations: Perthville from 1876, Wanganui in NZ from 1880, Goulburn from 1882, Lochinvar from 1883 and Westbury in Tasmania from 1887.

A visit to our Lochinvar archives netted me many treasures, including the souvenir booklet of my Congregation's Silver Jubilee from 1908, the year before Mother Mary died and the year my father was born. Before reading it, I simply assumed that it would be filled with accolades about our early Sisters and the bishop of Maitland who had secured their services to begin a network of country schools in remote places. I did find some of this, understandably enough. However what took me by surprise was the easy, friendly and highly complimentary remarks included in the booklet, not only about Father Woods, but also about Mother Mary, about the core significance of the initial founding at Penola and about the life and continuing mission of Sisters belonging to the original Congregation. It was as if the celebration of the Lochinvar Congregation's first twenty five years was also cause for celebrating not just the beginning of the Josephite Sisterhood but the continuing story of the Brown Congregation. I found no overwhelming sense of narrow provincialism here.

"The Very Smallest Convent in the World"

Let me quote one instance of this booklet's surprising freedom in utilising examples from one Congregation to shed light on another. The extract is from the writings of a Mr W. Redmond MP, a visiting member of the British House of Commons, representative of an Irish constituency. Somewhat ironically, the excerpt concerns Sisters far away in Nymagee, deep in the back country of NSW. I say "ironically", because Nymagee had a checkered history in the overall Josephite story. It was one of the early foundations from what had become the diocesan institute at "The Vale". In 1887, a change in Church boundaries caused Nymagee to become part of yet another diocesan group in the newly established Wilcannia-Forbes diocese. However, when this Congregation foundered, in 1902 twenty Sisters from Bourke, Nyngan, Balranald and Nymagee chose to be amalgamated with the original Josephite Congregation.[12] The comments of Mr Redmond from the period around Lochinvar's jubilee in 1908 would have applied to the life of women who used to be Black Josephite Sisters but were now Brown Josephites.

> Not far from the church, and separated from the town by a wide stretch of bare red soil, there is a small convent where four Sisters of the Order of St Joseph live. This is, I verily believe, the very smallest convent in the world; such a tiny little box of a place it is that the wonder is where the four nuns manage to exist ...
>
> It would be quite impossible to over-estimate the splendid work that the Sisters of St Joseph perform. Their special mission seems to be to follow the settlers into the remote districts, and right out in lonely bush localities they establish themselves, sometimes in little houses which look like toy houses, they are so small, and wherever there are children to be taught they teach them…
>
> In many places these nuns are extremely poor, but they are as well supported as the means of the people will allow…
>
> I visited the little schools of Nymagee and Nyngan, and it was a pleasure to see the bright and happy faces of the children and to notice their evident affection for their teachers.[13]

A Tradition Shared

Apart from the symbolism of the grave of Sr Teresa MacDonald at Perthville it would be hard to find a more telling reference than this one about Nymagee to the lives of early women, caught up in the consequences of events beyond their control, but committed above all to getting on with the job of transmitting the founding vision to others. As to my reference to Sister Teresa MacDonald, she was one of the original Sisters from Adelaide, one of Mary's right hand women, the one who was faithfully at her side so often, including on her knees beside her at the time of her excommunication. It was she who said to Mary "Wherever you go we will follow."[14] She was the first superior of "The Vale" and she died there early in 1876, just before the time which has come to be called the "split". She was buried as a member of the Original Congregation, but she lies amongst those who came from Ireland and from the goldfields, railway camps, farms and townships of the mid-west of NSW to join the diocesan Congregation of Perthville. Her grave, like the Convent of Perthville itself, is testimony to a history shared, and, I believe, a tradition shared.

Before the Recovery

This "split" in the Josephite Sisterhood in 1876 at "The Vale" in the Bathurst diocese has been explored recently in a most engaging fashion by Marie Crowley, the historian of the Perthville Sisters' story.[15] Before reading our souvenir book, I would have imagined that this "split" would have created a type of hiatus in tradition in a Congregation like Lochinvar established seven years afterwards. Or, at least, one might have imagined that a Congregation in such circumstances might have focused more narrowly on its own establishment from Perthville in 1883. I admit to assuming these things, because that was the sense I had of my Congregation when I first joined it, just as the Second Vatican Council was beginning.

At that time it was rare to find pictures of Mother Mary on our walls, unlike today. In fact, there were only a few fairly unattractive ones of Father Woods in evidence. (My personal view is that we have still not developed an appropriate way of portraying him and his significance.) In my first years in the Congregation I remember few references to Mother Mary and no details about Father Woods, apart from the clear fact of his being known as "Father Founder". Along the way I also heard that there was a book about him we were not supposed to read. There were occasional mentions of Perthville, but, by and large, the wider Josephite story was not on our active agenda. What was uppermost in our minds, instead, was the understandable pride and relief experienced in the Congregation's recent gaining of Definitive Approbation as a Pontifical Institute. To join our group at that time was to feel part of a real powerhouse for mission in school education and in music teaching in the local area of the Maitland diocese and in a few places in the Lismore and Sydney dioceses.

In those days we heard stories of earlier times when the Sisters struggled to make ends meet, close to the circumstances of the people amongst whom they lived and worked. There were tales from country boarding schools, mining settlements, farming townships and the city communities around the steelworks of Newcastle. There was the yarn, for example, about a statue of Joseph left out overnight by the Sisters in Denman to protect their home from the rising flood waters of the Upper Hunter. They awoke in the morning to see Joseph bobbing his way down the road, safely high on the floodwaters. Above all in those days, there were references to great women who had led us in lean times, relying on Providence and being saved from trouble just in the nick of time. For many of us too, there was the feeling of belonging to something good when we gathered for retreats and sang together Dom Moreno's "Lochinvar Hymn", composed especially for St Joseph's College, Lochinvar, from amongst whose ex-students the Congregation has drawn most of its members over the generations.

Recovering our Roots

Then there was change. In the year of my profession the Vatican Council called all religious to return to our roots, to recover our authentic founding charism. Together with the other Black Josephite Congregations the Lochinvar group willingly embraced the task of forming the Federation of the Sisters of St Joseph of Australia and New Zealand as early as 1967. From then onwards we began to speak and write our story. We came to notice what linked us and to realise all that had been passed down through the simple medium of the Sisterhood's "passing on the baton" from the beginning, in spite of what had happened on the larger stage concerning co-founders and bishops at different times.

Around our centenary year in 1983, most of the Lochinvar Sisters went on a series of pilgrimages to Penola and Adelaide. I think we restored within ourselves some of that inclusive vision expressed in our Silver Jubilee souvenir booklet of 1908. In many of my Sisters' estimation, I believe, these pilgrimages to Penola have provided the most formative experience we ever had for being Sisters of St Joseph. We not only saw places significant in the story and touched the wood of the Penola school house, but we encountered that story embodied in the hospitable welcome we received wherever we went from the Brown Josephites of the Province of South Australia. There was, and still is, amongst these Sisters a special interest in Father Woods who worked and rode and wrote among them. This meets half-way the Black Josephite who, in pre-Vatican days, had grown up with the inspiration of his words from "The Explanation of the Rule" as virtually her only guide for the founding vision, apart from its embodiment in her Sisters.[16]

"I will bring them into their own land"

In both inner and outer journeying, around Penola, Mt Gambier, Robe, Naracoorte, Bordertown, Clare, Sevenhill, Norwood, Kensington and Morphett Vale, we experienced a type of homecoming. As we came into Penola itself, some women cheered and then we all fell silent, as each of us in her own way took in the significance of the moment. This experience was made all the more real for me when I participated in a further pilgrimage with representatives of most of the Josephite Congregations during the centenary year of the death of Father Woods in 1889. On this occasion we arrived at the chapel at Kensington in Adelaide just in time for Mass on the feast of the Sacred Heart. Without a chance to prepare, I was asked to proclaim the first reading. I soon found my voice unsteady as the significance of Ezekiel 34:11-13 struck me:

> For thus says the Lord God: I myself will search for my sheep, and will seek them out. As shepherds seek out their flocks when they are among their scattered sheep, so I will seek out my sheep. I will rescue them from all the places to which they have been scattered on a day of clouds and thick darkness. I will bring them out from the peoples and gather them from the countries, and will bring them into their own land; and I will feed them on the mountains of Israel, by the watercourses, and in all the inhabited parts of the land.

The Banyan Tree and a Living Tradition

Scripture's call to bring home again those who have been scattered, finds companionable resonance with a further beautiful extract from Lochinvar's souvenir booklet of 1908. Here the Josephite Congregations are imaged wonderfully as a living, expanding tradition:

> There is a product of tropical forest, famed in Indian story, known as the banyan tree. When a branch, bending from above, touches the earth, it sends out roots, and forthwith a new tree grows. Where a single tree stood, in time there stands a grove, each member of which still shares the life of the parent trunk.
>
> From the original institute of the Josephites have sprung other institutes in Australia. They retain the name, they follow the rules in the main, of the parent Order. They are scattered all over the continent. If these are reckoned in, there is no State of the Commonwealth – Tasmania and Western Australia not excluded – which is not blessed by Josephite self-devotion and by Josephite zeal. [17]

These are the words of Monsignor O'Reilly, a former Archbishop of Adelaide whose perspective obviously did not include New Zealand! What is quoted is part of an address he delivered somewhere else on some other occasion, but I found it printed in full in our booklet. Edited by "a priest of the Maitland diocese", the booklet's contents offer an interesting window into the world of how both the Archbishop and the editor saw the earlier groups of Josephite women in relation to each other. Presumably the leaders of the Lochinvar Sisters would also have agreed to what was included in their booklet, so I am assuming that they too were confident at that time in seeing themselves as both inheritors and transmitters of the original Josephite tradition.

The Hopes that Matter

Before concluding, I want to reflect on something I have learnt from daily life over many years, since it helps me make meaning of the Josephite story, especially the painful parts of it that can be disillusioning. I refer to that awareness that grows in us that, as human beings, we find ourselves constantly working towards, rather than fully achieving, all the good to which we aspire. As Paul says in Romans 8, we "groan" as we wait in hope for the completion of God's ways among us. The way forward is ours to co-operate within, but the Spirit's to carve out. In the disappointment we sometimes feel about the gap between what we aspire to and what we actually live, we face several challenges, I think: to remain compassionate in judgement about the messiness of elements of our collective story; to keep ourselves open enough to learn wider perspectives on it; to be honest about what we need to face; and finally, to be hopeful enough to believe both in ourselves and God's Spirit, so that, in fidelity to what constitutes a living tradition, we can take new steps in history to be more fully who we have always been meant to be in the world and Church on this part of the earth.

Beyond these hopes for the collective Josephite tradition I register a personal one. It is the hope that someone reading this chapter might recall seeing somewhere a personally inscribed navy-blue, kid-leather, gilt-edged, Douai version of the bible, about 6 inches wide by 10 inches long by 2 inches thick. Amongst other treasures, such a bible disappeared from my family home at Saratoga in late 1960. Whoever removed it probably never realised its significance, but this bible is important to my family. It was given by Mother Mary of the Cross to my grandparents on their wedding day. She wrote and signed a greeting on the inside page. I would love to touch again that gift, a very personal link with the co-founder of the Josephite tradition to which I belong, with the early Sisters of the Congregation in which Mother Mary lived and died, and with my ancestors for whom she was an esteemed mentor and friend.

A Final Say

Since my family's tradition gave me my first appreciation of Mother Mary of the Cross, I will let it speak the last words in my tribute to her. Jack, my father, used refer to her often. She was top of his honour list, above the pioneering Duracks, Sidney Kidman (the "Cattle King"), Les Darcey (the boxer), and even that cricketing legend, Victor Trumper! I encouraged him to write down what he had been telling us about Mary all our lives. I quote some of his words, spelling amended, since the Brown Josephites of his school days never succeeded in regularising his uniquely free way of committing words to paper. He begins with his own sense of inheriting and passing on a tradition:

> As told to me by my mother and father, here is some of the history of Mother Mary, in later years to become a legend as a citizen, and above all, a religious of the highest order.
> When professed, she became known worldwide as Mother Mary of the Cross. She was the foundress of the Order of the St Joseph Nuns. This was a teaching order in outback places.

> The Sisters were carers of isolated bush women and their children. They were the solace of the expectant mother, black or white, no matter what religion, or perhaps none.
>
> In Mother Mary's early days there were cases where she and her company not only brought children into the world, but laid them out and buried them. (I can remember them doing that.)
>
> Mother Mary moulded her co-Sisters and her own work to soothe troubled waters, so much so that the toughest of men loved her and almost sat at her knee seeking her counsel on all the troubles of life.
>
> Mother Mary had many "brush-ups," so to speak, with a lot of narrow-minded people. So much so that she made a trip to Rome to see the Pope and won her cause 'hands down'.
>
> Mother Mary was a great sport, a light hearted girl, my father used to say.
>
> Mother Mary was a courageous, broad-minded and magnanimous woman. She was, although a woman of great piety, a great realist, with the ability to grasp the way in which the people of the world had to grapple with life.

In his cattle yard, surrounded by his horses, our father died late in 1983. My brothers and I gathered from all the places where adulthood had scattered us. Gaining strength from our mother we stood around him needing to connect with him across the suddenness of his leaving us. This need moved me to take off my Black Josephite cross and pin it onto the "brown habit" in which he had been clothed for his journey, just as his father had been before him. Knowing he would now understand all my meanings, I said, "Here is something for you from Mother Mary."

Endnotes

1 The Central Josephites – the Sisters of St Joseph of the Sacred Heart – wore brown habits from 1867, hence the name, "Brown Josephites". The Australian-New Zealand Federation of the Sisters of St Joseph is composed of autonomous Congregations. As a distinguishing mark they wore black habits – hence "Black Josephites".

2 J.J. O'Donovan, *The History of the Catholic Church in the Brisbane Water District, 1842-1942*, (Printed September 1942. No other publication details available), 15.

3 This Monogram was drawn from the personal seal of Father Julian Edmund Tenison Woods, the co-founder of the Josephites. He drew this directly from the seals used by the Marist Fathers amongst whom he had been a novice in France early in his life. Besides the A+ M on the Monogram, there were three letters "J" in honour of Jesus, and Joseph and John the Baptist who were special patrons of the Congregation.

4 Acts of the 24th General Chapter, Sisters of Saint Joseph of the Sacred Heart, October 5th to October 15th 2001, 4. Used with permission of the Trustees of the Sisters of St Joseph, North Sydney, NSW.

5 Ibid.

6 Acts of the 24th General Chapter, Sisters of Saint Joseph of the Sacred Heart, October 5th to October 15th 2001, 5.

7 Ibid.

8 Ibid.

9 Ibid.

10 Acts of the 24th General Chapter, Sisters of Saint Joseph of the Sacred Heart, October 5th to October 15th 2001, 7.

11 Acts of the 24th General Chapter, Sisters of Saint Joseph of the Sacred Heart, October 5th to October 15th 2001, 8.

12 Marie Crowley, *Women of The Vale, Perthville Josephites,* 1872-1972 (Richmond, Victoria: Spectrum Publications, 2002), 84-5.

13 A Priest of the Diocese of Maitland, ed., Souvenir of the Silver Jubilee of the Sisters of St Joseph, Lochinvar, NSW, (Westmead, Sydney: The Boys' Industrial Home, 1909), 86. Used with permission of the Trustees of the Sisters of St Joseph, Lochinvar, NSW.

14 Crowley, *Women of the Vale, Perthville Josephites,* 1872-1972, 20. Words recorded by Sr Mechtilde Woods.

15 Crowley, *Women of The Vale, Perthville Josephites,* 1872-1972.

16 This "Explanation of the Rule" is, I believe, basically the same document as "The Book of Instructions" within the Brown Josephite Congregation.

17 A Priest of the Diocese of Maitland, ed., Souvenir of the Silver Jubilee of the Sisters of St Joseph, Lochinvar, NSW, 66.

A 'Saint' for Australia

Mary Cresp rsj

The veneration[1] of people or places seen to have a special relationship with the holy, is a phenomenon common to all civilisations.[2] The Judeo/Christian world shares this tradition, and Old Testament stories support it in recording how people maintained and visited shrines to commemorate an encounter with God. The site of Jacob's struggle with the angel (Gen 28:10-22) is one such example. Moses was honoured by the Jewish people as having no equal, one who had known the Lord "face to face" (Deut 5:4). However, unlike figures of other cultures whose veneration often led to their being made gods, neither Moses nor other "holy" ones such as kings or prophets could claim virtue in and of themselves.[3] For Israel, as for later Christians, it is God who is honoured through the saints. Those who reverence God's action in the lives of these saints are challenged to respond to that same graciousness in their own lives.[4]

Whether or not Christians were influenced by pagan practices with regard to the cult of saints – be its roots in ancestor worship, magical attainment to the power of the godhead or whatever – for Catholicism at least the cult is integrated with its belief system and is secondary to the Church's understanding of the centrality of Jesus Christ. Through Christ, the Christian is brought into union with God. In his humanity, Jesus not only reveals the divinity but is himself revealed as Son. His union with God is ultimate. Through their incorporation into the body of disciples, his followers thereby enter, through adoption, into a like relationship with God. All who are thus bound to God in Christ are bound to one another.

From early times, this relationship has been described as the "communion of saints". Used at first to emphasise the union between the different local churches and the universal Church, the concept has also traditionally recalled the ongoing union between the living and the dead. One corollary of this union is the ability of the one to intercede with God in prayer for the other. Martyrs were regarded as having attained perfect union, and prayer made to them to intercede for the forgiveness of sins was a common practice in the early days of the Church. Later, honour was paid to "confessors" and others whose lives of virtue had likewise witnessed to Christ. Between the sixth and tenth centuries the need for regulating the public acclamation of "saints" became apparent, especially when abuses led to legendary figures being held up as exemplars of the Christian life. The approval of Bishops, and eventually the Pope, was gradually required, and, while the acclamation of the faithful was still deemed necessary, it became but an adjunct to a compulsory, meticulous examination of the candidate's life. The stages of this examination were marked by the bestowal of a series of titles such as "Servant of God", "Venerable", "Blessed" and, finally, "Saint". This procedure was fairly well established by the Middle Ages, and, while not central to the Church's doctrine, the cult of the saints certainly had the effect of "incarnating" the experience of what living in Christ meant for this and subsequent eras.

With the colonisation of Australia in 1788, many victims of religious persecution were shipped to these shores and with them their belief systems. This was a time when, as a consequence of persecution especially in Ireland, Catholic devotionalism was especially strong. Opportunity to take part in the religious rites of the Church was often denied, and yet through the recounting of stories from the Bible and from popular accounts of the lives of the saints, a certain level of education in the faith and of relationship with Christ was fostered. Meanwhile, Aboriginal Australians preserved only with great difficulty their collective memory of encounter with the transcendent. Since European settlement, the telling of their "Dreamtime" stories, the visiting and care of places marking these encounters and the rituals through which they entered into relationship with the sacred were belittled and trivialised by the incomprehension of non-aboriginal society.

It was into this setting that Mary MacKillop, daughter of migrant Scottish parents, was born in Melbourne on January 15th 1842. Although the relationship was apparently often strained (Mary describes her home as "a most unhappy one"), both gave to their children a deep appreciation for God's loving care and providence in all aspects of their lives. This appreciation was based on relationship rather than on mere knowledge. Prayer, even in her infancy, was for Mary a matter of conversational listening and speaking to God.

Mary was eventually joined by seven brothers and sisters. However, Alexander MacKillop was not a good provider for his family. After a promising beginning he suffered financial loss, and from then on the family continually found themselves in want, often depending on relatives for material support. Nevertheless, Mary received a thorough education which equipped her well to take on a series of professions – governess, shop assistant and teacher – when, between the ages of sixteen and twenty-four, she assumed what she herself calls "the principal care" of her large family.[5]

In 1860, while acting as governess for her cousins in Penola, South Australia, Mary came into contact with Father Julian Tenison Woods. Faced with the pastoral care of a scattered parish about the same size as Sicily, Julian had a dream of providing catechetical and formal education for outback children. Mary's desire to "devote (herself) to poor children and the afflicted poor in some very poor Order"[6] thus found an arena for action. Six years later Mary returned to Penola at Father Woods' request to take over the Parish school in a refurbished stable, and the dream became a reality. On March 19th, 1866, Mary donned a simple black dress, marking what is now regarded as the birth of the Sisterhood of St Joseph.

Circumstances provided for the rapid expansion of the Sisterhood. Father Woods, appointed as Director of Education in the Diocese of Adelaide, called Mary (now "Sister Mary of the Cross") and her companions to the city to take over the schools and to establish other charitable institutions throughout the State.[7] It was not long before other Bishops invited the Sisters to their dioceses. However, misunderstandings, libellous rumours and outright hostility against the Sisters soon began to plague Mary's life.

This "cross" was to remain a factor for Mary until her death. It was composed of a series of tragic events which left her confused and deeply hurt. In 1871 she was excommunicated from the Church by Bishop Sheil;[8] at the same time he expelled forty-seven of her companions from the Institute and some of these never returned; Father Woods took exception to Mary's agreement to Roman changes to the Rule and ended their friendship, never forgiving her even though Mary tried to make reconciliation with him until his death; an investigation into the lives of the Sisters was conducted in Adelaide and Mary, unknown to her, was wrongly accused of drunkenness and embezzlement; Bishop Reynolds, at first a supporter, tried, like Bishops Matthew and James Quinn, to assume diocesan governance of the Sisters and expelled Mary from South Australia; in 1885 Mary was advised by Cardinal Moran to vacate her office as Mother General of the Institute purportedly because she bad been wrongly elected to leadership for more than the legal twelve years but more likely "to placate the bishops with regard to a woman who had a bad record for resisting attacks on her Institute's rights"[9]; the same prelate arranged for her successor, Mother Bernard, a kindly but incompetent leader who caused Mary much embarrassment and frustration, to assume office for what would have been a period of seventeen years had she not died suddenly in the twelfth year; during all this time Mary suffered the normal sorrows of strained relationships[10], family troubles and the death of loved ones – especially of her mother drowned in a shipwreck while travelling to see her daughter; further, throughout her life Mary was the constant victim of ill health caused by violent period pains, harsh living conditions and eventual strokes.

Yet by the time of her death on August 8th 1909, this nun was venerated by the general public as a woman of great vision, of heroic character and outstanding holiness. Cardinal Moran visited her at Mount Street, North Sydney in her last illness and declared, "Her death will bring many blessings .... on the whole Australian Church." On leaving the convent he added, "I consider I have this day assisted at the deathbed of a saint"[11] Her Sisters, now numbering over one thousand, were ministering on a wide variety of fronts throughout Australia and New Zealand. It was recognised that Mary and the Josephites had played a major role in the transformation of Catholic Education in Australia.[12] Notice of her death was featured not only by the Catholic press but also the secular press. For her requiem Mass the Church was filled to overflowing, and people crowded both sides of the street as the funeral procession wound its way to the Gore Hill cemetery. Her successes had been many. However, as one of her early companions testified, "the reason the Sisters looked on her with veneration and the outside world had such an interest in her was her personal virtue rather than her achievements."[13]

In January 1914, the body of Mary MacKillop was translated to the newly built Memorial Chapel at the Mother House in Mount Street. Since that time, a continuous stream of pilgrims, many from overseas, have prayed in intercession and thanksgiving at her tomb. The official process of inquiry into her life and virtues opened in 1926 at the instigation of Mother Lawrence, an early companion of Mary, and was headed by the Archbishop of Sydney, Dr Kelly. Proceedings were interrupted, however, when the 1884 report of Cardinal Moran exonerating Mary from the charge of intemperance could not be found. By 1951 the secretary to the 1926 proceedings, Norman T. Gilroy, had become Sydney's Cardinal Archbishop, and when he decided to re-open the Cause, that is, the "case for sainthood", he again requested the said report from Rome. It arrived by return mail!

With the transcript of the evidence of witnesses and other required documents completed in 1972, Mary was declared "Servant of God", marking the intention of the local Church to introduce her Cause to Rome. The preparation of the Positio, with its meticulous examination into every aspect of Mary's life, was completed in 1992,[14] and was accepted by an appointed body of theologians and then of Cardinals soon afterwards. The account of a miraculous cure of a young woman from leukaemia, together with doctors' testimony and medical records, was presented in 1993 as further indication of God's favour still shown through Mary. On June 6th 1993, Pope John Paul II signed the declaration indicating his approval that this woman should be recognised by the Church as "Blessed Mary MacKillop". On January 19th, 1995, he travelled to Sydney to preside at the official celebration of this fact.

One requirement of the process of canonisation, the acclamation of the faithful, has been an ongoing constant in the phenomenon of Mary MacKillop since her death. Involved in the decision of the Pope to hold the beatification ceremony in Australia was the fact that many ordinary people had written to Rome requesting this. Since the early 1990s, large numbers of pilgrims have come to the North Sydney Chapel to ponder and pray.[15] In 1970, during his visit to Australia, Pope Paul VI himself turned pilgrim and prayed at Mary's tomb, as, of course, did Pope John Paul II on the occasion of the beatification. The little town of Penola, while in proximity to tourist attractions such as the volcanic lakes of Mount Gambier and the vineyards of Coonawarra, has become the focus of much attention for no other reason than it having featured so prominently in the life of Mary MacKillop. Pilgrimages to the simple, unadorned Schoolhouse and the Interpretive Centre at Penola are constant. Other locations, such as the site of Mary's birth, 11 Brunswick Street, Fitzroy, Melbourne, and places in Adelaide frequented by Mary during her years there, have also become hallowed spots. In 1988 on the occasion of Australia's bicentenary, Mary was listed as one of the country's outstanding citizens. While best known in the Catholic world, she has become a permanent but living part of Australia's story.

For me, this is precisely the moot point – the figure of Mary MacKillop goes beyond its historical context to become a "living part" of that history, touching into our nation's mythology. As Diarmuid O'Murchu points out:

> There seems top in human culture a tendency to embody in a radical and profound way the values we cherish most deeply. Unconsciously rather than consciously, society "sets aside" certain individuals and groups, and endows them with intensive value-systems. It projects on to these liminal groupings its deepest hopes, dreams and aspirations and, in a sense, requests the liminal person or group to embody and articulate, for society at large, the deepest values this society holds dear and sacred.[16]

I propose that, for our society, Mary models those religious or spiritual values that are enshrined in the myth of what it means to be Australian. Max Harris, well-known writer and proclaimed agnostic, put it thus, "Mother Mary MacKillop gives us the chance to contemplate a wholly Australian mystery, to revivify a dormant depth in our culture."[17]

What, then, are the "Australian" spiritual values that Mary enshrines? In his study of the themes of spirituality in Australia, John Thornhill[18] develops certain concepts that are generally accepted as belonging to the Australian myth.

In Chapter Four, "The Ideological Factor: Shared Visions", he touches on the Australian dream of "utopia", an egalitarian society free of "the injustices and shortcomings of the old world."[19] When Mary MacKillop refused to divide her Sisters into "lay" and "choir" Sisters, she demonstrated the Christian virtue of belief in the dignity of all humans as made in the image of God. But this action is in sympathy with the Australian ideal of giving everyone a "fair go", no matter what their social status. In other words, it articulates the "dormant" spiritual basis for this aspect of Australian mythology. Mary's resistance to segregating paying students from non-paying students, and her reluctance to have her Sisters teach music lest they appear "above" the poor, belong to the same tradition. As thousands of letters written to the Pilgrimage Centre at North Sydney attest, Mary MacKillop and the Josephites are "for the poor". In nineteenth century Australia, the key to claiming one's dignity was through education. In making education available to the poor, Mary consolidated her identification by the Australian public as a hero, embodying the values of a society which would like to describe itself as "egalitarian".

The "legend of *mateship*" underlies for Thornhill, "the refusal of Australians to touch their hats to their superiors."[20] For many, institutional religion epitomises the type of overbearing attitude against which the legendary Australian struggles. That Mary found herself the victim of unjust ecclesiastical structures and that, on not a few occasions, she politely but firmly maintained her position before Church dignitaries makes her a credible hero even to non-believers. Further, as a woman, her access to decision-making power within Church circles was severely limited. According to Thornhill, mythology is a product of the drive within human beings to "make sense of experience and to describe its underlying principles."[21] Within recent years, more and more women comment on the inspiration they receive from reflection on Mary MacKillop's "mythical" ability to live with ambiguity; they can identify with her struggle to find the meaning of faith in a Church whose structures were so unattuned to the needs she observed and whose power systems placed her in such a position of vulnerability.

The story of the ANZACS is one which has become legendary in Australia. In the defeat of Gallipoli, it seems, Australia identified its soul. Not for us the loud boasting of the "self-made" character we praise; instead, the one who endures in adversity the "quiet achiever". As Thornhill points out, the stance of Australians is against "self-aggrandisement":

> Our national struggle was not one that ended in triumph; the prize more often than not was mere survival. And so ours is a strange catalogue of heroes - heroes who have won our admiration for the way in which they have conducted themselves when they were up against it.[22]

The "cross" that featured so much in Mary's life surely puts her into this category. In so many instances, her adversaries came out the "winners". Mary's refusal to further the evil by self righteous defence was often based on an acknowledgment of the legitimate role of authority figures especially in the Church, even though she could not agree with their actions. She had a wonderful ability to suspend judgement of the motives of these people. Moreover, on more than one occasion, we learn that Mary quietly replaced the evil with good. Cardinal Gilroy describes one such incident, "When the Secretary of the Commission that condemned her was himself suspended for intemperance, he went to her for help and she sold her own watch to provide him with a suit of clothes."[23]

The power of the landscape as an "icon" for Australians is another theme taken up by Thornhill. Further, this landscape is not that of urban Australia but rather of the outback. It speaks of isolation, ruggedness and strength, a stark beauty "defiant of all the traditional and established European expectations".[24] In presenting her case to Rome for approval of her Sisterhood in 1873, Mary had argued her case on the premise that "It is an Australian who writes this...." Only one brought up in the Australian setting can fully appreciate the peculiarities of this land and the needs of its people.[25] The fact that the Sisterhood founded by Mary has constantly been referred to as the "Brown Joeys"[26] is surely an illustration of the unconscious endowment on them of an acknowledgment of the unique relationship of the landscape to the spirituality of Australians.

In her endless travels in remote parts of Australia, Mary and her Sisters were deeply involved in the Australian encounter with the land. For many, Mary is a "Drover's Wife" character, experiencing the hopes and dreams of the pioneers as they carved out farms and mines in what was, to them, a "wilderness". She experienced nature's judgement on misguided agricultural expansion as the Sisters suffered with the people and were forced to withdraw, for example, from the ill-fated copper mining settlement at Blinman in South Australia's Flinders Ranges in 1875, or from the drought-affected farming community of Orroroo's marginal lands in 1885.[27] The Australian themes of blighted dreams and survival under hardship were part of the world into which Mary brought her practical brand of faith, a faith that stood her in good stead in her own hardships. It is this aspect of the folklore of Mary MacKillop that is most often referred to by those who write for prayers to the Mount Street shrine: variations of the phrase, "Please let this case be put into the special care of our Australian saint", imply that, even after death, Mary's background of having grown up in this country gives her a particular ability to understand the situation of tis people.

The reluctance of Australians to speak of such "deep" subjects as religion is the focus of Thornhill's last chapter. Whereas silence may indicate the stance of awe before what, in the end, is the mystery of life, the cause of this reluctance may well be the *pragmatism* that characterises many Australians and has become part of our mythology. Here again, Mary MacKillop touches a deeply held value. Mary was a "doer". Her practicality in identifying the crucial issues facing the Church and doing something about them appeals to the Australian imagination. Max Harris named it as "goodness". "Goodness is not a state of mind alone. It is a source for the most productive energies."[28]

It comes as no surprise to those who admire Mary that her first impulse was to "roll up her sleeves" and do something about the situation. When one of her Sisters was badly burnt at Port Augusta, she immediately caught the coach to Quorn, a town twenty miles from her destination, and was prepared to ride a horse for the remainder of the journey. Her practical kindness is legendary. Before leaving her Sisters in the isolated town of Arrowtown, New Zealand, Mary set up a fowl house and bought chickens to ensure ongoing nourishment for the community. Such "ordinariness" is constantly alluded to by those writing letters of intercession to the Sisters conducting pilgrimages at the site of Mary's tomb. People sense that this woman understands their homely situation. While many may write out of desperation — cancer victims having exhausted medical skill, relatives of hopeless alcoholics, long-term unemployed with no prospect of work — somehow, Mary has named for these people the truth that in the stuff of everyday life God is both involved and encountered.

In 1992, the Sisters of St Joseph held a consultation with a large group of people from various walks of life to discuss the implications of the deterioration of the buildings at Mount Street and especially of the area of Mary MacKillop's tomb. One option was to sell up the land and relocate the tomb elsewhere. A factor favouring this solution was the encroachment of the North Sydney Central Business District, which by now totally surrounds the Mother House. It was a group of Aboriginal people who opposed the proposal and impressed on us the importance of the "sacred site". Nothing can alter the fact that it was here that Mary MacKillop lived and died. It is here that the vitality of her spirit lives on. While all sharing the "communion of saints" may draw inspiration from her memory and may claim her intercession, Australia needs to see and touch those things that were seen and touched by Mary MacKillop so that, at last, we can say, `One of *us* is a saint!'

Endnotes

1 This article is a slightly adapted version, first printed in, and reprinted with permission from Australian Folklore, Journal Number 9, July 1994, pp 114-121.

2 *New Catholic Encyclopedia*, s.v "Pilgrimages, Medieval and Modern", by E. R. Labande.

3 Refer to incidents such as that described in 2Kgs 5:7 - `Am I a god?' Paul shows similar dismay when it seems he is to be honoured as a god, Acts 14:15.

4 As early as the fourth century we find warnings against the magical understanding of the cult of the saints.
Augustine warns, for instance, that it is not the pilgrimage of the feet that is meritorious but rather inner conversion which he calls the pilgrimage of the heart (*Epist 155.4.15; PL 33:672*).

5 Mary MacKillop to Monsignor Kirby, May 22nd I873.

6 Mary MacKillop to Bishop Sheil, September 10th 1871. This letter was written on board the steamer *Kangaroo.*

7 A house for the destitute, a home for reformed women, an orphanage and a reformatory for girls were among the early establishments of the Sisters. The visiting of jails and hospitals also became their responsibility.

8 Mary was excommunicated by Bishop Sheil on September 21st 1871 for "disobedience and rebellion." The issues around which this judgement was made concerned the opinion of the Bishop's advisors that the Sisters should have local, not central government (that is, they should be subject to the local priest rather than to Mary as the "Sister Guardian"), and that the Sisters should be ranked in "classes" of "lay" and "choir" Sisters. Mary was opposed to this division. While admitting his right to found an Order according to his likes, Mary had declared that she, vowed to live according to the present rule, could not agree to such fundamental changes and so would have to go elsewhere (Mary MacKillop to Bishop Sheil, September 10th 1871). The Bishop lifted the excommunication on his deathbed, six months later, admitting he had been badly advised.

9 Paul Gardiner, *An Extraordinary Australian: Mary MacKillop:The Authorised Biography* (Sydney: E.J.Dwyer, 1993), 327.

10 One that must have caused particular pain was the plotting of one of her own sisters, Sister Clare, to have Mary put in jail over an unpaid debt, incurred in buying boots for a community member. A friendly priest had Mary whisked away over the border to avoid answering the summons: and the debt was eventually paid.

11 Gardiner, *An Extraordinary Australian: Mary MacKillop: The Authorised Biography,* 479.

12 Edmund Campion, *Australian Catholics* (Ringwood: Penguin Books, 1988), 45-51.

13 Gardiner, *An Extraordinary Australian: Mary MacKillop: The Authorised Biography,* 482.

14 The official biography or Positio was prepared by Father Paul Gardiner S. J, who worked for ten years building on the research of his predecessors, especially of Monsignor Aldo Rebeschini, secretary to Cardinal James Knox in Melbourne.

15 In 2004, these numbers averaged 4,000 per month.

16 Diarmuid O'Murchu, *The Prophetic Horizon of Religious Life* (London: Excalibur Press, 1989), p.37

17 *The Australian*, April 13th 1985.

18 John Thornhill, *Making Australia: Exploring our National Conversation* (Newtown, Australia: Millennium Books, 1992),

19 Ibid. 64.

20 Ibid. 94.

21 Ibid. 45.

[22] Ibid. 128.

[23] Quoted by Paul Gardiner, "The History of the Cause of Mother Mary of the Cross", *Australasian Catholic Record,* Oct. 1991, 491.

[24] Brian Elliott, *The Landscape of Australian Poetry* (1967) and quoted by Thornhill, *Making Australia: Exploring our National Conversation,* 143.

[25] Mary MacKillop to Monsignor Kirby May 22nd, 1873.

[26] "Brown", the colour of the cheapest material available in the 1860s, was used for the Sisters' habits and obviously evoked the colour of the land. The slang form of "Josephite" is "joey"; in its rightful use the word describes a baby kangaroo.

[27] Marie Foale, *The Josephite Story.* (Sydney: Sisters of St Joseph, 1989), 226-227.

[28] *The Australian,* April 13th 1985.

Mary MacKillop and Joanna Barr Smith

Lady Mary Downer

Mary MacKillop and Joanna Barr Smith[1] first met in Adelaide in the 1860s. Joanna was a life-long friend and supporter of Mary and they corresponded with each other for forty years.

I am the great granddaughter of Joanna. My great grandparents were very early settlers in South Australia. Robert Barr Smith, or Robert Smith as he was then known, was born in Lochwinnoch, South of Glasgow. His father was a priest, initially in the Church of Scotland, but latterly with the Free Church, which he joined following some disagreements with the authorities. Robert Smith was a scholarly man and after he left university he went to work as a clerk, starting his own business in 1848. Through his partners he came in contact with the Elder family of which my great grandmother, Joanna, was a member.

In 1854 he asked Joanna Elder to marry him but, driven by a business decision, he went to Melbourne and was then persuaded by Joanna's brother, Tom Elder, to join him in his family business in Adelaide. So it happened that in 1856 Joanna, who was then aged twenty, sailed out alone to Melbourne to marry Robert, itself a great act of courage.

They moved to Adelaide shortly after their marriage and quickly established themselves as successful members of society. Robert's business interests prospered and he and Tom Elder became wealthy through the exploration and development of copper mining in Wallaroo, South Australia.

Joanna, like so many women of that time, spent much of the early part of her life bearing children and between the ages of twenty-two and forty-four she gave birth to thirteen children. Robert Bruce was born in 1857, followed by George Elder in 1858, Neil in 1860 (he lived about a month), Mabel in 1861, Tom Elder in 1863, Jean in 1864, Joanna in 1866, Marjorie Erlistoun in 1868, Hugh in 1870, Ida in 1871, Robert Barr in 1872, Ursula in 1876 and Dorothea in 1879. It was the tragedy of Joanna's life that by the time of her death out of the original thirteen children, only four survived, which as you can imagine was heart-breaking for both her and her husband.[2]

Personally I knew Aunt Mabel very well; Tom Elder was my grandfather; Jean lived in Brougham Place, North Adelaide; Joanna was my godmother and lived in England. Every birthday she sent me an English five pound note, which I always remember was worth seven Australian pounds and five shillings. A very different exchange rate now!

The Barr Smiths – as they became known, using Robert's middle name - but without the hyphen – lived in great style in South Australia.[3] They moved a number of times until they settled in the city in 1874, at Torrens Park, a large Gothic style stone residence which is now the home to the central part of Scotch College, and in the country, at Auchendarroch in 1880, which was an old coaching inn in Mount Barker, about twenty miles from the city in the Hills where many Adelaide families had summer houses to escape the fearsome hot Adelaide summers.

The Barr Smiths travelled often to England, usually taking their entire family with them for extensive periods of time. Usually these journeys were caused by some business problem or opportunity that Robert needed to pursue.

The records left by the Barr Smiths were extensive because when they were apart which was reasonably often, because of Robert's business, they wrote to each other every single day and this was before the days of emails or faxes and much more simple methods of communication. Theirs was a true love and so we have quite a clear picture of these two people who left their mark in South Australia because of their philanthropic and generous nature. One of Robert's main interests was education and he provided large amounts of money to purchase the Library collection for the University of Adelaide, both during his lifetime and in his will. His son, Tom Elder, built the Library at the University as a memorial to his father and to this day it is called the Barr Smith Library and is a fine Neo Georgian building. Interestingly enough Robert Barr Smith also contributed the money to finish the building of the Anglican Cathedral in Adelaide, St Peter's, with the erection of two fine spires. And this from a man who was more a Presbyterian than an Anglican!

Not only was he generous in academic and church circles but also actually supported the working man by paying the accumulated debts of the Trades Hall, the home of the Trade Unions. His generosity and that of his brother-in-law, Sir Thomas Elder, was renowned. They formed the pastoral company Elder Smith & Co Ltd.

Joanna Barr Smith's generosity was as extensive as her husband's, within her means. On her death one obituary writer said, "Mr Barr Smith once said to me, 'You would hardly believe the number of begging letters I receive every day, but my wife receives more than I do, because she has the reputation of being more generous.'"[4]

It is this generosity which was demonstrated in her friendship with Mary MacKillop – a generosity not only of material things, but of spirit and time.

The friendship between Joanna, who was no doubt inundated with the needs and wants of her children, and Mary MacKillop, arose in the 1860s and there is no doubt that it was motivated by religious faith. In reading the letters that remain, it is quite obvious that Sister Mary wanted to win Joanna over to the Roman Church and spent many years working on her spiritual life. Joanna, in turn, was able to assist Sister Mary during her difficulties with the church, including the time of her excommunication.

It is worth pointing out the similarities in background between these two women. Mary's family too was Scottish, from the Braes of Lochabar, and her father, like Robert Barr Smith's, was involved in the priesthood – in fact he had studied for it in both Rome and at Blairs near Aberdeen. However, he decided against the priesthood and migrated to Melbourne in 1838, marrying Flora in 1840. Mary, their first child, was born in 1842. Alexander was unable to manage his affairs and his large family became very poor. Mary benefited greatly from her father's scholarship. She went to Penola in 1860 as a nursery governess and it was there that she met Father Julian Tenison Woods.

Both young women, Joanna and Mary, left home early in life, were both strong characters with the highest principles. Mary was very fond of Joanna. She wrote to her mother in 1873:

> They (the Barr Smith family) move in the highest society here

> and Mrs Robert Barr Smith is an elegant and accomplished Scotch lady. She is a woman of very superior mind, and why she should so singularly attach herself to me I cannot understand. Both she and her husband know that my earnest desire is for her conversion and I hope much good from her visit to Rome.... She has asked me to keep up a correspondence with her. Pray for her return to us as a Catholic, and if it but please God to grant this, the church in Adelaide will long remember her.[5]

Joanna replied to Mary MacKillop:

> Ah if I could believe in the efficacy of prayer, how much have I to pray for? .... But you know my hard unbelieving spirit, I seem to get worse every day. I wonder you can take the very faintest interest in me for I must continually wound your spirit and vex your heart – you fancy these are germs of grace in my heart! Alas, so choked with the weeds of worldliness and selfishness, they have no room to spring up into the goodly flowers or fruits of faith.[6]

As you can see Joanna had a wry honesty. She relished conversation and ideas. Mary and she became friends when Mary first came from Penola to Adelaide and was struggling to set up a school for impoverished illiterates.

Joanna tried hard to attain religious faith but there were, for her, too many unanswered questions. She admired Mary for her tenacity through all her quarrels with the Catholic bishops, and her excommunication but showed an exemplary adherence to poverty. She was admiring of Mary's courage and faith through all these setbacks and wanted the faith in order to experience the comfort derived from it, particularly following the deaths of her children.

Mary was very grateful for help from this wealthy "elegant and accomplished" Protestant who made great contributions to the building of the Josephite Convent in Kensington, Adelaide. Mary urged the Sisters to remember to pray for their kind benefactors to whom they owed so much. Mary discreetly hoped that some Catholics might be encouraged to donate money to allay the costs of the building and announced that the newly-completed convent was due to the 'liberality of a non-Catholic friend'.[7]

The tone of many of Joanna's letters is very self derogatory and much of the time she criticises herself for being too greedy, selfish, intolerant and she wishes she could derive the satisfaction and solace of a stronger faith. She was too questioning, doubtful and pragmatic for the enlightenment she hoped for. Her faith in Robert's goodness remained her inspiration and example.

As Robert was dying, Joanna allowed no clergy to visit him but said afterwards in a letter to her son, Tom, my grandfather:

> I sometimes feared I did wrong not to propose visits (from the clergy). It does not at all matter any outside condemnation but I am jealous of any misconstruction of his personal religious feelings. I shall probably show the other members of the family his letter to Mother Mary, because it is such a decided statement of his faith and his happiness and his peace.

Interestingly enough, in 1869, Father Julian Tenison Woods, Mary's inspiration at the time, invited both Robert and Joanna to Mass. Robert very politely wrote, declining:

> My dear Father,
>
> I have been thinking over your proposal to perform mass at Mt Lofty and have come to the conclusion that it will be more proper to decline it. My wife has been the subject of much remark lately in connection with your church and there are now many people who will not believe when told she is not a Catholic.
>
> I do not think it is wise for a lady to provide such remark unnecessarily. You will agree with me.....[8]

On the death of Pius IX in 1878, Mary MacKillop wrote in a letter to two of the Sisters, that Mrs Barr Smith attended the Requiem Mass for the repose of his soul and "put on mourning for the occasion." Mary added, "Was it not nice of her?"[9]

Joanna was obviously the subject of some gossip because of her connection with Mary MacKillop in a conservative Anglican dominated South Australian society, so it proved both the strength of Mary MacKillop's conviction and the bravery of Joanna in defying general public comment.

In spite of all the gossip Mary MacKillop and Joanna continued to see each other when in Adelaide. Joanna travelled to Europe reasonably often while Mary in 1873, went on her first and only trip abroad to seek an audience with the Pope to establish the rule for the Josephite Order. Joanna spent the winter in Brussels in 1873 and wrote to Mary of her family in October, "My dear Sister Mary, we arrived here yesterday after a very stormy crossing at Calais."

In 1873 when Joanna was about to set off to England she asked Mary MacKillop to write to her, as she was passionately seeking spiritual faith. But for all Mary's efforts Joanna never slipped over to the Roman Catholic Church:

> I am sorry you did not give me the address of the young girl at Coblentz (sic) you wish me to see – as I am leaving this on Monday to run down to Wiesbadeen by Cologne and Coblentz to see if the Baths will cure our rheumatics. I am leaving the children with Miss Fickert at this hotel till I return. We have nearly fixed to stay the winter in Brussels. There is a school here where some members of my family were educated. I find I can get two floors in the next house with a door of communication through, which would be very nice for the girls going on comfortably with their lessons – they are all such ignorant little.... (the remainder of the letter is missing).[10]

I must add, the girls were never ignorant when I knew them!

Joanna wrote later in November 1873:

> My dear Sister Mary,
>
> I have been wandering over the face of the earth for many weeks, which must be my excuse for not writing to you. I have been all over Rhineland and have been trying the baths of Wiesbaden for my husband's rheumatism. Down also to Frankfurt on the Main and after that back on a visit to Paris. I have fixed all the children at school here in Brussels and my husband and I intend to radiate from this convenient centre all over Europe.
>
> I am in receipt of two letters from you. Very much thanks. I am much interested in all your proceedings. Your Scotch letter pleased me very much, i.e., it pleased me very much to think you were in the land of your father's folk. I have an extravagant love for Scotland. In going to Oban, which you did I suppose by one of the Clyde steamers, probably the *Iona*, you must have passed quite close by my summer home,

Knockdow, Argyleshire.

Your letter to Coblentz is too late, I have already been there. I was delighted with it. The old fortress of Ehrenbrechstein is magnificent. This mail's letter from Adelaide are all very satisfactory I fancy for us all. We have bought Briers, our last home in Adelaide – a place for which we have a strong affection. We are going to add to it and hope to go out next October. You will be out before us. I am quite resolved to be in Rome in Holy Week this year, but I fear you will be gone by that time. .... My husband is going over on a visit to Scotland in a week or two. Perhaps he may see you in Edinburgh. But his special homes are in Ayrshire and Renfrewshire. Be sure to let me know your future plans, dear Sister Mary.

What a daily, hourly cross I have to take up in my own family – a cross year by year getting heavier as my unfortunate son grows older[11] but you know my hard unbelieving spirit. I seem to get worse every day. I wonder you can take the very faintest interest in me.

We live her in the shadow of St Gudule, the beautiful old cathedral of Brussels. Its bells awake us and call to our daily duties. I always think of you whenever I look at it or hear the deep, solemn chimes,

Adieu,
Heaven keep you. Heaven keep us all.
Ever, dear Sister Mary, your friend, Joanna Barr Smith.[12]

Mary and Joanna both wrote with utter honesty and openness to each other. Mary wrote from Liverpool, England, to Joanna on October 17th 1873:

My dear Mrs Smith,

I did not answer your kind letter sooner knowing that I was too late for mine to reach you before you started for Wisbaden. I cannot tell you how much pleased I was to find that you wrote to me so soon. Ah my dear and much valued friend how much I wish that I could speak my whole mind to you upon the one thing which in your case so much absorbs my thoughts. Your last little note spoke volumes to me. Do tell me when you next write how your convictions now stand upon the one thing necessary. I cannot believe that your mind is at rest upon this point, and until it is, you know that the true heartfelt affection of my poor self for you will never be satisfied. ....

Please tell me one thing more. Have you sufficient Faith to believe that by praying earnestly, promising God at the same time to stop at nothing His holy Will may require of you, He in His turn will come to your aid, and grant you what your heart desires for your child Georgie? ....

There is one prayer more than any other which I would like to ask you to say, but it is one to the Mother of our God. I never knew an earthly mother to have to say that prayer in vain. Will you try to have Faith and say it, and then what is there that Jesus the Son of Mary can refuse to the Mother He loves? ....

But I must stop. Forgive me if I have said too much, you know I love your soul, and that I cannot be false to it.

Believe me dearest Mrs Smith,
Affectionately yours in JMJ,
Mary of the Cross.[13]

Mary MacKillop wrote to Joanna on November 19th 1873 and among other matters, shared her thoughts and feelings about Father Julian Tenison Woods:

My dear Mrs Smith,

I had sad tidings of the health of our dear Father Woods who was dangerously ill when the mail closed. You may imagine how anxious I am, and I am sure you can understand my sorrow if it has pleased God to take him from us. But in any case, the holy Will of God is welcome. He only knows what is good for us all. ....

Hoping that you are all well and that you will soon let me have one more letter from you, with kindest regards to Mr Smith, and much love to yourself, I remain, dear Mrs Smith,

Affectionately yours in JMJ,
Mary of the Cross.[14]

In January of 1874 Joanna wrote to Mary:

My dear Sister Mary,

Your letter received. Thank you very much. Did I tell you we lived in a house next to a *pensionnat* where my daughters

> are being educated? Well about a month ago fever broke out in Brussels. Two of the young ladies took it – and my boy Tom. I have been nursing him nearly three weeks, having sent all the other children and servants into the country to avoid infection. ... He has not got the turn yet but is going on favourably and will do well, please God. Last night we thought the Angel of Death would come for one of the young ladies whose lungs had been congested - in addition to the fever. But today she is a shade better and will, I fancy, pull through. A sister is assisting her mother to nurse her. I must make her acquaintance when I get the chance. Belgium is unhealthy, the convents are all nearly empty of Sisters, they being employed nursing the sick. I can only send you these brief lines, dear Sister Mary, and explain my sad position. I wish you a very happy New Year and a speedy reunion with your beloved helpmates in the South.
> Ever....[15]

Over twenty years later, in 1899, Joanna wrote a letter of congratulations to Mother Mary MacKillop on her election as Mother General of the Sisters.

> My very dear Mother,
>
> I think you know how very near to my heart was your election to the Mother Generalship and therefore you will understand the delight it was to receive Sister Annette's wire announcing it. I did not know where to address, otherwise I should have liked to wire my joy at once. It is the one place for you in life, my darling friend, and now you will spend and be spent in God's service and the whole community will rise and call you blessed.
>
> I wish I could have seen you ere I go hence, for oh dear me, I am going away full of misgiving and the future seems dark. My life is so much changed lately that my husband is quite sure I need a complete change. I get very down on my luck sometimes and in fact there does not seem anything now to live for. You will say this is very unhealthy and unholy attitude of mind. I grant this, darling Mother, but there's something fundamentally wrong with me in my mind and heart. Perhaps I'll be able to write a better account of myself in England. I think what is wrong with me is that I cannot

> fit in to my altered family relations – and I am discontented and unreasonable.[16] Joanna Hawker and her children go to England with us. She is going to marry again and has made an excellent choice this time.
>
> Won't you write me a little word of goodbye? I go to Melbourne on the 13th to take the *Oceania*. Farewell, my beloved friend. Ah, if things could have been different.[17]

Joanna was actually full of worries about the impending marriage of her daughter, Joanna Hawker, (a widow with two young children) to the Irish railwayman George Acres. Her depression and anxiety comes through quite clearly. The marriage was not a success and it was at her mother's suggestion that they divorced, quite a brave decision for those days. Her daughter reverted to the name of Hawker for the rest of her life, so Joanna's worries were quite justified.

Paul Gardiner writes in his book, *An Extraordinary Australian: Mary MacKillop: The Authorised Biography:*

> Mary MacKillop prayed for Joanna (Barr Smith) every day. .... The friendship was close enough to allow Mrs Barr Smith to remark to Mary that she did not think the Josephites had quite the same spirit of simplicity that was evident in the early days. She (Joanna) was still open-handed, and responded generously to a request for help in furnishing the chapel of St John's.[18]

In 1870, Mary wrote a spiritual message, *An Appeal of the Sacred Heart to a Weary, Disappointed Soul.* In March 1907 she sent copies of this to the Sisters and, as well, to Joanna. Joanna wrote in reply:

> Ah, dearest Mother Mary, we are all weary and disappointed when we get old. Well for us if we have some hope of life beyond this. I like your little paper so much. It speaks to my heart and I envy you the life you have been able to live.[19]

But there was another more cheerful side to Joanna and it seems she laid her soul bare when she communicated with Mary MacKillop. Robert and Joanna were obviously a romantic couple in spite of the restrictions of the Victorian age.[20] Every day they were together Robert picked a posy of flowers for Joanna from the garden. One of the stories I remember came from a good old friend of mine Molly Bowen, whose father, Archdeacon Clampett, used to go and stay with the Barr Smiths at Auchendarroch. Molly Bowen died a couple of years ago at the age of one hundred and five. Molly used to go on the early morning walks with Mr Barr Smith and got to know him well. She noticed that instead of having a gold watch chain like most people, his watch was attached to his person with a piece of string. So she asked him one day, "Are you very rich, Mr Barr Smith?" He replied positively and so she continued with her line of questioning, "Why do you have a string for your watch instead of a chain?" He answered, "The string always seemed more practical than a gold chain." This gives you an indication of the practical nature of Robert Barr Smith.

I do have one direct memory of the Barr Smiths' generosity from a dear friend of my husband's Jack Duncan Hughes. He was born before the turn of the century and used to go to parties at Torrens Park. The Barr Smiths loved games and theatricals – they even had a theatre built at Torrens Park. At this particular party there was a game with prizes and he played appallingly and won the booby prize. He often told the tale that the booby prize turned out to be the best pair of gold cufflinks he ever owned!!!

I well remember a famous anecdote about her ordering Tom Smith crackers. These crackers made by the firm Tom Smith were still being sold when I lived in London in the 1960s and our family always liked to use them because of the association with Joanna. Year after year Joanna would order vast quantities of these crackers not only for herself but also for other family members. One year the management wrote to her asking whether she owned a shop because she was buying such a huge number of crackers.

I should mention that the Barr Smiths were also friendly with the Downer family into which I married in 1947. My husband's father, Sir John Downer, was Premier of South Australia before the turn of the century and the Barr Smiths admired him a great deal. Sir John Downer's first wife died and he remarried in 1900. In my dining room at home I still have the silver rose bowl which the Barr Smiths gave to Sir John Downer and his second wife Una as a wedding present.

My mother, Joanna Gosse, was devoted to her grandmother after whom she was named and often talked to me about her with great affection. She died five years before I was born and unfortunately I never knew her.

The relationship between Mary MacKillop and Joanna Barr Smith was a close one, and was based on shared experiences of a Scottish background and the forging of a life for themselves in a new country. The spiritual journey on which Mary MacKillop accompanied Joanna may not have had Mary's wish fulfilled, in that Joanna did not become a Roman Catholic, but their friendship was obviously sustaining for both of them. Joanna's final gift was the marble slab for Mary's tomb in the Memorial Chapel in North Sydney.

Joanna's final letter to Mary MacKillop is a noble testament of their friendship:

> Oh, my dear friend, I wish I could see you again or hear your voice. .... Living or dying, my beloved friend, I am ever the same to you and am proud to look back on nearly forty years of unbroken friendship. My husband and I send dearest love.[21]

Endnotes

1 A public lecture, entitled "Joanna Barr Smith", given by Lady Mary Downer on March 30th 2003 at Mary MacKillop Place North Sydney NSW, forms the greater part of this article. Additional material has been included as indicated.

2 Robert Barr Smith died in 1915 and Joanna in 1919. Mabel, Tom, Jean and Joanna survived them – they lived to eighty-five, eighty-three, ninety-seven and ninety-seven respectively.

3 Robert Smith's mother was Marjorie Barr.

4 Fayette Gosse, *Joanna and Robert: the Barr Smiths' Life in Letters, 1853 – 1919* (Adelaide, South Australia: The Barr Smith Press, 1996), 256.

5 Mary MacKillop to Flora MacKillop, January 21st 1873.

6 Gosse, *Joanna and Robert: the Barr Smiths' Life in Letters, 1853 – 1919*, 33.

7 Paul Gardiner, *An Extraordinary Australian: Mary MacKillop: The Authorised Biography* (Australia: E.J.Dwyer, 1983), 475.

8 Gosse, *Joanna and Robert: the Barr Smiths' Life in Letters, 1853 – 1919*, 28. Robert Barr Smith to Julian Tenison Woods, circa January 1869, 28.

9 Mary MacKillop to Sister Josephine McMullen and Sister M. Josephine, February 25th 1878.

10 Gosse, *Joanna and Robert: the Barr Smiths' Life in Letters, 1853 – 1919*, 32. Joanna Barr Smith to Mary MacKillop, October 11th 1873.

11 This was their son George who was fifteen at the time. He was retarded and lived until he was fifty-six.

12 Gosse, *Joanna and Robert: the Barr Smiths' Life in Letters, 1853 – 1919*, 32. Joanna Barr Smith to Mary MacKillop, November 30th 1873.

13 Mary MacKillop to Joanna Barr Smith, October 17th 1873. The initials, JMJ, stand for Jesus, Mary and Joseph. Material added by the editor.

14 Mary MacKillop to Joanna Barr Smith, November 19th 1873. Material added by the editor.

15 Gosse, *Joanna and Robert: the Barr Smiths' Life in Letters, 1853 – 1919*, 33. Joanna Barr Smith to Mary MacKillop, January 6th 1874.

16 This was the time when Joanna and Robert lost two of their youngest children, both about the age of two.

17 Gosse, *Joanna and Robert: the Barr Smiths' Life in Letters, 1853 – 1919*, 188.

[18] Gardiner, *An Extraordinary Australian: Mary MacKillop: The Authorised Biography*, 404.
[19] Gardiner, *An Extraordinary Australian: Mary MacKillop: The Authorised Biography*, 477. Material added by the editor.
[20] Gosse, *Joanna and Robert: the Barr Smiths' Life in Letters, 1853 – 1919*. This title carries their story.
[21] Gardiner, *An Extraordinary Australian: Mary MacKillop: The Authorised Biography*, 484. Material added by the editor.

Unless a Grain of Wheat

Marie T Foale rsj

Jesus said: I tell you most solemnly,
unless a grain of wheat falls on the ground
and dies, it remains only a single grain;
but if it dies it yields a rich harvest

Jn 12:24

Ten years have passed since Mary MacKillop's beatification amid scenes of great rejoicing. She was honoured as a woman before her time, as one who had dared to found a radical new Religious Congregation of sisters to work among the poor and outcast, especially those living in rural areas. She had lived simply, frugally and celibately, and was single-minded in her service of God. She had an unfailing trust in the loving Providence of God and a great sense of God's presence.

Yes, Mary is a saint and is worthy of the honour the Church has bestowed on her. One does not become a saint, however, unless like a grain of wheat, one falls into the ground and dies. It was in the hard school of pain and suffering that Mary learnt to place her confidence in God in the many and varied circumstances of her life. She received her first lessons on trust in God at her mother's knee and never forgot them. As she wrote soon after her religious profession in August 1867:

> Dearest Mamma, you ever taught me to look up to and depend on Divine Providence in every trouble and when you saw me dull or unhappy you always had the same sweet reminder for me. Ah, do not forget what you were the first to teach me (sic).[1]

Family Life

Mary's early life was one of "hardship, poverty and even want."[2] As the first of the eight children born to newly arrived immigrants, Alexander and Flora MacKillop, she was conscious of their struggle to make their way in a new country. She dearly loved her father, who had spent his youth studying to become a priest and found it hard to make a living in business or on the land. Ultimately, even his best efforts were unsuccessful because he suffered from a compulsive idealism, which alternated with periods of discouragement and depression of spirit. Nevertheless, she always acknowledged the great debt she owed him.[3]

As a result of Alexander's inability to support his wife and children adequately, money was always tight and they enjoyed few material luxuries. They seldom had a home of their own and often they were forced to seek refuge with relatives. At such times, they relied on the charity of these relatives for food and shelter. This was never easy especially when some of the people concerned were impatient with Alexander for his apparent neglect of their needs.

On one occasion he went overseas with a friend who wished to visit the old country before he died. He left behind his wife with five young children, including a babe in arms, to manage as best they could until his return. To finance his trip he mortgaged their house with his brother Peter, in the expectation that Peter would not mind if he was late getting back. When Alexander did not arrive on time Peter foreclosed and tried to evict Flora and the children.

Flora, who knew nothing of the arrangement, refused to budge, even when Peter moved in with his wife, Julia, who appears to have been quite a formidable woman. Everyone was afraid of her except ten-year-old Mary. Her sister Annie described the situation as follows:

> Peter said he required the house for himself as it was conveniently situated for his wife. (Her sister had a home nearby). It was a very unhappy home for all as our mother would not leave, and Aunt Julia always remained in her room, seeing no one but Mary who brought her food etc.[4]

Mary was the one who kept the peace with her aunt and the family stayed on until their Uncle Donald MacDonald came to the rescue and took them to his place, where they stayed until Alexander's return.

One can well imagine the scene when, after an absence of seventeen months, he arrived home. What happened then may have been one of the events that caused Mary to write, "My life as a child was one of sorrows, my home, when I had it, a most unhappy one."[5]

It seems, however, that Flora and Alexander soon made it up, because young Donald was born before another year was out. Mary was there to help when he arrived. She noticed that the nurse her parents had engaged to care for both mother and baby was not only incompetent but also intoxicated. On her own initiative, she dismissed this woman and, to everyone's amazement, cared for the new arrival in a very able manner.

For many years Mary had been convinced that God was calling her to religious life although just how she might answer that call was unclear, especially as, by the time she was sixteen she had become the family's principal breadwinner. From then until she was twenty-five, she carried this burden which weighed heavily upon her. Above all else, her aim was to keep the family together and she struggled to do so even when her work required that she live away from home. During this time she held various positions including those of shop girl at Sands & Kenny's stationery business in Melbourne, governess to the children in a number of families in Western Victoria and south-eastern South Australia and teacher in the Catholic denominational school at Portland in Western Victoria.

Towards the end of this period, the family enjoyed a happy interlude when the parents and children were all together in Bayview House at Portland. This situation was short-lived, however, mainly because of her father's lack of tact and sense of family honour. At the time Mary was teaching in the local Catholic Denominational School. She was an excellent teacher and, when the Inspector came to examine the school, the headmaster, Mr Cusack, took into his class her well-prepared pupils and gave her his less able ones. Alexander was furious at what he felt was a slight on his daughter and his family as a whole. Thanks to his intervention, she was blamed for this fiasco, lost her job at the school and was ostracised by many members of the local Catholic community.

Then, as Annie put it, "Pa and Ma disagreed"[6] and the family Mary had worked so hard to keep together split up finally and irrevocably. Her parents now realised they could no longer live together in peace and harmony. Acting on Father Woods' advice, her father moved to his brother's property near Hamilton while her mother and the younger children found alternative accommodation.

This was a difficult time for Mary, who felt that God was calling her to join Father Woods at Penola and become the founding member of his proposed new Religious Institute, the Sisters of St Joseph. However, as in many of the other events of her life, there was no thought of self-pity or loss of faith. Instead, she simply let go of what had been, trusted in her God and waited until she was free to follow that call. She always had a keen sense of what was right even when it put her in difficult situations. As she put it:

> (God) gave me a keen sense of duty, and in the discharge of what appeared to be my duty, I felt it impossible to pause or consider my own feelings. …. For all that, my good God watched over me and guarded me when I did not try to guard myself.[7]

Finally, by the end of 1865, Mary and her two sisters, Annie and Lexie were able to accept Father Woods' invitation to go to Penola and take charge of the Catholic school there. The way was now open for the founding of the Josephites.

Family Tragedies

From her earliest years, tragic loss was something to which Mary was no stranger. She was five when her much loved grandfather MacDonald drowned in the flooded Darebin Creek near her home. His death and that of her baby brother, Alick, which occurred in the same year, both had a profound effect on the little girl and she never forgot either of them. In their old age, Annie commented that:

> It was while living there (Darebin Creek) that Mary had her first great grief. She loved him (her grandfather) very much and even last year reminded me with tears in her eyes of his birthday. Mary always remembered every incident of his loss with sorrow.[8]

The family broke up in 1865 and then, in December 1867, Mary's brother John, the fine, "strong, independent, loyal young man"[9] who had converted the Penola stable into a schoolroom for her, died in New Zealand after a fall from a horse. He was twenty-two years old and was doing what he could to help support his mother and younger brothers, even if from a distance.

Then, less than a year later Alexander died at Hamilton, aged 56 years. Mary was in Adelaide at the time and was unable to be with him, but was consoled by the fact that her mother was at his bedside at the end.

During the next fifteen years, three more of her siblings died. The first was twenty-nine year old Maggie, the sister closest to her in age. Maggie had suffered from rheumatic fever as a child and had never fully regained her strength. Next to go was Peter, the youngest, who died in Melbourne in 1878, aged twenty. Then, four years later, thirty-two year old Lexie, who was a Good Shepherd sister, died at the Convent at Abbottsford in Melbourne. After her death, Mary commented sadly to Donald that now there were only three of them left out of eight.

Then came what could be described as the bitterest blow of all. In May 1886, seventy-year-old Flora drowned in a shipwreck near Eden on the South Coast of New South Wales. Mary had invited her mother to Sydney to help with a bazaar she had organised there. She and the Sisters were eagerly awaiting Flora's arrival when, instead, they received news of her death. Mary's anguish and grief were compounded by the knowledge that she had put some pressure on her mother to make the trip to Sydney. She wrote to her sister as follows:

> My dearest Annie, God help us all. The hand of God is heavy upon us, but his holy will must be done. Oh, Annie, I had so yearned to see her again and all the sisters were planning to make her visit a happy one. Poor, dear, long-suffering Mamma. I am sure she has gone to a well-deserved rest and will no longer have to feel her dependent position.[10]

Her brother Donald, who was a Jesuit, was overseas at the time and Mary grieved for him too. She wrote:

> My dearest brother, how can I write. You must ere this have heard from Adelaide of our sad, our terrible loss. Everything was too bewildering at first, then the efforts to recover the dear remains, the funeral, and then came the reaction. Between all, you, for whose sorrow my heart ached, have been seemingly neglected by me. ... I cannot now attempt to describe the dismay with which I heard the sad news. It was too terrible to be true, but its truth was too soon proved.[11]

Only someone who has suffered a similar tragic loss can fully appreciate the pain suffered by Mary, Annie and Donald at this time.

Life as a Josephite

Yahweh said to Abram:

Leave your country, your family and your father's house,
for the land I will show you.

I will make you a great nation;

I will bless you and make your name so famous that it will
be used as a blessing.

So Abram went as Yahweh told him and Lot went with
him.... They set off for the land of Canaan, and arrived
there.

Gen 12:1,2,4,5

A home life marked by hardship, poverty and even want, and the loss of many family members, some in tragic circumstances, were not the only sufferings endured by Mary. In order to follow her call to be a Josephite, Mary, like Abraham, left all that she knew and loved and moved to a place that God showed her.

Her first major move was from Portland to Penola to take charge of the catholic school there and to become the first Sister of St Joseph. This was a big change but she was already at home in Penola. She had spent two years there, working as governess to the Cameron children. Her sisters Annie and Lexie were her assistants in the school. Father Woods was her director, as he had been for several years, and she knew the families of many of her pupils.

This situation did not last, however. The bishop was so pleased with the school in Penola that he appointed Woods to Adelaide as Director of Catholic Education in the diocese. She stayed behind until Woods realised that he needed Mary's help in setting up his and the bishop's new education system. Hence, he invited her and some of her assistants to leave their familiar setting and come to his aid.

This was a big move indeed, perhaps the most radical of all that she ever made, because she had to leave a place where she felt at home and go to where she had never been before. It was a leaving of her country, her family and friends, her securities, and, like Abraham, stepping out in faith into the unknown. For her Adelaide was a strange city. She had not been there before. She did not know its people. She had no guarantee that she or the Sisters of St Joseph would find acceptance there.

Yet when the call came in June 1867 she left everything and went willingly. One can only imagine her feelings as, after having said goodbye to her friends at Penola and Mount Gambier, she made the journey to Port MacDonnell and turned her face resolutely towards the ship waiting for her out in the bay. Once aboard there could be no turning back.

She arrived safely and the people of Adelaide welcomed her warmly. She quickly became involved in the schools and charitable works that Woods and his fellow priests asked her and the new sisters to undertake. Initially, everyone treated the sisters with kindness and respect and they received more applications for admittance than they expected.[12] This quick expansion of the Institute and the work that the sisters were doing brought its own difficulties.

Mary was a good teacher and all her life she loved to be with children, to talk to them and give them little gifts. She had been in Adelaide for less than a year when she had to give up teaching and take on the training of the young sisters. From then onwards she was constantly on the road, visiting and supporting them in their work and writing countless letters to them after her return home. Never again did she have a school or a class that she could call her own.

In September 1871, Bishop Sheil made it known that he intended changing the Josephite rule he had approved less than three years earlier. Mary had committed herself to God under that rule. Hence, she believed that her only option was to leave the Institute she had founded and move on until she discovered God's Will for her. She was at the point of leaving all she knew and going out into the unknown once more.[13]

The new place that God showed her was different from anything she could have imagined. Instead of going of her own free will, in control of her own destiny, she was sent away - excommunicated and banished from the Josephite community and the Church she loved so dearly. When she walked out of the Franklin Street convent chapel on that Friday morning she had nothing with her beyond the clothes she was wearing. Like Jesus, she had nowhere to lay her head. The bishop had threatened that, should she communicate with her sisters or her Catholic friends, they too would incur that same sentence of excommunication.

One brave woman risked all to support her and give her temporary shelter. She was Geraldine Woods, wife of Father Woods' brother, James. Geraldine took Mary into her home and allowed her to stay there for as long as it was safe for her to do so. When the news of the excommunication became public, Mary moved on to ensure that the Woods family did not suffer for having helped her.

After five long hard months, the bishop lifted the excommunication and restored Mary to her position as leader of the Institute. The bishops who came shortly afterwards to examine the state of the Adelaide diocese declared her innocent of any wrongdoing and confirmed her in that position. Her advisers, Fathers Reynolds and Tappeiner SJ, realised that other bishops might treat the Josephites in the same manner if the sisters did not measure up to their expectations. Hence, they decided that it would be wise to seek papal protection for the Institute.

This meant that Mary had to go to Rome, to leave her homeland and travel alone to a place where, once again, she was asked to let go of much that she held dear. This time it was some of her understandings about the Institute. In the light of what had happened in Adelaide, the Roman authorities decided to change the rule of poverty that was so important to her and her long time friend and mentor, Father Woods. Mary accepted the altered rule in the spirit of obedience, seeing it as God's Will for her and the Institute. She did not hesitate, even when her decision to accept the Roman ruling meant that she lost his friendship and support. As he saw it, this was a fundamental change to the spirit of the Institute and he could not accept it. Mary and he were never fully reconciled.

There were times when Mary had to let go of her good name. Bishop James Quinn of Brisbane believed that all religious communities in his diocese should be under his control. He accused her of being headstrong and refusing to consider the real needs of his people. He was angry because she defended the Roman Constitution with its emphasis on central government and removed sisters from places where the clergy were not providing them with even the basic necessities of life.

This was a difficult time for Mary as she struggled to balance the needs of the sisters against those of the poor children. Eventually, she felt compelled to withdraw all the sisters without having any guarantee that their good work would be carried on after their departure. Quinn blamed her for all the difficulties and misunderstandings that accompanied their removal, and demanded that she state publicly that she alone was responsible for their going. She refused to do so, because she believed that such a statement on her part would be a denial of the truth.

As the sisters began their journey southwards, they faced an uncertain future, as they had only enough money for their fares to Sydney. Imagine their joy when the Archbishop of Sydney and the Bishop of Armidale invited them to take charge of some of their schools. Mary gladly left the sisters in what appeared to be very promising conditions and returned to Adelaide where she faced a particularly difficult time.

She had been a healthy young woman but, over the years, she endured many bouts of ill health. She was often forced to take to her bed with severe headaches and period pain. Some sisters claimed that she needed so much bed rest because she was a drunkard and often had a hangover.

At the time the community was in debt. They had only a very limited income, the cost of living was high and Mary had incurred significant travelling expenses, especially during her frequent visits to Queensland. As this debt increased, some sisters accused her of using convent money to finance her habit. They reported her to the bishop who decided that she was unfit to govern the Institute and ordered her to leave Adelaide permanently. Until the end of her life, she had to live with the repercussions of that accusation. These included losing her position as Superior General, seeing the Congregation in the hands of an incapable leader and being unable to do anything about it.

At various times she fell victim to other illnesses. All caused her a great deal of pain and inconvenience but initially none was so bad as to prevent her from carrying out her duties as assistant to Mother Bernard or, subsequently, as leader of the Institute. Then, when she was sixty years old, and half way through her second to last term as Superior General, she travelled to the thermal baths at Rotorua in New Zealand for a course of treatment for severe rheumatism. She was looking forward to returning to Australia and resuming her duties with renewed energy. Instead, she suffered a stroke and was confined to a wheelchair for the rest of her life.

During the seven years remaining her, this independent woman was unable to move about freely and relied upon others for all her needs. Always a prolific letter-writer, especially to her sisters, she felt deeply her inability to send them more than a few scraps from time to time and visitation of their communities was virtually out of the question. She had to rely on her assistant to manage the day-to-day business of the Congregation, something very hard for a woman who preferred being at the helm.

Early in 1909, Mary wrote to her friend, Sister Annette Henschke:

> It is just seven years since the hand of God was laid so heavily upon me, and I often wonder how long more I shall be left in this weary world, but a thousand times welcome be His Holy Will.[14]

During those years when her enforced idleness gave her time to reflect, the grain of wheat that had fallen to the ground and died so many times, sprang to new life and bore a rich harvest, one that is still being gathered in our own day. The final letting go took place, "calmly and peacefully",[15] at half past nine on the morning of August 8th 1909.

Mary MacKillop endured the same kinds of hardships, struggles and tragedies as many people do. Her family seldom had a home of their own, had very little money and often had to turn to relatives for aid. At an early age she became the family's principal breadwinner and so was unable to continue her education. Her parents separated. She mourned their deaths and those of most of her siblings and suffered deep shock and a feeling of guilt at the news of her mother's tragic death. As a Josephite she was excommunicated from the Church, suffered the loss of her good name, was deposed from a position she was filling more than adequately and, in her final years, became totally dependent on others for all her needs. Throughout all her life, however, she maintained a sense of God's abiding presence and accepted God's Will in all things.

She was a true saint indeed!!

Endnotes

1. Mary MacKillop to Flora MacKillop August 21st, 1867. The letters of Mary MacKillop to her mother, Flora, are published in McCreanor, Sheila, ed. *Mary & Flora: correspondence between Mary MacKillop and her mother, Flora MacDonald MacKillop.* (Sydney: Sisters of St Joseph of the Sacred Heart, 2004).
2. Mary MacKillop to Flora MacKillop, November 27th 1866.
3. Mary MacKillop to Flora MacKillop, June 6th 1870.
4. Paul Gardiner, *An Extraordinary Australian: Mary MacKillop: The Authorised Biography* (Sydney: E.J. Dwyer, 1993), 31.
5. Mary MacKillop to Monsignor Kirby, Ascension Thursday 1873.
6. Gardiner, *An Extraordinary Australian: Mary MacKillop: The Authorised Biography* 49.
7. Mary MacKillop to Monsignor Kirby, Ascension Thursday 1873.
8. Gardiner, *An Extraordinary Australian: Mary MacKillop: The Authorised Biography,* 29.
9. Gardiner, *An Extraordinary Australian: Mary MacKillop: The Authorised Biography,* 34.
10. Mary MacKillop to Annie MacKillop, June 1st 1886.
11. Mary MacKillop to Donald MacKillop sj, June 17th 1886.
12. Mary MacKillop to Flora MacKillop, August 21st 1867.
13. Gardiner, *An Extraordinary Australian: Mary MacKillop: The Authorised Biography,* 100.
14. Gardiner, *An Extraordinary Australian: Mary MacKillop: The Authorised Biography,* 478.
15. Gardiner, *An Extraordinary Australian: Mary MacKillop: The Authorised Biography,* 480.

Young Australians: Journeying with Mary and Accepting the Challenge

Ann-Marie Gallagher

As we celebrate and acknowledge ten years since Mary MacKillop's beatification, we are reminded of the rich legacy she has given to all Australians. Her inspiration touched many in her life time and her memory will continue to do so for years to come. For young Australians we are reminded through her life story, that anything is possible if we allow ourselves to be open to the challenges and opportunities that our various communities provide.

Mary experienced many forms of community throughout her life and these influenced her. We need only look at her initial exposure to community in the family unit to gain a sense of her character. The eldest of eight children, born to Scottish immigrants, Alexander MacKillop and Flora MacDonald, Mary experienced impoverishment as a result of her father's inability to manage their finances and his unsuccessful attempts to provide for the family. This brought many struggles to the family and left Mary responsible for finding work in order to provide financially. In doing so she sacrificed much of her youth as she assumed responsibility for providing for the family. Mary expressed the experiences of her childhood in one of her letters, "My life as a child was one of sorrow… a most unhappy one".[1] Here we find her reflecting on the hardships she encountered, the reality of many families of our day.

It is obvious that Mary valued her family and was committed to supporting them to the best of her ability. Her example to the younger generation of today invites us to look at how we might support our own families in times of poverty, not only in the financial sense, but perhaps emotionally and spiritually as well. All too often we can neglect those closest to us because we can easily get caught up with other facets of our lives. Mary was dedicated to her family and took on the responsibility of meeting their needs. Her example provides us with a sense of what it means to be committed to our loved ones, regardless of our past experiences.

Further to being born into the family of the MacKillops and the MacDonalds, Mary Helen became a member of the Catholic community when her parents presented her to be baptized on February 28th 1842. From this moment on she would be part of a faith community which would impact on her life in ways beyond her imagination. Her passion for teaching led her together with counterpart, Father Julian Tenison Woods, to open a free Catholic school for all children in Penola. This in itself was a great achievement and provided a much needed service to those families who suffered from the extremes of poverty and isolation. She was meeting a basic need of the community in which she taught, and at the same time, was promoting the importance of an egalitarian society for all. This raises the question for us in the 21st Century, those who are the "school children" of today and are called to serve others.

Mary's enthusiasm and devotion towards the younger generation is noteworthy, in that she educated children regardless of their background. As a young adult herself she experienced a desire to meet the needs of those in the community she served. This led her to co-found the religious institute of the Sisters of Saint Joseph of the Sacred Heart in 1866. Mary did not let her age be a barrier in fulfilling her heart's desire and was consequently able to use her youth positively. This serves as a reminder to the younger generation of today that anything is possible, if we allow ourselves to be immersed in the opportunities that present themselves to us.

In establishing the Order she had a clear mission in mind. It was to bring hope, relief, encouragement and most importantly, an encounter of God's love to all Australians. In choosing the vocation of religious life she would be challenged by both clergy and laity; would be accused of things of which she was not guilty; and worst of all, be wrongfully excommunicated. The excommunication sentence was later lifted. In all of this we cannot help but be inspired by her because she never blamed those who brought her down in spite of their unjustified behaviour, but instead continued to love and see the goodness in them. Most importantly she took these challenges as opportunities to grow closer to her God who sustained her through it all. In a letter to her Sisters she said, "God will carry you safely through every struggle." This reflects her faithfulness and dependence on Him. Her strong belief in God's Providence enabled her to confront the difficulties with love and be assured that, "all in the end will be well."[2] For young Australians we can only sit in awesome wonder at how Mary applied herself to the circumstances that were presented to her. There is a big learning to be gained from this, in that we are able to recognise that we too can allow ourselves to be optimistic in our own situations and although we may feel burdened by a "death" experience, there will indeed be new life generated from it also.

Writing in 1873, Mary outlines the main premise of the motivation for the foundation of the Order, "The Institute of the Sisterhood of St Joseph of the Sacred Heart was established to meet the many wants of the Australian Colonies." She continued by saying, "It is an Australian who writes this, one brought up in the midst of many of the evils she tries to describe."[3] Here we find Mary revealing something of herself as a woman who was in touch with the needs of the nation (Australia being only a number of colonies at the time), and able to relate her own experiences of what it meant to live through the hardships. She could have entered another religious Order to fulfil her desire to serve God, but she knew she needed to do more than this so that the needs of the Australian people could be met.

Those who entered the Sisters of St Joseph were from different backgrounds and were classed as equals, unlike other religious Orders of the day who had choir and lay nuns. This was similar to that of her school students, with no preference given to pupils because of their financial or social status. Mary did not favour people because of their rank in society but rather she accepted and loved them as being equal in the eyes of God. All too often it is easy to get caught up in our modern consumerist world which is driven by greed, power and the need to control. When we look more closely at the behaviour and trends of people we see that many are only concerned with how much income they receive, how many shares they have on the stock market, which suburb they reside in and what sort of car is parked in the drive way. The message for us in all of this is to take a reality check of how we treat others in our own lives and how we would like to be treated ourselves. This comes down to the two Commandments given to us by Jesus himself when he said, "Love the Lord your God with all your heart, with all your soul, with all your mind, and with all your strength. The second most important commandment is to Love your neighbour as you love yourself" (Mk 12:30-31). Mary MacKillop was true to this and lived her life from the very core of what it meant to embrace people as she herself would like to be treated. Her example invites us to take a moment to reflect on how we interact with others and the importance of accepting people where they are in their lives.

It is evident that Mary placed a great value on every human being from all walks of life regardless of their position. She embraced all people who came from different faiths and cultural backgrounds such as friend Joanna Barr Smith who was a Protestant and Emanuel Solomon, a Jew who assisted her during her excommunication. Although an Australian by birth, Mary was proud of her Celtic origins and never lost sight of her rich heritage. She invites us to value the diversity of Australia today and the people who represent our multicultural society. In a letter to one of the Sisters her message is to "be kind to the poor foreigners. Remember I was a poor foreigner once and, as such was never laughed at or unkindly criticized".[4] In this we find Mary's sensitivity to those who are new to the nation and so desperately desire to make it their home. This message rings clear for us today, inviting us to be like Mary and embrace the "foreigners" with open arms. In particular we are reminded of those who have come to Australia in hope of building a better life for their families, such as the Sudanese, the East Timorese and others who seek refuge and asylum status. Mary promoted the human dignity of each person and desired to see their needs being accommodated. As Australians we are called to embody what Mary envisaged our nation to be, that is, a society which voices the right to justice for all.

One can only be inspired by the life of Mary and how she relied solely on her God to sustain her through the trials and tribulations. She did not have the resources which are so readily available to us today, instead she placed a great faith and trust in the Providence of God. She dedicated herself to promoting a sense of Christian community in all aspects of life and brought a sense of Christ's presence to those she encountered. In looking at her commitment to this, she encourages us to search for the way we can best live in relationship with God. The love of her "Spouse" was central to her life, and she was strengthened through him in embracing every situation presented to her. We can learn so much from how Mary related to her God as we belong to the same Christian faith which was integral to her life and one which requires us to also bear witness to the Gospel values. We are invited to respond to where God is in our own lives as we strive to be true to ourselves and give all we have to offer in using our gifts and talents.

Mary belonged to many communities in her life - as a member of the MacKillop family, as a Catholic, as a Sister of Saint Joseph and as an Australian. As young adults we each walk different journeys but what unites us is the common foundation of searching for what we really desire in life so that we can bring life to others. Mary's example leaves us asking ourselves such questions as: how do we relate to our own family, friends, colleagues and those we meet? How do we respond to others and bring out the positives in each of our communities? This is something upon which to reflect.

For young Australians and those young at heart, we need to apply ourselves to the common good of our nation and be strengthened by the vision which Mary had in her life mission. She gives us a sense of hope as we strive to live in this modern world of ours and encourages us to trust in God's Providence in the various communities to which we belong. Wherever we are we can live in God's awesome presence in our lives and so bring that Presence to the lives of others.

Mary's spirit will continue to radiate in our precious country and in the places we visit if we allow ourselves to be like her and see the inherent goodness in all things and encounter all situations with love. Her life provides a blueprint upon which to pattern our thoughts, our motivation for our actions, and how we relate with all life around us. Mary stood up for what she believed in, regardless of the many hardships she encountered and was committed to the promotion of justice for all. It is in the ordinariness of her life that we are challenged, inspired and motivated in the way we relate to God, our family and friends, and the rest of society. Mary dared to be different and for this reason she encourages each of us to take up the challenge. She leaves us with one final thought to contemplate, "Have courage and patience and God will help you in all things."[5]

Endnotes

1 Mary MacKillop to Monsignor Kirby, Ascension Thursday, 1873.
2 Mary MacKillop to Julian Tenison Woods, November 20th 1870.
3 Mary MacKillop, *Necessity for the Institute,* August 1873. Resource Material from the Archives of the Sisters of St Joseph of the Sacred Heart, Issue No. 3, January 1980, 49.
4 Thorpe, Osmund, CP. *Mary MacKillop.* Revised with endnotes, (Surry Hills, Sydney: The Generalate, Sisters of St Joseph of the Sacred Heart, Sydney, 1994), 150.
5 Mary MacKillop to Sister M. Bonaventure, August 15th 1899.

Blessed Mary MacKillop: A Saint of Ordinariness

Joan Goodwin rsj

Pope John Paul II's words to the people of Australia as he left the Beatification ceremony of Mary MacKillop, were:

> Think of Blessed Mary MacKillop and learn from her to be a gift of love and compassion for one another, for all Australia and for the whole world.

Father Paul Gardiner in writing of Blessed Mary MacKillop commented:

> The Institute was a great undertaking requiring thinking and organisation, planning and governing but she was never absorbed in such matters. She did not lose touch with the people with whom the Institute was working. She governed from the kitchen, the washhouse, the chicken yard, the hospital bed side, the prison cell, the schoolroom, the slums or wherever her Sisters or those dependent on them were to be found.[1]

After Blessed Mary MacKillop's death many of the Sisters close to her and companions recorded incidents that revealed her doing ordinary things extraordinarily well. Almost as one voice they spoke of her kindness, charity, goodness, her humility. She was always bright and cheerful and had a wonderful sense of humour. The following stories are their recollections.[2]

Mary was always concerned about each Sister's well-being. When in New Zealand she was sent with two young Sisters to Arrowtown as Little Sister.[3] As they were engaged in teaching she willingly and cheerfully undertook the cooking and general housework. She delighted in having a tasty lunch ready for them when they returned from school. One day she was given some fish and her first attempt at cooking it ended in disaster with the fish falling to pieces. She sought the advice of the lady next door who came and gave her a cooking lesson so she was able to present a beautifully cooked meal when the Sisters returned to the Convent. She took her share in washing the dishes, sweeping, dusting and gardening, in fact she lent a hand in everything that had to be done. The Sisters felt a little shy at first living in a small community with the Foundress, but her simplicity and loving sympathy soon dispelled all fear and they felt in her presence as freely as they would have been with their Novitiate companions. She impressed on them the need to create a bright, cheerful atmosphere. Mary herself was noted for her bright cheerful smile and sweet affable manner especially to anyone in trouble.

Mary visited Port Chalmers, New Zealand, when it was first established. The Sisters discovered on returning from school that Mary, with the help of two postulants, had washed all the quilt covers and found her distressed that she hadn't got them all on the line before they returned. When staying at Waimate the Sisters were preparing the children for their First Holy Communion. On the first day Mary noticed a very poor, ragged boy in the group and fearing insults from the other children, Mary asked if she could take the child aside and prepare him for his First Holy Communion. This she did and he rejoined the group on First Holy Communion Day in a beautiful suit that Mary had purchased from her meagre funds, lovingly attaching his medal to the lapel. Mary's keen eye always sought out the less fortunate and if she couldn't visit the family, she would send her Sisters to see into the family's needs. A family had lost a small child in death and Mary sent two Sisters to visit them, giving them a sovereign to leave on the dressing-table.

After Mary's death a Sister was passing a Pawnshop when she noticed a large picture in the window of Mary MacKillop. She went in to enquire and discovered the picture was not for sale. The owner told her, "That kind and holy nun saved my wife and me from starvation. She came to us in our direst need and brought food and clothing. She obtained for me a good position in a warehouse and from that time we prospered." He remarked, "we are not even Catholics."

When the Sisters had the House of Providence in the Rocks area of Sydney, Mary's delight was to wait on the poor men who had spent the night in the park. They came to the Providence in the morning and the Sisters provided breakfast. When at home, Mary would be found with sleeves rolled up making sandwiches with the Novices. The food must always be served with a winning smile and a kindly word was her advice to those who served the poor.

The children at the Providence were her great concern. When she moved to North Sydney she kept in touch and when her Sisters reported a serious out break of an eye complaint Mary had the children moved to North Sydney and she took charge of their care. She had her bed removed from the main building to a room near the children so she could attend to them during the night. She nursed them and when all were well saw to their return to the Providence. In March 1887, Mary supervised twenty two boys from the Providence beginning a new life at Kincumber. Cardinal Moran had given her the property as he believed it was a more suitable place to bring up children. Mary hoped that in their new surroundings the boys would be able to learn trades that would fit them to work in the world. Kincumber was very dear to her heart and she visited as often as possible.

On April 21st 1899 she received word that one of the boys from Kincumber, Philip O'Brien, was close to death. He had made a request to see Mother Mary. Mary was in Sydney so she caught the first available steam train to Woy Woy. By the time she reached the wharf where she was to meet the boys the weather had changed. The boys were to meet her here and row her across the Brisbane Waters. This was a job where there were plenty of volunteers as oarsmen. Their reward was the sweets Mary carried in her pocket. The weather had turned foul and it was too dangerous for the boys to row across. One of the local Bourke boys offered to take her across. It was a terrible trip, the howling wind and driving rain making the crossing difficult. She was drenched by the rain and the water splashing the side of the boat. She knew Philip needed her so the weather wouldn't stop her. On entering Philip's room she heard a weak voice say, "I knew you would come, Mother Mary." Mary stayed with Philip until he died in the early hours of the morning and then attended to his funeral arrangements as there was no priest available. During the burial service a storm broke out. Later the boys were asked if they were frightened and their reply was, "No, Mother Mary was with us."

Mary was visiting Kincumber on another occasion when she heard a knock at her door. She called out, "Come in" and a small boy appeared before her. She could tell by the look on his face he was in trouble. Upon enquiring she was told that he had stolen a bun from the bakery. Mary asked him if he was hungry and he replied, "Yes Mother." "Well go and tell Sister to give you two buns." A very relieved, happy boy skipped out of the room that day. Mary has recorded in her diary many events and visits from the boys at Kincumber and you will find, "Boys visited today, gave us a concert." "Boys here today, took them on a picnic to Mosman." "Boys stayed overnight."

Many years after Mary's death the Sisters and boys sought Mary's intercession in their time of need. One particular time was when two of the boys were dying from Diphtheria. The doctor had said that there was nothing that could be done for them and they would most likely die during the night. The Sisters and boys gathered in the Chapel and prayed to Mary. Later in the night the boys fell into a peaceful sleep and awoke the next day well on the way to recovery.

The sick it can be said had a "key" to Mary's heart. If her Sisters were sick she did everything possible to make them comfortable. When a sick Sister was brought down from the country Mary insisted that she be given her bed. She slept on a mattress in the corner of the room partitioned by a draught screen. Under Mary's care the Sister improved and Mary said she was to have meat, even on Friday and to take the stimulants the Doctor ordered. The Sister protested but Mary's answer was, "There is no pledge in the Convent and obedience is better than sacrifice."

Distance was no impediment for Mary when there was a need for her presence. One of her Sisters was badly injured when putting out a crude kerosene lamp after evening devotions in the Church. The lamp exploded and the Sister was engulfed in flames. She lingered for several days in great agony and kept asking for Mary. Mary set out at once for Port Augusta. There was no boat for a week so she took the train to Mt Remarkable where it terminated. Mary made a fruitless effort to get driven further and made a final plea in the Hotel where she said, "Gentlemen, my Sister is dying at Port Augusta and is asking for me. If I could borrow a horse I could ride there." The result was that two or three men jumped up, got a pair of horses and a buggy and drove her that afternoon. Mary arrived in time to console her dying Sister.

The care of the sick extended to anyone in need. Sister Rose Lehane recounted the story of her mother being very ill and being unable to go to her. Mary went herself, stayed all night with the sick woman, attending to her needs and then the next morning cooked breakfast for those in the house before she returned to the Convent. In the early days at Kensington a poor woman was very ill. Mary sent two Sisters to nurse her and they remained in the house until the patient was fully recovered.

One day, Mary with a companion set out to visit an elderly sick gentleman. She hadn't gone far when she remarked to her companion that they had nothing to take to him. She felt in her pocket and found a penny. At a shop nearby Mary purchased a pennyworth of sweets. The shop-keeper gave her a generous supply. The old man was delighted with the gift and Mary's companion remarked, "You would think Mary had given him a five pound note!"

Mary inculcated the greatest respect and veneration for priests and would tolerate nothing to the contrary in the Sisters. She hated to refuse a request for Sisters, especially if the place was poor. She never saw a priest in need without helping in some way. Mary once met a priest who had developed consumption and was obliged himself to supply the bread and wine for his Masses. Mary learnt he had no means to do this so she supplied them out of her own meagre finance.

A priest who had been bitterly opposed to the Sisters was silenced by the Bishop. He had a stroke and was being cared for by some women. When Mary heard of this she rented a cottage and had him removed there. She sent two Sisters to look after him. They cooked and washed for him, tended and nursed him. Mary had him reconciled with his Bishop and the Sisters looked after him until his death, which was a holy, happy and peaceful one. Many priests knew the "motherly" care of this woman in their time of need.

Those in need who encountered Mary's generosity were numerous. A daughter who was looking after her frail, sick father was having difficulties in paying the rent. Mary paid the rent for a long period while they stood in need of it. Another family, because they were unable to pay their debts were visited by the bailiffs, who took all their possessions including their furniture. The next day Mary went into the city and purchased beds and other necessities for the family. Later on when the family was able to pay their way, they repaid Mary but she did not expect any return. Even the shoes on Mary's feet weren't safe. Mary noticed that Sr Kieran's shoes were worn and broken and she called to her, "Sister, take these shoes of mine, your old ones will do me very well."

Mary heard of a family newly arrived on an immigrant ship. The mother was very sick and the family was in want. Mary asked the Sisters if they had any clothing they could spare and took it to them. She visited the mother in hospital but despite all care she died, leaving behind four orphaned children. Mary took the children to the House of Providence and there they were cared for until they were able to leave and work for themselves.

Mary had an extra-ordinary gift to forgive. One day as she was about to catch the ferry at Circular Quay she noticed in the crowd an old, ragged, crippled man. The face was very familiar. It was Mr Cusack her old headmaster of Portland days. Mary had lost her job through his dishonesty. Mary could see he was in need and went over to him and offered to help him.

On another occasion a woman who professed friendship for the Sisters, and Mary in particular, turned against her and did all she could to injure her. Some time later the woman fell on difficult times and came to Mary for help. Her daughter was suffering from a mental complaint and she was penniless. Mary took the daughter and placed her in the care of her Sisters and gave the woman money on a number of occasions to get her back on her feet.

Sometimes Mary was compelled to reprimand wrong doers but it was done in a kind, motherly way that the one corrected would feel as a child, who knows all would be forgiven and forgotten and a new kind of love established.

Mary excelled in charity. Sr Ethelburg, Mary's nurse said:

> I never knew her to speak an unkind word to anybody. Neither would she permit any Sister to do so in her hearing. She was very forgiving. One day I witnessed an instance of this, and I said to her, 'Mother, how is it that you are so ready to forgive those who give you pain and trouble?'
>
> Her reply to me was, 'My child, as I hope to be forgiven, so do I forgive.'

Sr Eulalie recalls a time when she saw an instance of Mary's supernatural charity in the case of a Sister who had been disloyal and wronged her. Mary treated the Sister with great kindness and showed that she still had confidence in her. Mary never gave a correction in anger nor would she ever reprimand in an overbearing manner. Sr Irene told of a time when Mary sent for her:

> 'Do you want me, Mother?' she asked.

'Yes dear.' was the answer.
'I want to beg your pardon for the impatient way I spoke to you when you came to me this morning. I fear I have given you pain and I am sorry for having done so.'
Mary may have felt irritable and thought she had betrayed it in her words or manner, but I had no knowledge of it and told her so for she had been most gentle and kind to me.

Equality was an essential element in the Sisterhood of St Joseph. Mary lived this to the full never considering herself greater than the humblest Novice. When the Sisters first took up residence in Sydney they had no beds and slept on a mattress on the floor. Mary like the rest slept on the floor. Her remark was, "It is better than the hard wood of the Cross on which the Lord was suspended by the nails." When Mary was making the first foundation at Numurkah in Victoria she remained with the Sisters for a few weeks. On washing mornings she would go into the kitchen and prepare the breakfast for the Sisters. In the days when butter was regarded as a luxury, a supply was placed near Mary's place at the table. Mary at once passed it on and gave orders that in future no butter was to be served to her unless there was sufficient for everybody.

Mary attended an annual concert at Granville in Sydney. While the Sisters were engaged in looking after the different items Mary kept the children interested, so they could be easily found for their items. Mary's secret was the lollies in her pocket. The morning after the concert, as there was no Mass, she told the Sisters to have a sleep in and she brought to each Sister a cup of tea. When on Visitation to the Convents Mary would not allow any fuss to be made or anything special got for her, but she enjoyed the common fare with her Sisters. One day when Sr Bride was assisting in the kitchen, she mistakenly sent a dessert to the infirmary that was meant for Mary. The Cook was very annoyed and sent her to beg Mary's pardon. Mary commended her for what she had done and told her she was a good child and said the sick Sisters needed it much more than she did.

When Mary moved the Novitiate to Dean Kenny's house in North Sydney she and the five novices depended on supplies from the Providence and sometimes these were not forthcoming. Bread and dripping would often form the main meal. Never a murmur was heard from Mary's lips, only a thanksgiving that Jesus had allowed them to share His poverty. She would tell her novices, "This is a sure sign that God loves us and that the Institute will prosper." Years later some novices were sent to her by the Novice Mistress who had caught them cooking eggs they had found in the garden. Mary told them to sit down on the floor and eat the eggs. She told them how hard she had found it to get enough food for them, and how the Sisters went to bed sometimes hungry in the early days of the Congregation. Mary had them in tears but she embraced them and sent them off without a penance but with a greater love for her.

Mary opened a Boarding School in one of the Sydney suburbs. After it was furnished there was no money left. The only money coming in was the money from the fourteen boarders, so they could hardly make a living. The house was comfortable but Mary said there was one thing missing – a crib for Christmas. Mary had said to the Superior, "It's near Christmas and I don't think I'll be happy till I get a crib." The Superior tried to get Mary to put the idea out of her head as there was no money for one. Mary was not content, "I'll write and ask the price of a crib." A week later a crib, packed in a box was brought to the door of the Convent. The Sisters were very concerned. "What are we going to do with it?" they asked. Mary said, "I'll unpack it." This she did and set it up beside the altar. The cost of the crib was forty pounds and they had no money to pay for it. Mary said, "Never mind. St Joseph has sent it and he will send the money too." Later a gentleman came to inspect the place and the children's work. He was very pleased and satisfied with what he saw. Before leaving he handed Mary an envelope which she placed in her pocket with other letters. Later in the day she sat down to read the letters, and on opening the gentleman's letter she discovered a cheque for forty pounds. What a delighted Mary! St Joseph had not let her down. Mary's words to her Sisters were, "I told you St Joseph would send the money for the crib."

When the Sisters were in Queensland there was a day when they had no food. Mary placed the statue of St Joseph in the window asking him to provide some food. A lady was out shopping and a thought passed through her mind that the Sisters might not have anything to eat. She purchased some provisions and took them around to the Sisters. Her gift was the answer to prayer. This lady kept up this practice as long as the Sisters were in that part of Brisbane.

Mary needed the permission of Cardinal Moran on an undertaking involving some expense. She took Sr Ildephonsus with her as companion to see the Cardinal. The Cardinal appeared to be dubious of its success and asked Mary what expectations she had. "I trust in Divine Providence, Your Eminence," she replied. The Cardinal smiled and rejoined, "I think you presume too much on Divine Providence." "He has never failed me yet," was Mary's answer.

In the early days at North Sydney there was a wooden structure of two rooms and an old stone building behind. There was no space and when the paddock at the back was to be sold, Mary set everyone praying that she might secure it. She had no money and her Sisters didn't share her simple faith and thought their prayers useless regarding the block of land. On the morning of the sale Mary sent a Novice to tell the owner of the land that the Sisters wanted to buy it but they were not well off and asked if the price could not be too high. The Novice didn't like the task but obeyed. The gentleman saw how confused the Novice was but listened attentively and then sat back and roared laughing. He said, "What beautiful simplicity! Where does this woman come from?" When he found out Mary was of Scottish descent, he told the Novice that he was too and said, "I hope your Mother Mary gets this land." Mary did get the land and reproved the Sisters for their want of faith and trust.

One evening at recreation Mary told this story about when she was in Italy. She had paid her fare to a certain town but didn't know what she was going to do when she got there as she had completely run out of money. She pondered and prayed for help. "An elderly grey-headed man, not so tall but very venerable looking, came up to me and presented me with all the money I needed until some arrived from Australia." She firmly believed it was St Joseph as he became lost to her view and everything happened so suddenly that Mary did not know who he was or where he came from.

Mary's confidence in God was remarkable. She once said, "When I want something very much, I thank God beforehand, for I feel He will certainly grant what He has already been thanked for."

From childhood days Mary had a great love of animals. She was an excellent horsewoman and had no fear when riding the horse, Donkey, whom Donald, her brother, described as, "a brute, known for bolting." When on the farm her Grandpa McDonald had given her a cow which later had a calf that Mary called, Blorac. One day she came home to discover that her father had sold off some calves and amongst them was her pet, Blorac. She quickly found out who had purchased him and as there was no money in the family to buy him back she set out for Grandpa MacKillop's farm to see if he could give her the money. Her Grandpa seeing her so distressed gave her the money and she was able to purchase the calf.

Among the Sisters' reminiscences there are stories of Mary's love for animals and concern for their welfare. Two of her Sisters recounted this tale:

> They were travelling with Mary on a Cobb and Co Coach. It was a very hot day and the coach had its full complement of passengers. They came to a very steep hill and Mary thought it was too much for the horses. The three of them got out of the coach, much against the will of the other two Sisters. The hill was very long and steep, and to make matters worse she asked them to join in the Rosary for the driver. He was a very unpleasant man who was swearing at his horses most of the time. Mary walked to the top of the hill in the best of spirits and then provided the driver with some refreshments.

On another occasion, Mary was on Visitation to one of the convents. When the Sisters came home from school they couldn't get into the Convent. They could see Mary busy inside but she wouldn't let them in. When she finally opened the door they discovered that she had been making a bed for the cat that was sick and had been mewing about her. At another time there was a dog tied up outside in the rain. Looking out the window Mary noticed the dog and asked one of the Sisters if she would go and let the dog off the chain and find it some shelter.

During the last years of her life she had as companion a little dog called 'Bengi'. One evening she asked Sr Colette to feed it. Sr Colette collected the dog's dish and placed the food in it. Mary had noticed that she had placed the food in a dirty dish and reprimanded Sister. Sr Colette made sure the dish was clean when she fed the dog in the future.

Mary's Sisters described her as kind and gentle. She had a charming manner, a personality that drew people to her. She had only to smile and a gentleman would get her a chair, or a lady would offer her a rug or a book, children would be drawn to her and in a few moments she would be at home with everyone. She had a hearty laugh and was always bright and cheerful. When the holidays came she would send her Sisters off saying, "Now, my dear children, enjoy yourselves thoroughly, have as much fun as possible but don't neglect your prayers." Then she would add, "And keep a diary so that I can have fun afterwards."

After Dr O'Reily was consecrated Bishop of Port Augusta in St Mary's Cathedral he came to North Sydney to perform the ceremony of Profession for two Novices. After the ceremony was over he left his Bishop's robes in the sacristy while he went to breakfast with the other priests. The Sacristan, a bright young Novice, on seeing the beautiful robe, put it on and paraded along the verandah of the novitiate with another novice as train-bearer. When she returned to the sacristy who should walk in after her but Mary and Father Michael Kelly. When they saw the picture they took to a fit of laughing. The tale was told to the clerics inside, one of whom came and knelt at the Novice's feet for a blessing. The Bishop too enjoyed the fun. This little incident of the purple robes was not forgotten.

During the last years of Mary's life she was confined to a wheel chair. Those close to her were greatly edified by her patience, especially when her sufferings seemed almost unbearable. Whenever anyone remarked on this she would smile and say, "My dear child, it is nothing compared to what our dear Lord suffered for us. We must bear our crosses patiently." The Novices acted as Mary's "ponies" and would lift her chair into the chapel. She was often very ill and seemed in great pain; even the slightest jolt of the chair caused suffering but her lips moved in constant prayer and no matter how ill she always had a gracious smile of thanks to her "ponies". Throughout her illness she was very thoughtful for the Sisters on night duty and she would see that they had warm clothing and she insisted on their having plenty of rest.

Paul Keating, Prime Minister at the time of Mary's Beatification, said:

> The beatification of Mary MacKillop rings with significance for all Australians. The qualities she embodied - openness and tolerance, courage, persistence, faith and care for others are qualities for individuals, communities and nations to live by. We will serve Australia well if we allow the values which inspired and guided Mary MacKillop's work to inspire and guide our own.[4]

May this "Ordinary Woman" be our inspiration as we reflect on these words of Pope John Paul 11 at Mary's beatification:

God took this daughter of your land and made her a sign of spiritual greatness, a model of personal holiness and of service to the common good, to be contemplated and admired by all the people. Mary MacKillop's faith and commitment have become part of your Australian heritage, a faith immersed in the knowledge of God's hope, imbued with the presence of Christ, a love expressed by the selflessness of a sincere and undivided heart. Let her stir up in each of you the desire to be God's own handiwork.

Endnotes

1 Paul Gardiner, Cause of Canonisation of the Servant of God Mary of the Cross MacKillop (1842-1909), Foundress of the Australian Sisters of St Joseph of the Sacred Heart, Positio Super Virtutibus, Rome, 1989, Congregation for the Causes of the Saints. Vol 3, 29.

2 A Collection of Reminiscences of Mary MacKillop by some early Sisters. Mary MacKillop Archives, 9 Mount St, North Sydney, NSW.

3 "Little Sister" was the name give to the Sister in charge of the community.

4 Parliamentary Hansard, February 2nd 1995, 357.

The Unknown Journey

Sue and Leo Kane

She caught our eye in a little gallery we were browsing in one day last year. A whimsical, gentle - faced lady in a painting called simply *Unknown Journey*. Maybe it was the title that drew us in, but whatever the attraction, she now holds pride of place on the wall at home. Oddly enough, she inspires a jolt of recognition. Her thoughtful face, with its haunting, "I've seen a lot of life" eyes, tells of fullness of experience. The leaf that wafts gently, just beyond the reach of her outstretched hand, suggests a future that is elusive. She is calm, but diffident. She is us.

At some level, she reminds us that life is never quite the journey we think it's going to be. We've certainly found that to be true in our own experience. On another wall we have a different picture, one of Mary MacKillop. It shows her in three stages of her life, looking serenely to the past, the present and the future. It too suggests a journey through phases we all recognize. We've come to the conclusion that these two women share a common perspective. Certainly, as we look back over the paths we've travelled, we take inspiration and comfort from Mary MacKillop's journey. In the story of her life we find our story too, a gradual "getting of wisdom", though admittedly ours is a somewhat "pale" version of her growth in insight. Nevertheless, there are common human bonds that link us to her, as much as to the lady in our painting. Call it the human journey, if you will.

Like her, we began our journey unaware of the great changes, both inner and outer, that were to come. We were blessed then with the enthusiasm and certainty of youth. Those were simple days, when our spiritual backpacks contained little more than the Ten Commandments of God and the Six Commandments of the Church! There were plenty of road maps to tell us how to steer clear of such detours as sin, especially mortal sin. Roadside "billboards" reminded us constantly that missing Mass on Sundays and eating meat on Fridays were pitfalls to be avoided at all costs. Holy Communion was our food for the journey. However, woe betide if we broke the midnight fast by swallowing water while cleaning our teeth, and still went to communion. The road we knew then was straight and narrow, but the God to whom it led us was, for the most part, a source of fear, a punitive God. Nevertheless, we accepted and followed the road map that had been designed for us. Maybe we replaced the reality of faith with the illusion of certitude. For a while at least, it was sufficient. The resilience of youth kicked in. As we headed confidently towards the future, we didn't realise how blinkered we were.

Perhaps it was that we failed to notice that our personal life story and our faith story were taking us on two different journeys. Our spirituality separated the two, divorcing the sacred from the secular, the spiritual from the human. It lacked awareness of the way spirituality comes from within, from an inner journey where we could come to really know ourselves and the direction God was inviting us to go. It was so easy to emphasise the "otherness" of a God hidden in the tabernacle and fail to see God in the whole of life.

Mary MacKillop, though coming from the same Church subculture, was able to transcend it, and therein lay the beginnings of her greatness. Such was her spiritual insight that her faith journey became intrinsically her own personal human journey. She was able to find the treasure that lay hidden in the field of her own experience. While fellow travellers were busy avoiding demerit points, she was able to follow the sign posts that led to her love story with a God of Unconditional Love. Thus, she could state, often, and with great conviction, that "God is all Goodness and Love". Like all of us, she couldn't always see the road ahead, and at times did not know where the next step might lead. The thing she did know for sure was that she had discovered and experienced a love that cast out fear. This was enough to sustain her, although she knew what it was to feel vulnerable and helpless and even, at times, on the brink of despair. She writes, as she looks back over the years, of her encounter with the Mystery, "With this burning appeal of the Sacred Heart of Jesus came such a rushing of longing desire on my part to be Its lover...It deigned to raise me to It. Its love makes suffering sweet."[1] Clearly she did not feel she had to make the journey alone. The path led she knew not where, but her delight in encountering Jesus, and his love for her gave her the strength to follow him into the unknown. In this she never wavered.

She wrote, "When storms rage, when persecutions or dangers threaten, I quietly creep into its deep abyss, and securely sheltered there, my soul is in peace, though my body is tossed upon the stormy waves of a cold and selfish world."[2] Her conviction that a God of Unconditional Love went with her on the journey meant that she could empty her backpack of much that was unnecessary. We, on the other hand, being less discerning travellers, would often trudge along for days, weeks, years, feeling alone, forgetful of the Mystery, a Loving Divine Presence Who is always there for us. Needless to say, we sometimes lost our way. Gradually, our experiences along the road, and the fragility we found within ourselves, opened us up to truths she had internalised early on. Time and again in her letters to her mother (and others) she refers to her "good God", and assures her that she often loves "to think upon God's mysterious ways."[3] In her first letter from Scotland she reminds the Sisters "an ever-watchful Providence is guiding all things to our mutual good."[4]

Bishop Geoffrey Robinson, a fellow traveller, describes what it is like to try to lead a spiritual life without this relationship. "The truths of faith will become lifeless, the norms of living will be burdensome tasks and the worship will be empty."[5] Faith, then, as Mary discovered, has its foundation in a relationship with a God of Mystery and Unconditional Love.

So…the road stretched away before her, and Mary MacKillop had an inkling of the dispossession it would demand of her, but she never tried to walk it alone. She understood that the initiative was not with her, but with the One who guided her. She confides in her mother, "Is it not a great and strange work in which I am a poor worker. Great things are done in it but not by me. I am only a wondering looker-on."[6] It was not what she was doing, but what was to be done through her, that mattered. While she explored the path ahead, looking for God, it was really God who found her, and so she could have said, in the words of the poet, that "the paths of life have found us and we are led through into marvellous light."[7] The being "led" is crucial. Here we are, still journeying, still stumbling, and still trying to figure out what it is that holds and binds us. For we can't really go where we are "led" unless we understand what stifles our freedom.

Mary could take the fast lane because she knew that she was accompanied at all times by a God of Unconditional Love. The wisdom into which she grew along the way, her own process of continuing conversion, convinced her of this more and more. The God she went with was not a God of soft love, but One who challenged her in the way of the cross and who was always with her – no matter what! The One who held the lantern to light her way was not removed from life, not an imagined God of her own making, like a kind, old man who lived in the sky, but the Great Loving Reality behind the little realities of each day. Mary understood that as daily happenings unfolded, they revealed something about that other, deeper journey which we all travel. She never spoke of an authoritarian, legalistic God. Her spirituality was always in touch with life and the Mystery of life with all its ambiguity and suffering, and often, lack of resolution.

We now understand, at this point in our own journey, that we never do finally arrive, but we are always arriving - even if only in spurts, like the poet James McAuley:

> Bored in my self-prison,
> I doubt uneasily;
> But the times I get out,
> I know you have risen.[8]

It has so often been within the spaces of our lives that revelation has come! To be "Between Towns",[9] that is, to be nowhere in particular, can, ironically, be the dislocation that opens the way to grace. All that we have is the present moment, and we must live that fully, trusting and letting go, experiencing whatever the journey brings, rather than looking to the destination.

It's a bit confronting to realise that, because we take ourselves wherever we go, the journey inevitably brings us back to the truth of who we are. We must face the folly and nobility of our own humanity. Mary could accept this, and still cast herself into the mysterious but loving arms of her God on the unknown journey that we all have to travel.

It's not easy to look within ourselves, as the journey demands. Is there still a niggling residue in there of the desire to be perfect? Many of us set out burdened by this expectation. Gradually it dawned that we don't grow spiritually by looking for something "out there", to be someone we *ought* to be – the good spouse, the perfect parent, the always-available Good Samaritan. Hopefully, life has taught us not to fall into the trap of being governed by "oughts". (Spiritual writers refer to this as the "hardening of the oughteries").

Do the signposts point us down the track of becoming the person we think we should be, rather than the person God calls us to be? This false spirituality involves control and a lack of openness. Mary saw it for what it was, and honestly analysed her own situation. "I may indeed be mistaken; I may think that I have done God's will and all the while have been following my own."[10] She understood that we can put ourselves at the centre, rather than allowing God to take the driver's seat. It can be so tempting to become the back seat driver, full of suggestions and theories about how the journey could be better negotiated! Maybe the driver just wants us to rest easy and trust?

Certainly, in Mary's spirituality her good God was at the centre, and she "did not surrender to some lesser version of herself."[11] She was always open to what was asked of her. Her great desire was to respond in love and generosity. Much of this came from her close relationship with her mother, whom she regarded as her "Mistress of Novices".[12] She wrote, "You used to tell me to love the Will of God - and to submit to it in all things. Your words still often ring in my ears."[13]

Her spirituality may sound simple, but it's not so easy, especially for us as spouses or parents in today's complex, western world. We tend to get hooked on speed as the road signs urge us to go ever faster, to "put our foot on the gas" in order to keep up. The car stereo pounds out a message that we need a functional, controlling, assertive approach to life. It's easy to get caught up with wanting to drive a limo, rather than being happy with a VeeDub. We must take time, as we travel along, to be open, reflective and relational with our spouse, our children and our God. Do we at times believe we always need to be in control, making decisions about the many problems that crop up in a working family? It's so easy for us to put God in the glove box somewhere out of sight and fail to be open to the Transcendent Mystery in our lives. Speed humps that slow us down could well be a blessing in disguise! They give us time to stop and think about the many different hands dealt to us each day. It's hard when our children embark on their own unknown journeys, especially the roller coaster road of adolescence, a road we need to travel with them. Sometimes, alas, they might even want to get out of the car and hitch hike! But Mary reminds us that we find God, not in the hand that we'd like to get, but in the hand we're actually dealt each moment. In Mary's words, "Believe me, an ever-watchful Providence is guiding all things to our mutual good."[14] So, maybe we hoped for a Speedy Gonzalez and we ended up with Mr Magoo. No matter. Experience has taught us that being grounded in everyday realities will set us on an authentic spiritual path. Mary captured the essence of this, with both its simplicity and complexity.

Geoffrey Robinson writes:

> God didn't create us haphazardly. He made each of us for a purpose and He is determined that we accomplish that purpose. He does need, however, our co-operation and when we give him our goodwill and open our hearts to Him (which is really all we have to offer) he sets in motion all the machinery we need to fulfil the task He has planned for us.[15]

Even our everyday journeys can have a way of confronting us with unexpected and challenging situations. We still enjoy the precious memory of the time we boarded a train, with two toddlers, and then discovered that we'd be facing backwards for the whole fourteen hour trip! There were other times, such as when our car broke down on a country road, the kids were carsick, we had a minor accident, lost our way, found ourselves seriously delayed, arrived at a crossroads and couldn't decide which way to go…. all a mirror of life really, and showing us how difficult it can be to control what happens. But when the smooth bitumen gives way to a gravel road, as it does in all of our lives, we know it's time for a reality check. The road will take us to our shadow side. Every journey we make, if we attend to what is happening, has an inner component. And going within ourselves honestly will inevitably confront us with our own lack, the brokenness we all share. Mary was not afraid of this. She could see that it had the potential to become a source of blessing, for it could point in the direction of radical dependence on God. In his intolerance and hypocrisy the Pharisee couldn't begin the first step of the journey. Not so the Publican. He recognised and owned his shadow side. It was an essential part of his relationship with God. Mary was at ease with the truth of this. Her advice to "never expect perfection and bear gently with defects"[16] shows how compassion for fellow travellers is often born out of acceptance of one's own limitation. Self knowledge leads to a puncturing of the heart when one meets fragility and vulnerability in another.

The journey led Mary to know and own her shadow side. She reveals herself in a letter to Fr Woods:

> Will you pray that, if it please God, I may have a little more

> confidence than I have got in other fellow creatures around me. All seems false and I am tempted to think everyone is an enemy. Whilst my sisters think I am full of charity, my mind is full of poison, and everything, thank God, is a trouble and a cross.[17]

Coasting along cheerfully for the whole trip is not an option for anyone, not even a saint! This has thrown quite a bit of light on our own struggles! We've had to think, long and hard, about our need to refocus. For the journey thus far has shown that there is an element of surprise in God's dealing with us. Noel Rowe's poem "The Structure of the Real" aptly captures this:

> There was a time, too, when expecting stones, a crowd
> got instead some bread and fish. I heard a thief steal
> his way back to paradise. The structure of the real
> is mercy. Having seen so many reversals,
> I should have known he would test his muscles
> on the stone, and walk away from the dazed
> grave, leaving its mouth open and amazed.[18]

In the world's terms, much of Mary's life seemed absurd, for her living into the Cross exemplified failure. Her journey was laden with paradox. The normal standards of success counted, in the end, for nothing. Hers was the poverty of lack of certitude, reflected in her admission to one of her Sisters, "I am not a moment sure of myself."[19] There were times when she was even tempted "to fly from you all."[20] She learned, as we all do, that the journey of life is spiral rather than linear, in that, as we noted earlier, it brings us back to the truth of who we are. To truly live the human journey, we have found, is to come to know, in the depths of one's being, the truth of T.S.Eliot's insight that:

> We shall not cease from exploration
> and the end of all our exploring
> shall be to arrive where we started
> and know the place for the first time.[21]

There are many "small deaths" along the way, calling us to be compassionate with ourselves. We need to remember that falling down and getting up again is part of the journey. Exploring our shadow side isn't a time for an analytical, negative introspective examination of conscience leading to shame and self-destruction. Rather, it's an occasion for personal growth and a meeting place with the Loving Gracious Presence. When we feel we're just about running on empty, our shadow side can be our greatest treasure. It tells us how much we need this Loving Divine Presence in our lives. That is what it meant for Mary, "I do want with all my heart to be what God wants me to be."[22] When we face ourselves and submit to the truth of who we are, rather than pursue the illusion of what we are not, then "we will know the truth, and it will set us free" (John 8:32). The shadow side can provide us with the opportunity to be more response-able, to get out of the ego and into our real self, the person God calls us to be in love and service of others. Usually it's in our companions on the journey, especially our spouse and children, where God is disguised, waiting to meet us around each bend - if we stay alert!

Mary, no stranger to negative feelings, uncertainty, doubts and helplessness, was not a mere do-gooder, but one who walked into suffering through self-emptying. Every so often she "cried herself to sleep. ......weary of the struggle and felt so completely alone."[23]

And she could acknowledge that "there are times when the effort is too much and I break down and am quite helpless".[24] Hers is the story of each one of us if we are prepared to look within and know ourselves better. Her whole being was fully engaged in the journey she was on. She did not flinch from clasping "to her soul the sacred illness."[25] We all know this aspect of the journey intimately, for it is our way of the cross. For Jesus, as for Mary and for us, there was no miraculous deliverance from the painful path. The death in life mystery resonates universally.

In the isolation and ambiguity of it all Mary, wounded as she felt, chose still to respond in an unwavering trust that said "yes!" to a seemingly absent "good and loving God." She was often on the cross with Jesus, not fully understanding what was happening. But she continued to trust - no matter what, in a God who seemed far away, "Our good God, whom you always taught me to trust in, has never deserted me."[26]

She came to know herself as personally called and loved by this God of hers and despite the mystery of it all and a heartbreak that almost drove her to give it all up, she lovingly embraced the Cross. It was to become central to her understanding of what it means to undertake the human journey, "My name in religion is Mary of the Cross. No name could be dearer to me."[27]

It was the name Fr Woods encouraged her to take, overriding Mary's personal choice of Mary of the Sacred Heart, a name which revealed much of her own intimate relationship with God. She showed this intimacy, and her response to the Cross, especially in her many very human and personal letters to her mother:

> So long as we do God's will – that is all we want. I am sure you will look for no other happiness in this world than that of serving God in any way he pleases. 'Tis useless my trying to explain what I feel, but I think God can make us very happy even in this world, that is, when he gives us opportunities of suffering cheerfully for Him'.[28]

She knew, as Pope John Paul 11 would later claim, that "in suffering there is a concealed power which draws a person closer to Christ."[29]

Mary's journey within took her through her suffering, living the mystery and ambiguity of it all, to discover her own resurrection. From her we learn the wisdom of Meister Eckhart's observation that "all ways are of God."[30] We fellow pilgrims grasp this slowly, tending to be more like Jonas and to run from God when the journey takes a direction we prefer not to take.

Life, of course, eventually catches up with us as we get older and have to let go of images of ourselves as young, always healthy and even very successful. We pray now that Mary will continue to walk with each of us on the unknown journey. The road can feel uphill a lot of the time. If we look within we can recognise ourselves tending to get lost in security and routine, perhaps striving for status and more money or power. As we face the cross in the form of daily stress and crisis, it's easy to forget the Loving Divine Presence inviting us to be more compassionate and less self-centred, more patient with less self-pity. The lady in our painting has the pared - down look of someone who's tossed away encumbrances. She seems contented with her simple life. We must learn, now, in Daniel O'Leary's word, "to travel light."[31] Ultimately all we can do is "humbly wait and put our trust in God."[32] There's not so much use now for the backpacks, the road maps and such.

Mary MacKillop didn't know the journey ahead, or where it would end but she, full of hope, trusted in the seemingly slow work of God. She took comfort in the thought that "all will be right with time and a little patience."[33]

We can but try to do the same.

Endnotes

1 Lesley O'Brien, *Mary MacKillop Unveiled* (Melbourne: Collins Dove, 1994), 253.
2 O'Brien, *Mary MacKillop Unveiled,* 254.
3 George O'Neill, *Life of Mother Mary of the Cross* (Melbourne: Pellegrini & Co, 1930), 179.
4 O'Neill, *Life of Mary Mother of the Cross,* 179.
5 Geoffrey Robinson, *Travels in Sacred Places* (Blackburn: Harper Collins, 1997), 77.
6 Mary MacKillop to Flora MacKillop, December 19th 1871. The letters of Mary MacKillop to her mother, Flora, are published in Sheila McCreanor, *Mary & Flora,* (North Sydney: Sisters of St Joseph of the Sacred Heart, 2004).
7 Michael Driscoll, "The Pardon" in *Anthology of Australian Religious Poetry,* ed. L.A. Murray (Melbourne: Collins Dove, 1991), 131.
8 James McAuley, "Epilogue" in *Anthology of Australian Religious Poetry,* ed. L.A. Murray (Melbourne: Collins Dove, 1991), 165.
9 David Malouf, "Between Towns" (poem).
10 O'Neill, *Life of Mother Mary of the Cross,* 126.
11 Anthony Kelly, *A New Imagining* (Melbourne: Collins Dove, 1990), 8.
12 Mary MacKillop to Flora MacKillop, June 6th 1870.
13 Mary MacKillop to Flora MacKillop, September 14th 1869.
14 O'Neill, *Life of Mother Mary of the Cross,* 179.
15 Robinson, *Travels in Sacred Places,* 110.
16 O'Neill, *Life of Mother Mary of the Cross,* 358.
17 O'Brien, *Mary MacKillop Unveiled,* 82.
18 Noel Rowe, "The Structure of the Real", in *Anthology of Australian Religious Poetry,* ed. L.A. Murray (Melbourne: Collins Dove, 1991), 146.
19 O'Brien, *Mary MacKillop Unveiled,* 153.
20 O'Brien, *Mary MacKillop Unveiled,* 152.
21 T S Elliot, "Little Gidding" (poem).
22 O'Neill, *Life of Mother Mary of the Cross,* 180.
23 O'Brien, *Mary MacKillop Unveiled,* 129.
24 O'Brien, *Mary MacKillop Unveiled,* 204.
25 Francis Webb, "Epilogue", in *Anthology of Australian Religious Poetry,* ed. L.A. Murray (Melbourne: Collins Dove, 1991), 165.
26 O'Neill, *Life of Mother Mary of the Cross,* 179.
27 Mary MacKillop to Flora MacKillop, August 21st 1867.
28 Mary MacKillop to Flora MacKillop, November 27th 1866.
29 John Paul 11, The Christian Meaning of Suffering, 1984 (quoted in Sydney Morning Herald 9/4/2005).
30 Richard Chilson, God Awaits – Based on the Classic Spirituality of Meister Eckhart (Notre Dame: Ave Maria Press, 1996), 163.
31 Daniel O'Leary, *Travelling Light* (Dublin: The Columba Press, 2004).
32 Mary MacKillop to a Sister, October 17th 1871.
33 Mary MacKillop to the Sisters, December 23rd 1873.

Mary MacKillop: Practical Mystic and Contemporary Educator

Professor Terence Lovat

Introduction

Mysticism is about faith and about inner knowing. Practical mysticism is about putting these into practice. It entails an intense knowing of God and self that impels action, practical action for good. I want to begin this exploration of Mary MacKillop as a practical mystic and contemporary educator by exploring ways in which the particular mysticism that Mary practised led naturally to a practical approach to her lived out faith, an approach that eschewed piety in favour of doing. It is this kind of mysticism that has too rarely been hailed as the most authentic of Christian mysticisms. We see it in Jesus and his early followers. We see it in Francis and Thomas and, more latterly, in Dietrich (Bonhoeffer), Bede (Griffiths) and (Mother) Teresa. Yet, too often we still hold sainthood to be about the pious and the impractical. By exploring Mary's life in terms of practical mysticism, her influence becomes perennial, timeless in the best sense. As a result, we are able to speculate with some certainty about the approach she would take to the issues of contemporary education, were we graced with her presence.

Mary MacKillop, Practical Mystic

Early Influences

One would only need to see that Mary was a Scottish Catholic, whose chief inspirational figure was an English Catholic in what had increasingly become an Irish Catholic world, to understand that things were never going to be easy for Mary MacKillop. The eldest child in a sincere but partly dysfunctional family brought early hardships and no doubt reinforced a characteristically tough Scottish determination. She is described early on as a 'holy girl', a description that seems to go beyond pious devotion to capturing something of her reaction to her adverse circumstances. In a situation where many young people would have rebelled or at least complained on a regular basis, the testimony is of persistent respect and love for her parents whom she might have blamed for depriving her of a normal childhood. Instead, she demonstrated quiet resignation to her reality, including being rock solid and effective in the actions she undertook to wrest her family away from abject poverty. For Mary, this was what God wanted of her at the time, her own more personal ambitions needing to take second place.

The testimony therefore is of someone who could balance her dreams with her realities. She felt the call early on to religious life but following the call then would have thrown her family into an untenable situation. While there were apparently some who encouraged her to follow the call as a priority, for Mary this would have been the antithesis of responsible action before God and would itself have negated the dream. Holding the dream but staying the dream became the eventual substance of the dream, and certainly the substance of a lifetime of patience and forebearance against the onslaughts of ill health, betrayal and maleficent employment of church authority. For Mary, in these formative years, to have gone against what she felt most earnestly to be right and to be God's way for her would have weakened the fabric that eventually became the Mary we revere now.

The testimony is also of one not given naturally to disobedience; far from it. She grew up in a world where one respected and obeyed one's elders even when one might have one's own thoughts about them. Her natural cultural dispositions in this regard were clearly fortified by her experience of the Australian Catholic Church of the time. Here we find one of history's all-time instances of church and family ties, of a Church that had more effective control of the behaviours and practices of ordinary members than had existed in Europe for centuries, and that had designs on controlling their innermost thoughts as well. It would never be easy for Mary to disobey or even seem to be disobeying. At the same time, the early Mary had a long way to travel, and the fairly simple forms of acquiescence to church, family and state authority would be tested sorely before the story's end. Her early belief in proper authority was a necessary grounding but hardly sufficient to carry her to where she ended up.

One of the first real challenges to her early innocence was in the form of Julian Tenison Woods, the former monk turned parish priest In order to appreciate fully this influence, we need to look at the wider world in which the Church of the time was functioning and how the Church was responding. Mary's Church was in a state of reaction to the challenges of science, nationalism and protestantism, to name just a few. After early attempts in the century to deal with some of these influences, the church slipped in 1846 into the long and very conservative reign of Pius IX. This was the era which saw the Church react to everything modern in the "Syllabus of Errors" and saw it claim the Pope to be "Prisoner of the Vatican" as an expression of protest against the loss of temporal power for the papacy.

These were both expressions of a Church in retreat, a Church searching for an identity many would claim was well past its "use by" date. It was the era that would go on to produce the doctrine of papal infallibility, symbolic of a Church seeking solutions to its challenges by ramping up hierarchical control. Globally, this led to a narrowing of some of the moves towards reform that had characterized the Church in the early part of the nineteenth-century. This included a narrowing of priestly formation in an attempt to stamp out the increasing tendency for priests to get caught up in scientific debate, nationalistic movements and, most distasteful of all for some Church authorities, ecumenical dialogue with the Protestants. Rome was attempting to put a halter on clergy worldwide and to stamp them as dependent agents of a Roman agenda.

Julian Tenison Woods, liberal theologian, scientist, naturalist and freelance clergyman, was a man caught between religious worlds, something of an enigma for his times. He was an unusual priest, a globe-trotting charismatic free-spirit, intellectual, creative artist and social hob-nobber. On the surface, he would have fitted the part better as a bishop of the establishment Church of England rather than a mere clergyman of the "Convict Church". Ironically, he was in many ways the kind of clergyman that Bishop Polding, the well-trained English Benedictine first Catholic Bishop of Sydney, had yearned for but never received in sufficient numbers, the kind that he thought Catholicism needed if it was to outgrow its convict church beginnings. Even Polding would likely have been out of place in the increasingly Irish Catholic Church to be found in Australia in the 1860s and '70s. Certainly,

Tenison Woods was well out of place.

Tenison Woods was a formidable challenge to Mary's far simpler and more straight-up-and-down upbringing. He brought the world to Mary in all its complexities and convolutions. He himself was an enigma and, on the surface, not the kind of man that Mary would be likely to trust. There was an element of vanity, of arrogance and of dismissiveness of authority. None of this was what Mary had been reared to respect. Most enigmatically, there was a partial disposition towards the kind of mystical piety of which Mary was most suspicious. If anything was going to break the trust between them, it would have been their different understandings about mysticism.

Biographers ponder therefore on just what it was about Tenison Woods that captured Mary's trust and affection. Some suggest it was fascination about someone so completely out of any mould that Mary had experienced, and no doubt there could be an element of truth in this. However, I prefer the view that what Mary found in Tenison Woods amounted to three things that suited her own growing knowledge of herself and how she wanted to spend her life, namely, his intellect, his devotion to the poor and, above all, his unshakeable faith that his God was a personal God who was guiding his every move, even those that brought him into conflict with his church. It was this latter feature that would go on to influence so powerfully the course of Mary's life.

The Excommunication Influence

For all the influence that Tenison Woods had on her, Mary eventually outgrew it. This is the way it is with those who finally claim their own mystical status. It is a claim that cannot be borrowed. It must be staked on its own. As with all of those who finally achieve the mystical state, Mary's did not come without a struggle, for her the defining struggle of her existence, and not one that she would ever have chosen had there been a choice. For Mary, this defining struggle was found ironically but not unusually for saints in her formal severance with the Church through the experience of excommunication. She survived this unthinkable moment to be able to say:

> I do not know how to describe the feeling but that I was intensely happy and felt nearer to God than I had ever felt before. I can only dimly remember the things that were said to me, but the sensation of the calm, beautiful presence of God I shall never forget … I did not feel alone, but I cannot describe the calm beautiful something that was near.[1]

While in some respects, Mary might have blamed Tenison Woods for the free-spirited influence that led to her excommunication, blame was not in her lexicon and, furthermore, she could see beyond the event of the moment to a greater good to come. She had learned to live with the enigmatic, the ambiguous, and, through Tenison Woods, to trust in God as a personal God who loves and guides even in one's darkest moments. This could apply even when faced with rejection and exclusion from what she had been taught from earliest days was God's own church.

For these capacities, she knew she had Tenison Woods to thank, yet at another level, the excommunication experience took her beyond his influence. After this, she realized that she had survived the loss of innocence quite beyond anything that he himself had experienced. She had not only survived the rejection and the exclusion, but actually was left with the self-knowledge that she had come through intact. She was now more certain of herself than ever before, including that God was with her even midst the unthinkable formalities of excommunication. While Mary would continue her fond and respectful relationship with Tenison Woods, in a sense, from this point on, she was on her own and she knew it. She had staked her own claim to mysticism and, from this time forward, it could never be a pietistic mysticism. Mary had seen all that for what it was. From now on, only a very practical mysticism, of the kind bound to make a difference, could match Mary's understanding of God's will for her.

Achieving her own Mysticism

Mary's excommunication experience was a test, in the way of a prophetic trial. She came through it not only exonerated but re-shaped, enhanced in charity and fortitude, more certain of her destiny and what had to be done than ever before. Part of the test, and part of the self-knowing that resulted was around the foundations of her thought and spirituality. From the time of her meeting up with Tenison Woods, much of Mary's earlier thinking and spirituality had been under revision. To what extent was she the compliant Catholic of her youth or to what extent was she a liberated Catholic with her own free-spirit? The excommunication experience confirmed that she was both, that she had conjoined the opposing forces of her upbringing to issue in a new forceful self-identity.

So we find Mary confiding to Tenison Woods not only about the above experience of feeling liberated at the time of excommunication, but she also wrote:

> I seemed not to realize the presence of the Bishop and priests … but I felt, oh, such a love for their office, a love and sort of reverence for the very sentence which I knew was being in full force passed upon me. I do not know how to describe the feeling but that I was intensely happy and felt nearer to God than I had ever felt before.[2]

To be feeling liberated yet attached, free but captive, beyond the power of the bishop to carve a wedge between her and her God and yet to succumb to the action, to even "love" the action is either the stuff of madness or the stuff of mysticism. At this point, Mary called on all of her foundational formation, in all its mixed and variegated forms. They were what pulled her through, and yet she was, from this moment, beyond any and all of them. She had changed forever. She was both the compliant Catholic and the free-spirit, yet she was more again. She had passed the ultimate test, ironically but not unusually encased in an ecclesial act, and she had broken through. There would now be no stopping her. From now on, her agenda was practical action for change, a living out of her faith in a way that had to make a difference.

Mary knew now that there was far more to being a compliant Catholic than simply submitting to the will and whim of the local bishop or parish priest, and so there would be battle royals in that department. At the same time, she could see the need to moderate some of the free-spiritedness of Tenison Woods and this became the substance of the gentle but firm discipline that she brought to her Sisters of St Joseph as they grew increasingly beyond her day-to-day overseeing and control. Living out her practical mysticism and seeing out the dream midst an increasingly hierarchical church were going to require a toughness and regimen of her troops that were beyond what she came to see as the slightly naïve form of trust in God portrayed by Tenison Woods. "God helps those who help themselves" became part of the new toughness and the commitment to get the job done.

Practical Mysticism and Practical Work

So, from the excommunication point on, we see the major building work of the Order. There are confrontations with church and public authorities, no end of playing one part of the church or public against another, and huge pressure placed on a society to recognize its own educational needs. Throughout it all, Mary's practical mysticism held fast and ensured that a consistent, steady agenda was rolled out. The mission was all about education, especially of those who were otherwise deprived of it, and of other forms of social welfare unavailable in any other way. There was a special mission to the poor and to the Aboriginal population, and, while principally there for the Catholic population (for that was where most of those in need were), no-one was ever to be turned away.

Mary was hugely conscious that her essential mission could be disrupted by other agendas in the church if its control was to pass to the hands of church authorities. Again, her excommunication experience had made that particularly apparent to her. She therefore fought especially hard to maintain the form of control, allowed as an exemption by the Church, that saw many religious orders owning their own government. While quite common among the older male orders of Europe, it was relatively uncommon among the female orders, and especially the newer orders of the far-flung colonial world. This was, of course, the major source of contention between Mary and a number of bishops with whom she had disagreements. These bishops were happy enough to have the free labour of Mary's nuns, so long as they could control them. Australia's first Cardinal, Moran of Sydney, applied particular pressure on Rome to disallow the "Joeys" their own control. However, in 1888, Pope Leo XIII sided with the Order and the Sisters remained exempt from the control of bishops. Mary may have been lucky that it was the more progressive Leo, and not Pius IX, in Peter's Chair at the time.

So, I propose Mary as a practical mystic, standing proudly in the tradition of practical mysticism and a supreme emissary for it. Her mysticism was built on a knowing and a faith formed in the fires of torment, abuse and rejection, her faith well balanced between compliance and self-determination. Above all, hers was a mysticism that could not but be directed towards practical action, and for her the bulk of the action was in and around the overwhelming need for education, especially for those who were most in need of it. The results of her practical action were so profound and ground-breaking that they came to shape much of Australian education, both religious and public, as it would develop from her time to our own. Because of this, we can easily find threads of thought about education that stretch from those times to the present day. This makes it fairly simple for us to speculate on Mary's reaction to contemporary issues in education, and hopefully to take some light and guidance from her wisdom.

Mary MacKillop, Contemporary Educator

A Timeless Influence

Mary's practical work was principally that of an educator, a practical educator in that she was more interested in achieving the product than in speculating about it. There were thousands of others in the colony at the time who spoke about education, wrote about it, gave speeches about it in parliament, and even lobbied for it. There were few, however, who actually effected it in the way Mary MacKillop did, with such force in such varied circumstances yet with such consistency that it was recognized for its distinctiveness. What has always fascinated me about Mary, speaking as an educator, is the timelessness of her educational perspective. While not trained for it, at least in any fashion that would stand against current benchmarks, she had a natural sense of the essentials of good education, of its dynamics and its limits. In that sense, she provides a perennial yardstick by which any trend or development in education can be assessed. Just as people might ask of moments in nursing, "I wonder what Nightingale would make of this?", so we might say of any fashion in education, "What would MacKillop's take on this one be?"

Public and Private

For one, her reaction to some of the contemporary public versus private schooling debate would be interesting. The record would have it that she was a little wary of the developments in public education of the 1870s and '80s, but then again she was even more obviously wary of church officials trying to centralize and surround her schools with church bureaucracy and establishment politics. My own sense is that her problem with public schooling as she saw it evolving through the 1870s was in its bureaucracy and establishment politics, rather than anything inherent in the notion of public schooling. Having worked so hard to fill educational gaps in a land that she saw as devaluing the role of education, I sense she would have been delighted, and perhaps even felt a little vindicated, in the fact that the nation as a whole was finally catching up with her on this.

The two things that would have worried her, however, were firstly the potential loss of her strongly held belief that effective education could only be carried out by those who understood and connected with a local community. In other words, it could not just be run out of 'head office'. Second, she would have noted that public education was well and truly in the hands of the politicians and landed gentry, neither of whom would have left her brim full of confidence that it was going to be directed well towards her most passionately held and preferred clientele, namely, the poor and disadvantaged.

So, midst the debates about government funding and how it should be directed, and some particularly silly debates about religion and values and which system is handling them better, I think Mary would have cut through to say "where is education happening best 'on the ground' through connectedness to the community it is meant to be serving and where are the poor and disadvantaged getting the better deal?" On that basis, she would score certain public and private schools very highly while others on both sides would score poorly. Above all, I believe her inclusive sense would have deemed it an overwhelming imperative that educators strive to "bury the hatchet" regarding their marginal differences in the interests of the common fight to provide the best education, under whichever auspices, for the nation.

Standardized or Localized Control

Since the beginnings of formal education and, especially, since the challenging era of the 1970s, the debate around standardized versus localized (or "centralised" versus "situation-based") curriculum control has been a regular feature of the educational landscape. In other words, should the whole curriculum of a state be decided by one group in head office running out a standardized curriculum and assessment, or by those in the field and closest to their clientele? As is commonly the case, both sides held to their views passionately and sometimes in extreme form.

I believe the testimony is that Mary would have seen this debate from both sides and would have held to a negotiated position. On the one hand, she clearly valued the notion that the most effective education was carried out by those who knew their clientele best. On the other hand, she was one of the first Australian educators to enjoin a standardized approach to curriculum across a whole system. I believe Mary's educational wisdom was that good education happened when all teachers followed a standard set of basic requirements suitable to the broader clientele but, at the same time, each and every teacher worked closely with their own particular clientele to make sure the standardized curriculum was relevant and addressed to their own needs.

Religious and Values Education

Throughout the 1980s and 1990s, there was an explosion of interest in religious and values education and a return in the public systems to some of their own earlier agendas in this regard. The 1880 Public Instruction Act, for instance, was clear that public education should be marked by a strength in both religious and values education, agendas that were largely lost throughout twentieth-century forms of secularism and their impact on public education. As the world changed again and public education re-discovered these aspects of education, there was much debate about their suitability to public education, debate coming from within both public and private education quarters. For some within the public systems, it seemed like a rejection of the religious and values neutrality that they had come to "value" about public schooling. For some within the religious systems of schooling, it seemed that public education was "horning in on their territory".

Again, my sense is that Mary MacKillop would have taken the broader view. If one could be certain about anything in Mary, it is that she was not a bigot. Her own religious vision and her own sense of values was that good education was for all, that religious and values education was clearly part of that, and that it could be provided by any teacher anywhere provided the teacher was dedicated to their clientele and to the art of teaching. This is remarkably in tune with modern statements about the role of schooling provided by the Adelaide Declaration (1999) on the National Schooling Goals for the Twenty-first Century[3] and by the Australian Government's National Framework for Values Education.[4]

The Power of Teaching

The most prominent of today's issues in education concerns updated research that shows the undoubted power of teaching when performed well.[5] This research is unwrapped commonly under the title of "Quality Teaching", or is named more esoterically as "Quality Pedagogy". Its effects are best understood by comparing them to the most prominent beliefs about teaching of the recent past. From about the 1970s, generations of teachers and educational systems were guided in their thinking by research that seemed to show that teaching and schooling were fairly powerless to change the influences of a student's background. This was the classic "you can't make a silk purse out of a sow's ear" kind of pessimism that determined that a teacher could do little to impact on a poor start to life.

To Mary MacKillop, this would be the reddest of red rags to her bull of a Scottish disposition. She believed passionately that the teacher could make the world of difference to the story's end, regardless of its beginning. In this, she was as ever way ahead of her time, for now we have the almost definitive research on which the contemporary Quality Teaching agenda rests. The research that underpins Quality Teaching has illustrated just what extraordinary power the committed teacher possesses in order to make a difference, even in the face of some of the most extreme disadvantage, be it of socio-economic status, non-English speaking background or even disability. When mentored by the quality teacher, students from these backgrounds can achieve even faster than so-called regular students if the latter are not being mentored by a quality teacher. This would fit very well with Mary's fundamental hunch about the importance of education and the associated importance of having teachers who were dedicated to the art of teaching, well-trained, updated and, above all, committed to their students.

Teaching and Caring

Finally, Mary's natural sense about education has been vindicated by some of the most recent insights into just what makes for the quality teacher. In trying to search out and identify the characteristics of "quality" in Quality Teaching, whether it is the teacher's knowledge of content or the capacity to make for interesting and stimulating learning, recent research has uncovered a more important ingredient than either of these. Teachers "knowing their stuff" and being able to make things interesting are both important. However, we now know that the single most important feature in those classrooms where students thrive is that the teacher cares.[6]

By "care" is meant being fair and just in all the teacher's dealings with the students, as well as making them feel accepted, supported and encouraged. As most of those performing this kind of research will testify, this is not rocket science. When people feel cared for and good about themselves, they will bring out their best. Classrooms are no different, in this respect than anywhere else in life. However, in education circles, we sometimes become so preoccupied with other concerns, be they buildings, curriculum, class sizes or the latest in assessment regimes, that we forget the fundamentals. In her constant pairing of pastoral care with education, Mary never forgot that the most fundamental feature of all successful teaching is in the degree of care, compassion and inclusiveness extended to the student. Again, she was an educator way ahead of her time.

Conclusion

So, I propose Mary MacKillop as practical mystic and contemporary educator. Against the criteria prevailing in both fields in her own time, she was a giant, such a much bigger character than most with whom she dealt. In a day and age when so much of the religious agenda was carried by sectarian and denominational bigotry, she provided a model of true Christian forbearance, of knowing herself, knowing what God intended for her, and knowing what quality education was all about. In a day and age when so much of the educational agenda was dominated by ignorance and neglect, she carried a torch that lit up the pathway ahead. She laid important foundations not only for Catholic education but for all Australian education, foundations of thought about schooling, teaching and pastoral care that would eventually become part of the fabric of the public instruction acts that would guide Australian education into Federation and beyond. Of course, none of this came easy. Granted her fighting Scottish nature, and the fact that she did not resile from any of the fights, it is easy enough to see why sainthood would not come easily either. In many ways, it fits the entire story and witness of Mary MacKillop that sainthood would entail a struggle. In an ironic way, it is probably a good thing because it will be all the more celebrated and cherished when it does come.

Endnotes

1 William Modystack, *Blessed Mary MacKillop: A Woman Before her Time* (Sydney: Lansdowne Press, 2000), 67-68.

2 Ibid.

3 Adelaide Declaration, "National schooling goals for the twenty-first century", 1999. http://www.curriculum.edu.au/mceetya/nationalgoals/natgoals.htm

4 DESt "National framework for values education in Australian schools", (Canberra: Department of Education, Science and Training, 2005).

5 L. Darling-Hammond, *The Right to Learn: a Blueprint for Creating Schools that Work* (San Francisco: Jossey-Bass, 1997).

6 K.J.Rowe, "In good hands? The importance of teacher quality." *Educare News, 149:* 4-14.

The Providence Bag: Discovering the Treasure

Margaret McKenna rsj

It was a sunny June day in 1870 and Ellen Carolan watched as Sister Mary of the Cross taught some school children how to play a new game.[1] Ellen had joined a community of Catholic nuns newly arrived in Brisbane, the Sisters of St Joseph. This was almost five months ago, but she still felt a little homesick when she thought of her parents and brothers and sisters in Maryborough, a country town north of Brisbane. [2] Because it was customary for nuns to be given the name of a saint, she was now known as Sister Mary Josephine and she was happy to have St Joseph as her patron.[3] She remembered how Bishop James Quinn, a friend of the Carolan family, had told her that he had invited this new Australian sisterhood to work in Queensland and suggested that she should try to meet them.

On her first visit to the sisters' small rented house in South Brisbane, she felt so much at home with them that she asked to join them in community just to see if she was suited to their way of life.[4] Sr Mary of the Cross, the superior of the community, shared with Ellen how Fr Woods, a priest in South Australia, and she had founded a religious institute to teach in schools for Catholic children, especially those from the working class and those living in the smaller townships in the country districts. Ellen, a teacher herself, saw the need for such schools, and she liked Sr Mary who had welcomed her to the community of six Josephites. Today she was helping with a picnic in the grounds of St Mary's school in South Brisbane.

The children, about three hundred in all, from the three schools in Brisbane in which the sisters were teaching - St John the Baptist's, St Joseph's and St Mary's - had come together.[5] The sisters had organised a picnic to celebrate the feast of St John the Baptist, one of their special patrons. The new Sister Josephine and Sister Gertrude were organising the children under ten years of age while Sisters Augustine and Collette were looking after the bigger boys, and Sisters Clare and Francis de Sales the older girls. Sr Teresa was helping the mothers arrange the picnic lunch.[6] They all listened as Sr Mary told the children how to play a game called "The Providence Bag".[7] Sr Josephine had never heard of such a game. As she watched the children form circles, she wondered if this was a game played by the children in Adelaide because Sr Mary and most of the other sisters had come from there.

A hush fell over the children as they watched two boxes full of small parcels, one marked "Girls" the other "Boys", being carried on to the playground. A child from each group was asked to volunteer to be blindfolded. There was no lack of willing participants. The sisters gave a ball to a child in each group and asked that it be passed around the circle. The aim of the blindfolded one was to find the ball. Sr Josephine decided that this game was a combination of Blindman's Bluff and Lucky Dip.[8] Soon, within each circle, a child, arms outstretched, was wandering around trying to make contact with the ball. Each time it was within reach, the screams of the children revealed its whereabouts. Once the ball was discovered, the searcher was released from the blindfold and allowed to reach into one of the boxes and draw out a gift. Sr Josephine smiled as she heard the children's cries of "What did you get?" as the lucky player revealed the contents of the package - for the girls a handkerchief or a hair ribbon and for the boys a few marbles or a pencil. Such gifts were treasures to these children whose parents were struggling to keep food on the table.

The children, most without shoes, were now intent on the game and Sr Mary, free to talk, moved over towards Sr Josephine. These women had much in common. They were in their twenties but Sr Mary, Mary MacKillop, was eight years older than Sr Josephine. Both were school teachers and each believed that God had called her to dedicate her life as a nun. Their personalities, nevertheless, were more complementary than alike. Sr Josephine was an able manager, she had often accompanied her father and learnt from him how to conduct business. There would be times later when Josephine would feel obliged to offer Mary what she considered was timely advice. Although Mary had been the main breadwinner of her family, Josephine decided, when she knew her better, that she was a little too generous and trusting. Where Josephine in her directness could at times seem rather blunt, Mary was more gentle in her communication. It was a rare occasion when Josephine experienced any shyness in offering an opinion, whereas there were times when Mary had to struggle with feelings of reluctance in facing some situations.[9] Mary MacKillop recognised the strength of Ellen Carolan's character, but, at the same time, she was aware that the younger woman's directness and what could be experienced as insensitivity had the potential to create tension in her relationships.

Sr Josephine commented that the children were really enjoying playing the game. Mary agreed and told Josephine that this game was one of her teaching strategies. Josephine was puzzled, and just as she was about to question Mary further, both teachers were distracted by a call from some of the children near them that Tommy O'Leary was cheating by peeping under the blindfold. In her soft voice with its faint trace of a Scottish accent Sr Mary asked a defensive looking Tommy if it were true that he lifted the blindfold.[10] At first, he denied the charge despite the cries of "Yes, you did". After a second appeal to Tommy "to tell the truth" a repentant looking Tommy agreed the he had "only a little peep". He stood in the middle of the circle on one leg and then with bowed head turned slowly and returned to his place in the outer circle.

Both Mary and Josephine noticed the smiles of victory on some of the children's faces. It took less than a second before there was a chorus of "Sister, can I have a turn now?" It was clear that most were in agreement that Tommy should forfeit his chance of securing a prize. Sr Mary said "Let us think for a moment about whether Tommy should be barred from the game, or should be allowed to finish his turn". The suggestion that he might be allowed to continue caused looks of shock to cross most faces. Sr Mary continued, "What have we learnt about the messages God sends us in what happens to us each day?"

Within a second there was a cluster of hand-waving children eager to be chosen to answer the question. Sr Mary called on Peggy Hanlon who had been one of the most irate about the cheating. Peggy felt honoured to be chosen, especially as Sister Josephine was watching. "God has some gift for us in each happening. Often we can't find it at first, but if we search hard enough and ask for God's help we will discover it". Sr Mary congratulated Peggy on her answer, and Sr Josephine nodded in Peggy's direction. "Let's search for the gift God is offering in what has just happened", Sr Mary continued. "We feel angry that Tommy cheated and did not play the game fairly. Is there a secret gift in this for us?"

There was a pause as each child struggled with feelings of resentment and the desire to punish Tommy. Tommy, meanwhile, looked at the ground and made a pattern with his big toe in the dust. With some reluctance Peggy offered a response, "I suppose," she said "we should forgive" (she was reluctant to mention the culprit's name). Lucy Molloy, with a little more generosity, suggested that "We should let Tommy finish his turn, Sister". "Will we do that?" asked Sr Mary. There was a muted agreement, and Tommy, before he was blindfolded again, took a quick look around to see who held the ball. While the blindfolding was taking place, Sr Mary gestured to the children to pass the ball to the other side of the circle so that when Tommy rushed to where he had seen it, it was no longer there. He laughed and said "Aw, Sr Mary, you tricked me". Sr Mary responded with a smile, "Yes Tommy O'Leary, remember – no cheating". Mary and Josephine laughed, and the children broke into smiles. After all had claimed a prize, the game was over. It was time now for cakes and biscuits that had been provided by some of the mothers of the children. Sister Josephine had no need to ask Sr Mary to explain how this game was an educational strategy. She, as well as the children, had learnt a lesson about God's care.

After Sr Mary had assured Molly O'Brien, the little girl with the torn dress, that she would put the white hair ribbon that she had won in a safe place so that she could wear it on her first Communion day, she moved to where the parents stood. Meanwhile, the children collected any papers that had been dropped in the playground, said a "Thank you" to those mothers who had provided the food, and then all left for home. Sisters Josephine and Teresa walked with the children from St Joseph's to their school in Hubert Street. As they passed their home children left the group, and finally when they reached their school grounds the sisters farewelled those who were left. It had been a day that Josephine would remember.

That evening at night prayers both Josephine and Mary reflected on their experience of God's loving care. Josephine thought of the many times she had prayed to know if she should be a nun or stay at home to help her sister teach in the Catholic school in Maryborough. She remembered the day she met the Sisters of St Joseph for the first time. She had been teaching with the Sisters of Mercy in Ipswich and had come to Brisbane to sit for a teachers' examination. It had been cancelled and, because the Sisters of Mercy no longer required her services, she decided to return home to Maryborough and made the necessary arrangements for the journey. On the day before she was to leave Brisbane she decided to visit the new sisters. Her brother was also visiting South Brisbane and carried her case from the ferry up to the convent. Before they parted she told him, perhaps a little impulsively, that she might stay with the sisters, and that was what happened.[11] She marvelled that God had guided her so clearly, and she felt a little overawed by the thought.

Sister Mary noticed the fervour of Josephine and also remembered the Thursday afternoon that the young women from Maryborough knocked on the front door. On that Thursday Mary had felt so dejected. There seemed to be so many difficulties in settling into the ministry in Brisbane. She knew that the sisters were feeling lonely and disheartened also, and were missing the spiritual encouragement of Fr Woods. The bishop was away in Rome and Dr Cani whom he had appointed as the sisters' director, was reluctant even to hear their confessions. They had little money to buy food because a government directive forbade the payment of school fees and Dr Cani refused to allow the sisters to ask the people for help.[12] She told all her troubles to St Joseph and asked him to send someone to help them. Then Ellen arrived. What a surprise it was when she announced that she was thinking of entering the convent. Mary took this as a sign from St Joseph that somehow difficulties would be solved, and marvelled at God's care. She was filled with loving gratitude.

Mary's reflection also led her to repent of the times that she had not used the treasure that God had offered. She remembered the day she was returning home from St John the Baptist's, a school that the Josephites had opened in a poorer section of North Brisbane. It was a humid February afternoon and she and Sisters Clare and Francis de Sales walked to the wharf to catch the ferry across the river to their new larger rented convent - an old hotel. On their way they passed by a drunken man in the gutter. He was so drunk he could not even raise his head and was moaning in sheer frustration. A group of silent onlookers had gathered. Mary felt an urge to go to his assistance but her shyness prevented her from taking any action because she feared the laughter of those standing around. In a letter to Fr Woods she shared her thoughts about this experience. She felt disappointed with herself and was humbled that she had not responded to God's call. This was a lesson she was determined not to forget, and prayed that Jesus would help her always to mirror his tender love and care for all.[13]

Early in 1871 Sr Mary returned to Adelaide and by 1872 Sr Josephine was professed as a Sister of St Joseph. As the years slipped by she remembered the lessons of the "Providence Bag", and especially the instructions given by Sr Mary and tried to follow her example. Being of a very practical nature, she was sometimes a little sceptical when Sr Mary would suggest that the community rely on God's providence. She was quite prepared to say the prayer Sr Mary taught the sisters:

> Divine Providence can provide,
> Divine Providence did provide,
> Divine Providence will provide.
> O merciful and all provident God hear our prayers and grant our petitions.[14]

Mary told the sisters how her mother had taught her and her bothers and sisters to place their trust in God's care, especially when they were in a difficult situation. This was something that Josephine tried to depth in her life, too, and when she felt others needed a little sermon on the topic she would tell the story of the morning that a storm broke over South Brisbane:

> It was washing day. The bed linen, towels and tea towels and other clothes were sorted and ready to be put into the water in the 'copper'[15] in the back yard. The sisters took it in turns to do the washing. 'Imagine the consternation of the sister who was to do the washing that day', Josephine would say, 'when she turned on the tap to fill the bucket with water that she intended to use in the copper, discovered that the tank was empty, and the water carrier was away. There was not a drop of water!' Here Josephine would pause before she continued, 'Oh, well, no washing today I said to myself, as I hurried out the door on my way to school'.

Josephine continued after another pause.

> Then I remembered Sister Mary's 'Trust in God's Providence', and so did the sister who was to do the washing. She decided to ask St Joseph for help. By ten o'clock clouds began to gather in what had been a clear sky. Soon the rain was teeming down filling copper and buckets to overflowing. What a joy it was to hear the water gushing along the gutters on the roof and into the tank. By mid-day the sun was shining and the washing was well underway. Josephine would smile as

> she concluded her story with, 'Imagine the sisters' surprise and mine, too, when we returned to the convent in the late afternoon to find the washing folded and ready to be put into cupboards'.[16]

Josephine's audience was left to take the intended lesson to heart.

All those who lived with Sr Mary were struck by the way she seemed to be conscious of God's presence. When things went wrong, as they often did, Mary would assure the sisters that God would send help. It was a time to trust in "Providence". It was not that Mary did not take any action to remedy a situation, but she reflected on whether her actions were truly those of a Christian. Josephine tried to do the same, but there were times when she acted a little hastily.

One day, not long after St Joseph's school had been opened, Josephine was managing the ninety children in the one schoolroom because Sr Teresa was ill. The school was really a cottage with the partitions removed. A man came and commented on how the children were crowded together. Josephine was not pleased and replied that a proper school should be built. He looked surprised so she added "Send your wife here for a week and see if she would like to be in (this room) with seventy or more children".[17] That evening as she reflected on the happenings of the day she doubted that Sr Mary would have approved of her response, and she resolved that in the future she would think a little more before she spoke. Much to Josephine's surprise she was to learn that God can turn even our failings into something beneficial. The man whom she met that afternoon suggested to the priest that a new church be built and the school be housed in it. So, in January 1871 St Joseph's school moved from the cramped schoolroom to a much larger space in the new church building at the Kangaroo Point.

During the first ten years of the sisters' ministry in Queensland, Bishop James Quinn made it clear that he did not approve of the Josephite style of leadership. He did not think it right that the internal administration of the sisterhood remain in the hands of the sisters rather than under the control of the bishop of the diocese. He held this opinion even though the Catholic Church authorities in Rome had approved this style of government for the Josephites. Sr Mary realised that this was the main reason why the bishop allowed the priests to take such little interest in the sisters and in some cases deprive them of necessities. She believed that it was an attempt to dishearten the sisters and to compel her to remove them from the diocese.[18] She used to say "Surely he cannot be blind to the good they are doing for his people, yet his conduct is a mystery to me".[19] While Sister Mary found it hard to understand this and did not approve of such actions, nevertheless she was prepared to respect the role of the bishop in the diocese and that of the priest in the parish. In the face of such difficulties, Mary had to remind Josephine and other sisters to act with kindness and tolerance, but she admitted that sometimes they were provoked. On these occasions she defended the sisters and used every means to see that justice was done.

There was one scene from Josephine's days in Queensland that disappointment and grief had seared on her memory. How could she ever forget that day in December 1879. Sr Mary was standing on the wharf in South Brisbane with tears flowing down her cheeks, unable to continue her words of thanks to the people who had gathered to farewell the sisters.[20] Whenever Josephine remembered waving farewell to Mary and that first group of sisters to leave, a lump would rise in her throat. She felt both sad and angry. Bishop Quinn had told them to leave his diocese because he had other sisters to take their place. "After all we had done during the last ten years it had come to this", she used to say.

Memories crowded around this event. As though it were yesterday, Josephine remembered the afternoon she and her sister Collette, also a Josephite, had met with Bishop Quinn. Sr Mary had sent them to ask the bishop's permission to make a collection in the churches so that the sisters could pay their passages to Sydney. They did not have enough money. When he met them he told them how angry he was that they were not prepared to leave Sr Mary and join with him to form another community of Josephites under a Rule that he approved. Collette began to cry, but Josephine maintained her composure. He refused to give permission for a collection, so Josephine trying very hard to speak respectfully, as she knew Sr Mary would wish, responded, "Well, my Lord, you will not mind if we call in to the office of the *Brisbane Courier* and ask that an advertisement be placed in the newspaper inviting all our protestant friends to help us pay for our passage". There was silence. The bishop then said, "I'll give the permission". Josephine would finish her story by saying, "And that is how God provided for our passage".

It took Josephine and the other sisters a long time to discover the many treasures that God had hidden in their experiences during those first ten years in Queensland. Had it not been for the presence of Mary

MacKillop, her residence in South Brisbane, her many visits to the sisters over those years, her encouraging and understanding letters, some sisters may have given up the struggle. But it took time for the hurt and the sorrow to heal. There were times when all Josephine could manage to do was to sit with Jesus and hold out her feelings of anger and resentment and pray for the gift of healing. This she also learnt from Mary MacKillop as she watched her pray, and listened to her advice. As she planned the "House of Providence" that Mary had asked her to open in the Rocks area in Sydney, her awareness of God's presence in daily happenings grew. Gradually Josephine began to understand more clearly that somehow all fitted into the mystery of God's love. Sometimes, when she welcomed some old destitute person or an orphan child to join their "Providence Family", she remembered that day in Brisbane when she, too, began to learn the secret of the "Providence Bag":

> Divine Providence can provide.
> Divine Providence did provide.
> Divine Providence will provide.
> O merciful and all provident God hear our prayers and grant our petitions.[21]

Endnotes

1 Ellen Carolan (1850-1933) entered the Sisters of St Joseph of the Sacred Heart on February 2nd 1870.
2 Six Sisters of St Joseph arrived in Brisbane on December 31st 1869.
3 Josephine Carolan, *Memoirs of Queensland – 1870-1880.* Archival material. Sisters of St Joseph of the Sacred Heart.
4 Ibid.
5 Mary MacKillop to Julian Tenison Woods, Feast of the Visitation 1870.
6 Ibid.
7 *Brisbane Courier,* July 9th 1870.
8 Ibid.
9 Mary MacKillop to Julian Tenison Woods, January 2nd, February 21st, October 17th 1870.
Mary MacKillop to Josephine MacMullen, February 25th 1878.
10 Bridget Conlon, "unpublished diary", February 20th 1871. Sisters of Mercy Archives, Brisbane.
11 Carolan, *Memoirs of Queensland – 1870-1880.*
12 Mary MacKillop to Julian Tenison Woods, February 8th 1870.
13 Mary MacKillop to Julian Tenison Woods, February 21st 1870.
14 Prayer learnt from the early Josephites.
15 "copper – a large vessel (formerly of copper) for boiling clothes". *Macquarie Dictionary.*
16 Mary MacKillop, *History of the Congregation (1866-1900), 12,13.* Sisters of St Joseph, Resource material from the Archives of the Sisters of St Joseph of the Sacred Heart, Issue No 3, (Revised), August, 1984.

17 Carolan, *Memoirs of Queensland - 1870-1880.*
18 Mary MacKillop to Dr Grant, April 19th 1878.
19 Ibid.
20 *Brisbane Courier,* December 17th 1879.
Queenslander December 20th 1879.
21 Prayer learnt from the early Josephites.

Mary MacKillop: On Pilgrimage

Colleen O'Sullivan rsj

Introduction

A pilgrimage is both an outer and an inner journey. It is traditional in many religions, such as Islam and Christianity, where it often serves as a rite of passage. The idea of "Pilgrimage", as a real journey and symbolically as a life journey, is a term often used today by writers of both spiritual and mainstream literature. General Peter Cosgrove described his visit to Gallipoli as a pilgrimage – a journey made to honour the memory of those who died and to honour the sacred icon that is Gallipoli itself.

Literary works such as Salinger's *Franny and Zooey*[1] and the terminology of many modern spirituality texts, reflect the multi-dimensional sense of the term pilgrimage. A sacred pilgrimage, real or symbolic, has many facets. It is intentional, characterised by a sense of Presence and community. It takes us into sacred space and time but encourages us to remember who we are on that journey. A life pilgrimage is thus not only a linear journey but, as Margaret Silf writes, a deepening of our contact with God and a spiritual awakening so that when we reach the end of our pilgrimage, as Eliot says, we will find it to be the place from where we started and recognise it for the first time.

Guides are always significant in our spiritual life. Mary MacKillop is both guide and mentor on our life pilgrimage because she knew the joy and sorrow common to all humanity. But she also endured the temptation to despair known by many in the 21st century. In 1884 she wrote the sad words, "I feel as if death would certainly be preferable",[2] and yet she was always faithful to the God she "leant on" and encouraged her sisters "to lean on".

Mary's pilgrimage was for others and towards God whether she walked on Australian or New Zealand soil, on the Continent or in the British Isles. Like most pilgrims she drew others into her company and they struggled together to keep on the path Christ, their compass, indicated for them.

The Geographical Pilgrimage

The context of Mary's pilgrimage from the time of her birth was social and cultural change. Mary MacKillop's geographical pilgrimage began in Newtown, Melbourne in 1842 – the year the first Port Philip legislative council was constituted and separated from Sydney. In Australia the 1840s was a time of letting go of old connections. The people refused to allow convicts to enter Australia[3] and began the process of accepting social and political responsibility for themselves as a new country.

The MacKillops knew social change painfully. Alexander lost his home and money and by the time Mary was two he was declared bankrupt. The result was the family lived in a nomadic and dependent state, relying on relatives for most of Mary's life, until she grew old enough to discover ways to provide for it.

This unsettled existence actually began when Mary was four months old. The family moved from Newtown (Brunswick Street Melbourne) to Darebin to Portland, to Penola, and back to Portland. While this early part of her life caused Mary and her family suffering it was, for Mary, a preparation for her later travels as the leader of the Sisters of St Joseph. Mary and Julian's religious group were characterised by their ability to move around in small groups wherever and whenever a need called to them. This temporal and spiritual freedom lies at the heart of pilgrimage.

Mary's travels as a Josephite always involved the establishment and securing of the true Josephite spirit within this new country. After all her journeying she was to die at the Josephite Mother House at Mount Street, North Sydney – a place to which she had been exiled from South Australia and where she discovered that "the birds sing here as in Adelaide." God's voice and the work of the Kingdom were not bound by place or time, nor was the Josephite spirit restricted to a particular space or dimension.

The Inner Pilgrimage

The inner journey, the journey of the spirit, is the most significant aspect of any pilgrimage, however, and relates to the conscious integration of life. Factors which contribute to the wholeness of life are both within our control and outside it. Mary's case was no different from anyone else's. Her family, while financially unstable, nevertheless provided her with a context in which her faith in God and a loving compassion for others developed. Those men, who constituted the hierarchy of the Church she dearly loved, forced her to walk a way of the Cross. Her experience taught her what it was like to be ostracised and banished. Rejection and abandonment by Church authorities, her own friends and some Sisters, taught her a trust in God and not just in the human. As she grew older her inner world expanded and developed a depth of spirituality which led Fr Clune, who knew her later in life and at first hand, to describe her as a woman wrapped in God.

The Way of the Pilgrim

In the 1950s, J. D. Salinger wrote the definitive teenage angst novel, *Catcher in the Rye.* The success of this novel made it possible for him to choose topics on which he wished to write rather than those that might be commercially successful. As a result of this freedom, 1955 saw the novel, *Franny and Zooey* published. The book is based on a famous Pilgrimage guide printed in Russia called, *The Way of the Pilgrim.*

The *starets* – a wandering crippled monk – whose life call was to roam the world taught those he met how to respond to the Biblical plea to pray at all times. Franny describes him:

> Some Russian peasant apparently . . . He never gives his name . . . He just tells you he's a peasant and that he's thirty-three years old and that he's got a withered arm. And that his wife is dead.[4]

The monk is the image of the flawed human being who, while flawed, nevertheless seeks the presence of God on their life journey.

This little man is literally a perpetual pilgrim, as Mary was, as in many ways we all are. His life-work evolved after he met a holy man who taught him to pray the mantra, *Lord Jesus Christ, Son of David, have mercy on me,* and to pray it constantly. The theory is, if this prayer is said often enough the mantra moves through the lips to the heart and prays itself in the heart of the one using it. Any mantra if said often enough would have a similar effect, but this one has its derivation in scripture and is sacred to the Christian tradition.

There were many such perpetual pilgrims in the west during the middle Ages and in Russia until modern times. Today the great Pilgrimage sites in the British Isles and on the Continent, such as Canterbury, Croagh Patrick and The Compastella in Spain, are reviving the ancient walking pilgrimage as a sign of the more important inner pilgrimage that faith invites us to make.

Metaphor

Salinger's novel, *Franny and Zooey,* uses the pilgrimage as its key metaphor. This metaphor is a lens which allows us to view the different levels in which we live and move and grow. The lens both narrows and widens the idea of pilgrimage. Pilgrimage can be a sacred journey undertaken by a group to reach a particular place such as Lourdes and to go there for a particular reason. But it can also be the deepening of our understanding of the created world, or a journey of recognition of our own value and worth to the God who loves us unconditionally.

The notion of Pilgrimage in the Christian tradition has its roots in the scripture, beginning with the wanderings of the Jewish people and including the movements of those who followed Christ through the length and breadth of Galilee.

A pilgrimage then is a sacred journey which draws the pilgrim back always to the place where God is most constantly present to them – within themselves, within creation and within others. The heart of a pilgrimage is always awareness of the other/Other. By definition, a pilgrimage is always a long journey – a journey made in many ways - in sorrow and joy, in difficulty and ease, in loneliness or in companionship. It is made as T.S. Eliot says with the drawing of love and with the voice of its calling. It is an exploration and:

> We shall not cease from exploration
> And the end of all our exploring
> Will be to arrive where we started
> And know the place for the first time.[5]

Life is a pilgrimage – a constant movement from the known to the unknown. Our spiritual journey cannot be separated from any other aspect of our life journey. Pilgrimage is a journey through Presence to Presence, that is into deeper mystery and a deeper awareness of that Mystery. It is, however, a journey that must be made intentionally. A Pilgrimage is not a simple wandering in the desert - it is a movement in the desert towards a promise that is only vaguely recognised at times, but is never really lost sight of on the journey. In some ways Mary MacKillop is an archetypal pilgrim as she moves through loneliness, rejection and desert experiences, always towards a future hope grounded in God.

Rite of Passage

A Pilgrimage is, or can be also, a rite-of–passage - a ritualised pathway from one level of experience and growth to the next level. In such a rite there is a deliberate letting go of the old to put on the new. Often, however, the pilgrim experiences the unexpected and discovers that the choice ahead is not written in the guide-books. One such unexpected turn of events occurred for Mary at Penola. She became aware she would eventually have to let go of her mentor and Director. Her honesty in facing her real feelings around this circumstance prepared her for the reality when it took place. This pilgrimage milestone was a difficult one, but just one of many where the pilgrimage could have dissipated or stopped altogether, if she let go of the trust she had in the Spirit of God.

Mary experienced at first hand the power of an organised communal pilgrimage in 1873 when she joined the English pilgrimage to Paray-le-Monial. Father Christie, the Jesuit, encouraged her and saw that she was cared for on the trip. The pilgrimage made a profound impact on her. At one stage she got carried away with the excitement and was amazed at the response of the French Catholics to the visiting Belgium and English pilgrims:

> We saw more than I dare now to attempt to dwell upon, and I have got as a precious relic, one leaf from the tree under which our Divine Spouse told many things to Blessed Margaret Mary. Then there was the grand act of Consecration, then the sermon and Benediction, then another grand torchlight procession throughout the city joined by the French and Belgian pilgrims, singing hymns all the while.[6]

For the English Catholics this public celebration of their faith became in many ways a rite-of passage for Mary.

Mary waited for Rome's response to the rule and while waiting she travelled - visiting schools, convents, churches and Scotland, the place of her ancestry. But this public experience of church woke in her an awareness of the community of the Church at its grass roots. It was this Church to which her service and the service of the sisters was directed.

Mary's joy comes through her pilgrimage letters in a way different from her other correspondence. She stands joyfully in a long line of English pilgrims cheering the French and Belgian peoples who surround the group carried away by crowd excitement. Mary also excitedly points out to a group of people with her, the Bishop of Geneva and they surround and greet him exuberantly celebrating his presence with them. She joins with the group who spontaneously burst into singing the old hymn, *To Jesus' Heart all Burning*, in the streets of Paray-le Monial. This is a different but lovable Mary celebrating with joy her Catholicism.[7]

In a way this grass roots church was beyond written authority because each person was celebrating the memory of Christ interacting with Margaret Mary, at a personal level without mediation. The experience deepened Mary's own faith and she wrote about it at great length to the Sisters at home, wanting them to share in her experience, longing to let them know at first hand the value of the pilgrimage.

Awareness

There is always a danger of pilgrimages, such as the above, and stories like *The Way of the Pilgrim* taking on an exotic tinge rather than being grounded in reality and the everyday. Franny, heroine of the novel, becomes the image of those who go on pilgrimage for all the wrong reasons. She becomes lost in a judgemental stance and cannot let go of her own ego. Her pilgrimage is leading her down a blind alley because she fails to recognise the depth of love in the ordinary, and instead seeks some sterile perfection in the illusion she has about her own depth of spirituality. Many times she is recalled to who she really is and to where the sacred exists in her life. Her pilgrimage at times needs to be shocked into recognition of the truth of God's presence and love, found at home as well as in foreign places. The opposite can also be true and in some ways it was for Mary. The overseas experience deepened her faith and as her letters show, drew her closer to the people she left behind and to the work they were doing. She knew that "there where you are, you will find God and His work".[8]

Presence

In his work *Mary MacKillop: Made in Australia*, Daniel Lyne says of Mary that her life pilgrimage:

> Means a search into the heart of her trust and her faith in her God to see that in the midst of various circumstances of her life she always travelled two journeys. One was at the level of the immediate events and historical circumstances by which she was surrounded. The other, and more important journey for her, was the growth within her of a great trust and love of God from which radiated her true appeal.[9]

The inner and outer journey cannot be separated in anyone's life but distance can certainly grow between them; the outer world of action and doing can take over from the inner world of knowing and being and vice versa. Films, such as *The Love Machine, 1984* and *Six Degrees of Separation,* reveal the possibility of turning every person into an object and every action into a mechanical response. The protagonists in these films recognise no other point of reference except themselves. Robin, in the first film, is an extreme example of the one who manipulates. He uses every person he meets and despises those women who love him. He drives one woman to suicide and reacts to her death by attacking and almost killing a prostitute. He has no other frame of reference except himself. He is the anti-pilgrim in many ways. The reality is there is always some divergence between the inner and outer world of every human, but a pilgrim constantly seeks out what Thomas Merton has described as "the true North", that is, the direction that is even more exact than magnetic north which is always slightly off the true. Pilgrims are called to reflect on this divergence and to bring the outer and inner world into congruence.

Mary MacKillop had to grow spiritually by first reflecting on this divergence within her. The story of the rebuff she experienced as a young girl when faced with social rejection because she was a salesgirl for Sands and Kenny illustrates this.[10] Customers, who believed themselves a station above Mary and who had previously been served by her in the shop, attended a reception by the owners of the stationery emporium to which Mary was also invited. They refused to acknowledge the existence of a sales girl at the gathering. Mary's hurt pride caused her to run away and hide. When the other guests realised she had been treated badly they retaliated on her behalf. She was persuaded to come back and, as her brother Donald says, she would not have been human if she hadn't felt some satisfaction in the way events turned out. A growing point was offered here for the young woman! The extent of her growth in the area of forgiveness can be seen in the following letter written many years later to some sisters who had spoken untruthfully about her – perhaps a much graver offence than the above social slight:

> I excuse with all a mother's heart! I forgive. And as I freely forgive and wish to forget, so do I entreat you my dearly loved ones, to forgive from your heart any Sister who has pained you.[11]

Intention

All spiritualities begin with intention – a deliberate calling to awareness of the meaning of the journey and where the journey is taking the traveller, whether in light or darkness. Rupert Sheldrake in his work, *The Rebirth of Nature,* states that the primary factor in pilgrimage is intention:

> If we go as pilgrims to a sacred place, we go in the hope of being inspired and blessed, or to give thanks. We can inform our intention by learning the stories of the place and its spirit, and by hearing other people's experiences there. The journey itself is as much part of the pilgrimage as arriving and by remembering that we are not going for the sake of comfort, we are better able to respond to any difficulties we may encounter.[12]

Mary began her pilgrimage with an intention and a call. The intention was not articulated fully until she was in her late teens but was latent until the moment she realised her father had been in training for the priesthood and had left the seminary. In her autobiographical letter to Monsignor Kirby she stated that it was then she became determined to carry on in religious life where her father had left off:

> But from the time I came to understand that he had been intended for the Church and had not persevered, I began to desire that I could leave all I loved and live for God alone.[13]

This was not the same thing as Franny wishing to be something she was not. Mary's resolution described above, was the deciding facet of a call personally hers. The call was linked to Mary's sense of God's loving care of herself. This then enabled her to reach out to those around her knowing their need. Mary's stance was the pilgrim's stance described by Edward M. Hayes, even though she may not have described it in the same way:

> Sure Cleveland, Cairo, Tibet or Timbuktu, the place isn't important as the fact that you are on a journey that opens

> you to newness. You don't travel as a tourist but as a pilgrim. When you travel as a pilgrim the world is crowded with hidden shrines and with teachers who don't even know they're spiritual guides for you.[14]

Mary's movements were dictated by obedience and need, as well as by banishment from dioceses where authority saw her strength as a threat to its power. The lodestar in any change for Mary was the work she was called on to do for the Kingdom. Those who attempted to change her direction often opened spiritual doors for her unintentionally as Hayes says, and unwittingly became her spiritual guides.

Presence

Daniel Lyne, speaking again of Mary, says:

> We cannot look at her life, the life of any saint or even Jesus himself, and think that from studying these we can have an automatic blueprint of how to act, nor do we find a detailed roadmap that will give clear direction of the path to follow. Their life journey was theirs and our life journey is ours.[15]

If this is the case what does Mary have to offer us as fellow pilgrims? We learn not from her actions but from her attitude and the stance of her heart. Her faith is the key for modern pilgrims as it was for the little *starets.* The end of our pilgrimage is meeting – God and God's creation. It was this for Mary. The heart of our pilgrimage is presence leading to that meeting:

> This heart can feel presence at work in our times too, the presence of Christ in our relation with God. When presence to the heart is revealed to the eyes, it is 'coming'. That is the full meaning of *apokalypsis* and *parousia.* It is the meaning of the concluding words of New Testament, 'Come Lord Jesus'. Meanwhile, seeing conjoined with feeling, a knowing that is loving that is knowing, is aware of the presence at work in our times, like Brother Lawrence seeing the tree barren in winter and knowing that it would come alive in the spring.[16]

Presence, for Mary and for all pilgrims, is the motivating factor in journeying. One is lured on with the hope of encountering a fuller presence than that of present experience - to be drawn to that thin place between heaven and earth.

Presence is a gift. It is a gift given to us at different times in our lives. There are rare and special moments when we celebrate in creation this profound awareness of a Creator who calls us lovingly to enter and recognise Godself. Poets come to this place of Presence often even if they don't name God specifically. As Eliot says, it is the intersection of the timeless moment where we are with eternity. It is the thin space between places such as Iona and the Infinite. Gerard Manley Hopkins is such a poet who recognised presence by absence in his sonnets of despair.

Veste Fensternmaker captures some of this sense of presence in the following lines:

> To riddle out the koans of God –
> The light in a wave
> The curve of the bending grass.[17]

Unknowingly Mary was "rid(dling) out the koans of God" – those enigmas in life which both reflect and hide mystery.

Julian Tenison Woods understood this creative presence well as he stood at the edge of the Naracoorte Caves or on the coastlines of Tasmania. For Julian the presence of God shone through nature and through science:

> But these revelations, small as they are, stretch far beyond our comprehension. We learn that the dust we tread upon was once alive, that the rock on which we stand has lived and died . . . and this is a time which reaches so far back as only to be understood by the One who was from eternity… and we … are obliged to rest ourselves from the thought of the Infinite and to confess that, whether we search in earth, or sky, or sea, we are everywhere met by the visions of the Illimitable.[18]

But for both Mary and Julian the presence of God was most evident in the people and especially the children encountered on their journey. Mary MacKillop's sense of Presence was a gift she experienced from her earliest years.

> He gave me a sense of His watchful presence that I could feel myself reproved for my smallest faults. . . . He gave me a most keen sense of duty and in the discharge of what appeared to be my duty I felt it impossible to pause or to consider my own feelings no matter how much they had to be trampled upon.[19]

James Cuskelly in his book, *Walking the Way of Jesus,* sees Mary as a pilgrim who becomes a model for Australians – walking the way of Jesus, telling his truth and living his life. He quotes from the testimony of Fr Francis Clune cp cited in the *Positio*, "My first impression was that she was wrapped up in God. As far as a human being could be, she was wrapped up in God."[20] There is a sense here of Mary wearing the presence of God as a cloak wrapped around her as she travels.

Mary's sense of Presence was not strictly a poetic one but it was a sense of God being in relationship with her and wanting of her all she could give to others in the world of her family and in the world beyond. This was especially so as she came to recognise the pain and grief of those others. In some ways Thomas Merton describes the attitude Mary had when she dressed and looked after the small half-caste rejected child on the Cameron Station where she worked as a governess:

> I cannot treat others as persons unless I have compassion for them. I must at least have enough compassion to realize that when they suffer they feel somewhat as I do when I suffer. And if for some reason I do not spontaneously feel this kind of sympathy for others, then it is God's will that I do what I can to learn how. I must learn to share with others their joys, their sufferings, their ideas, their needs, their desires.[21]

One has only to read Mary's letters regarding the Bishops, priests, her own sisters and the laity to know how well she learnt the lesson of compassion and forgiveness during her life. Perhaps this lesson is the heart of what we learn as we travel our own life. In his travels Merton sought the great compassion - Mary sought the will of God. Perhaps these are two different ways of describing the same great love which drew Thomas Merton and Mary MacKillop on – mercy within mercy within mercy – the end of pilgrimage.

Sensitivity

Mary had a heightened sensitivity to the absence of faith in the lives of those around her. The reason for this was the sense of God guiding and directing her always. Mary was sensitively aware of God's presence from earliest childhood. In her moments of deepest pain this awareness surfaced and supported her:

> I have never felt such calm – such a sense of the Presence, the sweet Presence of God, as I have done since I left you at the Port Station just before we parted. I may say that it has never left me; it makes everything that is hard, easy. I just get a taste of bitterness in some things and then something calm and soft raises my mind above it all. I feel this Presence of God at

> all times – when talking to old friends, strangers, the Sisters or the Priests. Sometimes it comes, Oh so beautifully after a little struggle with something I do not like to do. It makes me see God – his Holy Will and immense mercy in everything.[22]

And again, after the excommunication, "I can only remember dimly the things that were said to me, but the sensation of the calm, beautiful presence of God I shall never forget."[23]

Journey Home

Margaret Silf in her work *Landmarks,* writes that the spiritual journey is anything but linear. For her there is a movement from the outer shell of our life to the central core. The outer shell is where we live out our physical life. The life movement is from the external place to a place where choice is confronted and decisions made – about friendship, life, religion. These two dimensions of our existence do not form the whole. Each person is challenged to move into the centre of the self where the encounter with God can happen. Only those who understand the spiritual nature of life are able to move into that place of encounter – what John Bell calls "the Touching Place". Prayer leads us there and our pilgrimage, our journey to the centre, relies on these moments of encounter. Gardiner wrote:

> The whole of Mary MacKillop's long life was a response to God's word spoken in her heart at an early age, a Word that grew ever more demanding. Her personal virtue, all the works she took up, her tireless activity, was an expression of her concern to be faithful to the Word.[24]

It was this dedication which allowed Mary to survive her personal pilgrimage and to encourage her Sisters to do the same.

Challenge

Mary's life pilgrimage is a challenge to all those seeking a deepening of the Spirit and all who struggle to find a meaning in their life. She shows us how to lean on God, something she encourages her sisters to do at all times. She reveals a way of encountering God in the everyday and every event of her life. Her journey encourages us to keep walking – the byways, incorrect routes - deviations ultimately are unimportant if the compass is true. Christ the compass she trusted refocusses our direction constantly.

As one Sister recently said, "Mary stood up to confront and knelt to serve!

She walked courageously to both places – the place of confrontation and the place of service led by her sense of God's presence, her compassion and her sense of duty."

Mary's last spoken phrase was to her sister, Annie, who was praying with her. "Go on," Mary said. Those words of Mary to Annie become a metaphor for those who travel as Mary did. "Go on" is the heritage she leaves behind - what better phrase could there be for those who walk in her spirit, in her land at this time.

Endnotes

1 J. D. Salinger, *Franny and Zooey* (New York: Bantam, 1985), 35.
2 Mary MacKillop to Sister Mechtilde Woods, April 16th 1884.
3 Transportation continued in some colonies until 1868.
4 Ibid.
5 T. S. Eliot, *Four Quartets* (London: Faber 1976), 59.
6 Mary MacKillop to the Sisters, September 25th 1873.
7 Ibid.
8 Sisters of St Joseph, Resource Material from the Archives of the Sisters of St Joseph of the Sacred Heart, Issue No 10, May 1988, 22.
9 Daniel Lyne, *Mary MacKillop: Made in Australia* (Sydney: Sisters of St Joseph, 1994), 6.
10 Paul Gardiner, Cause of Canonisation of the Servant of God Mary of the Cross MacKillop (1842-1909), Foundress of the Australian Sisters of St Joseph of the Sacred Heart. Positio super Virtutibus, Rome, 1989, Congregation for the Causes of the Saints, 106.
11 Mary MacKillop to the Sisters, December 14th 1890.
12 Rupert Sheldrake, *The Rebirth of Nature* (London: Rider/Random Century Group, 1990), 151.
13 Mary MacKillop to Monsignor Kirby, Ascension Thursday, May 22nd 1873.
14 Edward M. Hayes, *The Magic Lantern* (Leavenworth, Kansas: Forest of Peace Books, 1991), 207.
15 Lyne, *Mary MacKillop: Made in Australia*, 6.
16 John Dunn, *The House of Wisdom: A Pilgrimage* (London: SCM Press, 1985), 59.
17 Veste Fensternmaker, Writer's Digest (Ohio, 1993). This extract by Veste is taken from the winning poem in a competition run by Writer's Digest
18 Julian Tenison Woods, "Geological Observations of South Australia, 1862", in *Symphony of Life,* (McMahon Graphics Pty Ltd, Glen Innes NSW: Sisters of St Joseph, North Sydney, No publication date given), 37.
19 Mary MacKillop to Monsignor Kirby, Ascension Thursday, May 22nd 1873.
20 Paul Gardiner, Positio, Testimony of Fr F. Clune, 1466.
21 Thomas Merton, *New Seeds of Contemplation* (New York: New Directions, 1962), 76.
22 Mary MacKillop to Woods, March 6th 1869.
23 Mary MacKillop to Woods, September 1871.
24 Gardiner, Positio, 111.

Revisiting the Virtue of Humility with Mary MacKillop

Margaret Paton

The Need to Revisit Humility

If people today were asked what they thought the most important virtue was, they would probably select love, or faith, patience or courage. Humility would not rate highly, although it might be regarded as an optional extra for those who wanted to excel in virtue and piety. It was a different matter for Mary MacKillop, for whom humility was supremely important.

In this present age of self-expression and competitiveness, with its mind-set of individualism, focusing on the rights and entitlements of the individual, humility has become a neglected and unpopular virtue. Indeed, it is not clear how, in a society of noisy litigation there can be a place for humility. However, today's society is not solely to blame. Part of the difficulty is that humility has a history of misrepresentation. It is a fragile virtue, easily distorted and misunderstood. If we were to ask what humility means today, it would be connected in the minds of many with having a poor opinion of oneself and low self-esteem. If that were indeed the true meaning of humility, it would hardly be worth revisiting. As we shall see, Mary MacKillop did not necessarily connect humility with self-abasement. Recently, several notable spiritual writers, including Joan Chittister[1] and Esther de Waal,[2] have written to the effect that the true meaning of humility has been lost and needs to be reclaimed. Mary MacKillop would certainly agree.

The Importance of Humility to Mary MacKillop

It would generally be known that Mary MacKillop frequently wrote about the will of God, but not so well known that over the years, she devoted a considerable amount of attention to the virtue of humility. In a letter to Father Julian Tenison Woods,[3] written from Brisbane in

1870, she presented what could be described as a mini-treatise on the subject. Twenty years later (1893), her Circular to the Sisters for the feast day of the Institute's patron, St Joseph,[4] highlighted humility. In *The Book of Instructions*,[5] written in 1907, two years before she died, a substantial section is concerned with humility. Her view that humility was vitally important for the spiritual wellbeing of the Sisters had not changed for over almost forty years. It could be argued that humility used to be the hallmark of Josephite formation. It is not at all obvious that humility is central to formation today.

I shall address two questions in this short article, the remainder of which is divided into two parts. The first part deals with the question: Why did Mary MacKillop set such store by humility? The second part deals with the question: How can she help us to reclaim humility as an inspiring virtue for our lives today?

Mary MacKillop's Views on Humility

In her letter to Father Woods (1870), she distinguished between what she calls "true" and "false" humility, showing that she was well aware that some so-called humble behaviour was not an expression of genuine humility. As Father Paul Gardiner explains, "What she is saying is like saying 'there are two kinds of gold, fools' gold and real gold.'"[6] Mary MacKillop had a clear understanding of what might easily be mistaken for humility, but which on her reckoning was a counterfeit. She writes:

> (False humility)….seems to covet in its possessor every kind of opprobrium and censure from its fellow creatures, without the slightest regard to what it may cost many good souls, to entertain doubtful thoughts of another whom they would fain esteem, but whose actions and expressions they cannot understand.[7]

Her way of speaking does not resonate with today's idiomatic language, but it is not hard to understand what she is saying, if we consider our own experience. We have probably all come across people who tiresomely seem to enjoy belittling their achievements, in the name of humility. What they are actually doing, however, is drawing attention to them. Sometimes a person may receive an uncharitable or unjust slur from another, without making any attempt to correct the false impression because she believes it will keep her humble. It is more likely to lead to a loss of self-esteem, as well as perplexing others who do not know what to think. This so-called humility is "selfish.... cold....studied" (Mary's terms) because it is concerned with personal ambitions of reaching unrealistic pinnacles of virtue. Studying to present oneself as humble is inverted pride and is paradoxically self-defeating. What results is a grotesque parody. The prime example of this in literature is the character of Uriah Heap in Dickens' novel *David Copperfield,* who believed that by describing himself as "the 'umblest person going", and behaving accordingly, he would ingratiate himself with others. Mary MacKillop has rightly identified an attitude that is contrary to real humility because it masks pride and an inflated sense of self and consequently diminishes a proper sense of self and self-worth.

On the other hand, according to Mary MacKillop, genuine humility is grounded on truth and a truly humble person acknowledges her own self-worth rather than allowing others to labour under misconceptions about her. She writes:

> True humility.... is accompanied by a sweet and thoughtful charity....It troubles not itself about either the esteem or censure of creatures.[8]

True humility is inspired by charity and thoughtfulness for others. It is not concerned with self or one's failings or what others think about one. It is the antidote to both self-importance and loss of self-esteem. She acknowledged that there are different ways in which true humility might be expressed, but for the Sisters all behaviour that drew attention to itself was to be avoided.[9] However, humility is commonly associated with not taking any credit and taking the lowest position. Occasionally Mary MacKillop advised the Sisters to take the lowest position.[10] But in her letter to Father Woods, she was concerned with true humility as an inner disposition that was free from any illusions about self-importance, grounded in reality and an acceptance of the truth about oneself and others. For Mary MacKillop, humility brought freedom of mind by which she did not mean a *laissez-faire* attitude of thinking and doing as you please, but rather the ability to see things as they really are and to be grounded in truth which is consistent with the derivation of humility from the Latin *humus,* meaning ground or soil. It is the ground of a person's being, to adapt a phrase used by Tillich.[11] She regards humility as the selfless, creative environment of charity from which our true humanity grows. Humility or freedom from self-distortion is the fertile soil that ensures other virtues will take root and grow, because they are liberated from a self-centred preoccupation with "being virtuous", and so leave a person free to love and serve God and others wholeheartedly. Humility is far from being an optional extra in Mary MacKillop's view but is the necessary foundation for a well-grounded spiritual life.

How Can Mary MacKillop Help Us to Reclaim Humility as a Focus for Our Lives Today?

Mary's distinction between true and false humility is of major importance in helping us to unravel confusions in our thinking today about humility. A present day confusion that is similar to the confusion between true and false humility is between humility and humiliation, both of which are derived from the Latin *humus*. It is not difficult to see how the confusion has arisen. To humiliate means to bring another down. For example, the victorious side in battle humiliates the opposing side by defeating them. Similarly, an individual humiliates another by belittling or debasing him or her and metaphorically crushing the other to the ground. Unfortunately, there has been a mistaken tendency to think that one way of becoming humble is to suffer humiliation. A person may even relish humiliation, believing self-abasement would be spiritually beneficial but what results is low self-esteem and a poor self image which is not the true meaning of humility and is not, as we have seen, what Mary MacKillop understood by humility. Humiliation is destructive behaviour and is likely to be personally damaging to the one being humiliated, failing to encourage a properly grounded estimate of self.

Humility in its true sense, however, is already coming back into vogue. Joan Chittister, in her recent study of St Benedict's theory of humility writes, "Humility is the virtue of liberation from self that makes us available to the wisdom of others."[12] And Esther de Waal also maintains that humility is "having a proper sense of self. It means knowing and accepting my limitations, and not denying them."[13] Both writers recognise that humility is connected with the ability to have a well-grounded assessment of oneself in relation to others. This, I believe is how Mary MacKillop understood true humility, which is based on charity that diverts attention away from the self to love of others and God, as opposed to false humility which centres on self in isolation from others and ensures loss of perspective.

Josephite Humility - an Inspirational Virtue for Today

The virtue of humility has a long history of significance for the Congregation of the Sisters of St Joseph. It was central to Mary MacKillop's spirituality, as it is to Ignatian spirituality,[14] with which she was familiar.[15] The main reason for humility's importance to Mary MacKillop was the Founders' choice of St Joseph as Patron of the new Institute in 1867.[16] It is clear that Mary MacKillop wanted the Sisters to regard St Joseph as their model, particularly in relation to his humility. In her Circular to the Sisters for March 19th 1893 she wrote:

> This humility.... is something wonderfully beautiful in itself.... My Sisters, his was a quiet humility....a humility of heart, not of words.... a silent not a noisy humility.[17]

Why did Mary MacKillop regard St Joseph's humility as inspirational for the Sisters? What did she hope it would inspire the Sisters to do or be in their religious life? In the first place, St Joseph was the model of true humility that leads to an inner freedom of heart. Secondly, humility was the key to living life in a spirit of poverty; and finally humility was the means of preserving unity. What can we learn from her approach to inspire us to live well as Christians in today's society?

(a) Humility and Heart Freedom

The quality of St Joseph's humility that specially attracted her was its quiet hiddenness. There was nothing on show, it did not parade itself. St Joseph was the prime example of true humility. Elsewhere she writes, "St Joseph, our father, was humble and hidden."[18] St Joseph had an in-depth humility that was an inner disposition of heart or will. The humility Mary MacKillop so much admired was an ingrained tendency to look beyond self to the good of others, as Joseph looked beyond the opinions of others to his care of Mary and Jesus. It was St Joseph's selflessness that Mary MacKillop specially wished her Sisters to emulate, because it enabled a person to be authentic. This is further explained in the same Circular when she speaks of St Joseph being aware of "his own nothingness."[19] She did not mean by that, that St Joseph regarded himself as having no value or significance. What she meant is brought out in the following verse:

> A man that looks on glass
> On it may stay his eye;
> Or if he pleaseth, through it pass
> And then the heavens espy. (George Herbert)

When we look through a window we are not aware of the glass unless there is a mark or stain on it. There is a sense in which the glass is nothing or hidden and serves only to show the view beyond. Like a transparent windowpane, the Sisters' lives were to be selfless or free from self in order to be the clear medium through which people may glimpse eternity and divine love. To be humble, like St Joseph, a Sister must, through her selflessness, display the love of God in her actions and behaviour. No self-glory was to discolour the glass of her life and block the transparency. Selfish ambition would not have any place in a life that flowed from a liberated self, free enough to live solely for love of God and the good of others.

This Christ-like humility is a radical forgetfulness of self that goes beyond being a social virtue of unselfishness and consideration for others. It is the wellspring of the heart that creatively embraces the will of God as one's destiny. This charitable humility is as vital today as it was in Mary MacKillop's day. It is not for the faint-hearted but neither is it exclusively for Religious. It expands the understanding of what is humanly possible. It is a humility that takes risks and constantly adventures beyond the known. It is the stuff that saints are made of and is the doorway through which the divine can access suffering and affliction in the world. Josephites today are called to be pioneers in selflessness. People will always need to see that it is possible, to live beyond the parameters of self-interest and be inspired to try themselves, for by doing so they are free to engage with reality.

(b) Humility and Poverty:

Mary MacKillop saw an important connection between humility and poverty. Writing about the spirit of St Joseph that was to inspire the Sisters, she says:

> The spirit of the Sisters of St Joseph is a spirit of poverty.... Poverty and humility go hand in hand. If our poverty is not humble poverty it will not last... we must never consider ourselves, but only our work and be ready to do it wherever it is to be done.[20]

In society today, which is preoccupied with the standard of living, poverty like humility, is regarded as something to be avoided. However, by poverty, Mary MacKillop did not just mean financial poverty but rather being poor in spirit which meant the acceptance of complete dependence upon, and trust in, God. This poverty of spirit enabled them to have a grasp of reality.

She also connected humble poverty with the work of the Institute, which had been founded to be an option for the poor. As she herself declared, "St Joseph's schools are humble, intended only for the humble poor."[21] In her view, it was important that their poverty was humble, because unless it was, it would not last There were two points about humble poverty that she wanted the Sisters to grasp. Firstly, the Sisters were to be followers of the Jesus of humility, who himself thought nothing of becoming a servant and washing his disciples' feet. He responded to a real need with an actual loving act of humility, that went far beyond the habits and customs of the time and could well have incurred censure from his critics had they been present. Secondly, the Sisters' humble service of the poor called them to be one with the poor and to live alongside the poor. If they ceased to accept the reality of their own poverty and the needs of the poor they were to serve, Mary MacKillop feared the work would come to an end, for they would no longer be depending upon God but on themselves, nor would they be putting the needs of the poor first but rather government educational policy and aid. They were to be followers of Jesus, "who went to the poor like steel to a magnet (and) was poor himself."[22]

Mary MacKillop's connection between humility and poverty prompts us to reconsider our attitude to the poor today. The many kinds of poverty in the world are almost beyond comprehension. In the wake of disasters, natural and man made, people respond with generous financial aid out of their own affluence but the poor and destitute are a remote idea for many, or more concretely, pictures on the TV news. But images of the poor and destitute do not help us to be connected with real poverty. Helen Prejean speaks about the change in her life, when she heard a speaker at a meeting on justice quote the text, "I bring good news for the poor" (Lk 4:18), adding that the good news was that they would no longer be poor. Helen recognised a call to her to do something more than pray for the poor. She was being challenged to be with them in their poverty. This conviction eventually led her to "walk" with those on Death Row. A few individuals may be inspired to go and be with those suffering in areas affected by earthquakes and *tsunamis* but in general people continue to strive for success, power and status in a society where such things have priority. The poor remain images on our TV screens and continue to be idealised and kept at a safe distance.

Jean Vanier is today's prophet of humility and service of the poor. He points out that when Jesus called the disciples to take the lowest place, he was not just urging them to fight against pride and the need to be important. He was inviting them to sit with the poor, to become poor themselves, for there they would encounter the presence of God:

> Jesus tells us that by taking the lowest place we will meet the poor, the weak the crippled, the blind and the outcast, who are all signs of the presence of God. As we become their friends, we become friends of God.[23]

God still calls individuals today to stop climbing the ladder of promotion and striving for success and to mix with the poor, the oppressed, refugees and asylum seekers, and people with AIDS in Africa, for there they will surely discover the presence of God. Revisiting Mary MacKillop's understanding of humility can inspire us today to test just how realistic our attitude is to the poor in our midst and how prepared we are to be inspired by the Josephite charism, constantly and selflessly to serve and be with those who have been left at the margins of society.

(c) Unity – the Fruit of Humility

Frequently in her writings, Mary MacKillop connected humility with unity. In a letter written to the Sisters on September 30th 1873, she urges them, "Be faithful to your Rule, remain firmly united, diffident in yourselves."[24] Diffident is a word that is not much in use today. What Mary MacKillop meant by the phrase, "diffident in your-selves," was not to be overconfident but be humble, allow for the possibility that you could be wrong. A Sister did not have the right to criticise another and find fault, because to do so was to put herself on a pedestal thereby introducing division. There is a very plausible and practical connection between not thinking too highly of oneself and unity, in the sense that self-importance refuses to allow others to have their rightful place, which in turn causes resentment and disunity.

In her Circular to the Sisters for September 4th 1906, she wrote:

> Sisters of St Joseph should never love their own opinions.... Let us be ready to give way. We are never sure that we are right; and even when we are nearly sure let us not contend. When we have given our opinion humbly and quietly, let us sacrifice the rest for love of God.[25]

She knew very well how easily unity could be damaged in Josephite communities, through gossip, bickering, murmuring, criticism and fault finding.[26] Those who engaged in these "faults of the tongue" had an inflated sense of their own importance. They lacked humility and they were the cause of disunity. Over and over in her writings, Mary MacKillop urged the Sisters to maintain their unity, often asking them to be forgiving towards one another.

Of course, she is not saying that the Sisters are not to have opinions. What she is saying is that they are not be opinionated, that is, so attached to their own opinions and self importance that they cannot listen to the opinions of others. Humility teaches us wisdom to know that we can never be absolutely certain that we are right. Others have a right to their points of view. Sisters of St Joseph are to be ready to give way, not out of weakness, but for the love of God and the sake of unity. For many reasons, disunity is to be avoided. If there is no unity, firstly, the Sisters cannot live together in charity; secondly, their witness as an Institute is weakened; thirdly, they will be ineffective in their ministry; and fourthly, they will not be prepared to listen to others. However, when there is an attitude of humility that willingly allows others to express their opinions, the voice of God may be more easily discerned and disunity avoided.

Mary MacKillop gave practical advice on the importance of humility in relation to unity. Her advice to the Sisters to be humble enough and open to listen to others and be prepared to give way, is something we need to hear today and be able to apply at all levels of society, from the personal level of broken relationships, to a national level of finding ways to heal divisions within society between ethnic groups, those within the system and those who are excluded, refugees and asylum seekers, between weak and strong, rich and poor. There is a brokenness in today's society that cannot be properly addressed as long as self-importance and a competitive spirit are considered acceptable. We need to reconsider the virtue of humility as the antidote to self-importance and its consequence of disunity.

In today's pluralist society, in particular, there is an urgent need to listen to the "other", if there is to be peace between those of different religious persuasions. Tolerance is needed and also respect for those who are different from ourselves but humility is even more urgently needed, especially in relation to inter-religious dialogue, where there is the mutual need to learn from one another. Joan Chittister writes, "Humility lies in learning to listen to the words, directions and insights of those around us. They are the voice of God calling to us here and now."[27]

But we will not hear God's voice in the "other" unless we are inspired humbly to accept ourselves, others, and the reality of life as it is. Huston Smith writes perceptively about humility, "Humility is not self-abasement. It is the capacity to regard oneself in the company of others as one but not more than one."[28]

This modern definition of humility is in keeping with Mary MacKillop's aspirations for the Sisters regarding St Joseph's quiet humility that does not seek the limelight but is the answer to our self-importance that is so inimical to inner peace and undermining of relationships. In a society where relationships founder and are put at risk, it is surely worth revisiting a virtue that has been described as "the mortar of relationships"[29] which can have a healing effect in people's lives.

Conclusion

Joan Chittister writes, "The twenty-first century has plenty to relearn about humility."[30] Humility was of great importance to Mary MacKillop who spoke about it as "God's school".[31] The first thing we need to relearn is the true meaning of humility. Mary MacKillop can help us to do this by her distinction between true and false humility. St Joseph was the model of humility to whose selfless spirit of humble poverty she urged the Sisters to turn for inspiration. Humility is the great teacher of reality. It teaches us to be real about ourselves and others and also frees us from illusions about always being right. Humility teaches us about the reality of our own poverty and enables us to be in touch with the poor. Finally, humility is the ground from which unity within communities and society will be achieved because it fosters self-respect and respect for the other.

Mary's perceptive remarks about humility apply today and can inspire and challenge us radically to question the degree to which self-importance and competitiveness are admired in today's society. Just as she valiantly confronted disunity in her day, so Mary MacKillop can be an inspiration to us to ground our lives on the truth of who we are, and an acceptance of others who are different, as the presence of God in our lives, those whom we neglect at our peril.

Endnotes

1. Joan Chittister, *Twelve Steps To Inner Freedom, Humility Revisited* (PA, USA: Benetvision, 2003). Used with permission.
2. Ester de Waal, *Lost in Wonder* (Victoria: John Garratt Publishing, 2003).
3. Mary MacKillop to Julian Tenison Woods, June 3rd 1870.
4. Mary MacKillop to the Sisters, March 19th 1893.
5. Mary MacKillop, *A Book of Instructions for the Use of the Sisters of St Joseph of the Sacred Heart* (Westmead, Sydney: Boys' Industrial HomePrint, 1907), 25-29.
6. Paul Gardiner, Cause of Canonisation of the Servant of God, Mary of the Cross MacKillop (1842-1909), Foundress of the Sisters of St Joseph of the Sacred Heart. Positio super Virtutibus, Rome, 1989, Congregation of for the Causes of the Saints, 312.
7. Mary MacKillop to Woods, June 3rd 1970.
8. Ibid. The original Rule written by Julian Tenison Woods stated that Sisters were to, "consider themselves the least among all religious orders". The precise meaning is not known; but it may have been purely pragmatic – Australia was a young country, and the Sisters of St Joseph were a young Institute.
9. Paul Gardiner, *An Extraordinary Australian: Mary MacKillop: The Authorised Biography* (Australia: E.J. Dwyer, 1993), 402.
10. Mary MacKillop, *A Book of Instructions for the Use of the Sisters of St Joseph of the Sacred Heart, 7.*
11. Paul Tillich, *Courage To Be* (London: Collins Paperback, 1962), 153-154.
12. Chittister, *Twelve Steps to Freedom*, 23.
13. de Waal, *Lost in Wonder*, 82.
14. Karl Rahner, *Ignatius Loyola* (London: Collins, 1979), 23-24.
15. Gardiner, *An Extraordinary Australian: Mary MacKillop: The Authorised Biography*, 178. Gardiner refers to Mary MacKillop having studied Ignatius Loyola's *Letter on Obedience.*
16. Pope John Paul 11, *Guardian of the Redeemer, Apostolic Exhortation on the Person and Mission of St Joseph in the life of Christ and of the Church* (Boston, MA: St Paul's Books and Media, 1989). "St Joseph is proof.... it is enough to have the common, simple human virtues but they need to be true and authentic" (Quoted from Paul V1's Discourse, March 19th 1969, No 29).
17. Mary MacKillop to the Sisters, March 19th 1873.
18. Gardiner, Positio, 312.
19. Mary MacKillop to the Sisters, March 19th 1893.
20. Mary MacKillop, *A Book of Instructions for the Use of the Sisters of St Joseph*, 5.
21. Sisters of St Joseph, Resource Material from the Archives of the Sisters of St Joseph of the Sacred Heart. Issue No 10, May 1988, 30.
22. Rosemary Haughton, *The Passionate God* (Great Britain: Darton, Longman & Todd, 1982), 328.
23. Jean Vanier, *The Scandal of Service* (Great Britain: Darton, Longman& Todd, 1997), 51.
24. Mary MacKillop to the Sisters, September 25th 1873.
25. Mary MacKillop to the Sisters, September 4th 1906.
26. Gardiner, Positio, 32.
27. Chittister, *Twelve Steps to Inner Freedom*, 33.
28. Huston Smith, *The World's Religion* (New York: Harper Collins, 1991), 387.
29. Chittister, *Twelve Steps to Inner Freedom*, 58.
30. Chittister, *Twelve Steps to Inner Freedom*, 20.
31. Mary MacKillop, *A Book of Instructions for the Use of the Sisters of St Joseph*, 59.

Eucharist at the Heart of Mary's Life

Carmel Pilcher rsj

In his Apostolic Letter *Dies Domini*, the late Pope John Paul II wrote: "Sunday is a day that is at the very heart of the Christian life."[1] Each Sunday, continuing our rich and long tradition, Christians gather to celebrate the Eucharist on the Lord's Day. We live in an exciting time in our church's history. In the wake of the Second Vatican Council, (40 plus years is a short period in Christian terms), we are in the midst of liturgical renewal that has revolutionised the way we participate in our Sunday Mass. We are also experiencing a resurgence of devotion, where many are returning to adoration of the Blessed Sacrament at times other than during Mass. In some ways we are far removed from the Eucharistic experience of Mary MacKillop and the early Sisters' experience of the Mass and Sacraments, but in other instances there are striking similarities.

Eucharistic Practice During the Life of Mary MacKillop

Mary MacKillop lived in the second half of the nineteenth century, when devotion to the Blessed Sacrament was the hallmark of the faithful Catholic. Mary loved nothing better than be in the presence of her Lord, and invited her Sisters to do likewise. It appears that many who knew Mary testified to the many hours she spent in adoration before the Blessed Sacrament, and the frequency of her visits to the Blessed Sacrament, both before and after she became a Sister of St Joseph. While on visitation to a community of Sisters it was a common practice for Mary to spend one or two hours in the chapel each night after the other Sisters had retired. It was no surprise to her companions, that upon hearing devastating news about the shipwreck in which her mother was drowned, Mary's immediate reaction was to visit the chapel. As Mother Laurence recounted, "When she heard of her mother's death she went to the Oratory and spent two hours on her knees."[2] Her deep and personal relationship with Jesus in the Blessed Sacrament sustained Mary throughout all her life, and in particular, at times when none but her God could console or enlighten her.

Devotion to the Blessed Sacrament was a more familiar practice for Mary and her contemporaries than for most of us today. But then active participation in the Eucharistic liturgy was not possible for Catholics for several hundred years before the middle of the 20th century. Even the way Mary spoke about the liturgy reflects this. In her letters Mary never wrote about hearing Mass without separately naming the times that she also received Holy Communion. When visiting Loreto while on her travels in Europe Mary wrote to her Sisters, "I had the great happiness of receiving our dear Lord twice, and of hearing, I know not how many Masses."[3] That there appears a distinction between the Mass and Holy Communion appears strange to our ears but not to the Catholic at the time of Mary MacKillop. The offering of the Holy Sacrifice of the Mass had become the exclusive action of the ordained. The laity came to *hear* Mass being *said* by the priest. The role of the laity focused more on the devotional aspect of gazing at the consecrated host rather than sharing in the Eucharistic Banquet. The receiving of Holy Communion by the faithful often occurred before or after Mass, if at all. Frequent communion at Mass was the exception for the faithful at the time. Not until the time of Mary's death in 1909 at the insistence of Pius X, did Catholics begin to return to a regular practice of receiving communion during Sunday Mass.

Evidence of an expectation that frequent communion was to be the normal practice of the Sisters of St Joseph was written into their Rule and instilled at the direction of Father founder, Julian Tenison Woods. It appears that where possible Mary and the Sisters did communicate regularly. On numerous occasions Mary urged the Sisters to offer Holy Communion for one another, or for a particular intention, for example, the election of Superiors at the first General Chapter.[4] We know too, that this was Mary's practice from her assurance to them:

> I ... will continue my old custom of daily praying at Mass and Holy Communion for any Sister or Sisters whose feast falls on that day or whose death it may be the anniversary. Years ago I made this special intention renewing it daily, for by such means alone could I make sure of not neglecting any of my Sisters. [5]

It was the usual practice of the Sisters, and Mary herself, to attend Mass not only weekly, but also daily. At least on one occasion Mary implored the Bishop to say Mass at Surrey Hills, Auckland, to save the Sisters having to endure the hardship of travelling in inclement weather to the church of St Benedict.[6]

Mary had a deep love of the Mass. At the same time she readily travelled to isolated parts of the vast land where regular Sunday Mass was not possible. Nor did she hesitate to assign her Sisters to remote areas where no priest was in residence. As already noted, the original Rule required the Sisters on Sundays to hear Mass and take Communion, and to spend the rest of the day attending to the spiritual lives of the children. In commenting upon the observance of this Mary MacKillop reservedly remarked to the authorities, "The 7th chapter, that on Sunday Observance, is one, the teachings of which the Sisters earnestly wish to uphold, but which to the letter they are not in many places able to put into practice."[7] Mary states that where the Sisters were deprived of regular Sunday Mass, and the pastor could only visit once a month, or once in three months, they still observed the Lord's Day by gathering the people together for Rosary and meditation.[8] That this continued to be a regular situation is evident from one of her circulars, where Mary acknowledged that those Sisters who lived in places where there was no resident priest should move to a convent for part of their holidays where they would be able to hear Mass more frequently.[9] Sadly in our own time the lack of active ordained priests is causing a similar situation where Catholics and the Sisters who serve them are again deprived of their right to regular Sunday Eucharist in parts of Australia, New Zealand and beyond, but Mary wills us to endure this hardship.

Celebrating Eucharist Today

The most significant difference between Eucharistic practice before and after Vatican II, between the period in the life of Julian and Mary, and our own time, is the ability of the faithful People of God to participate in the Mass. The reform of the liturgy challenged the whole church to "full, conscious and active participation" in the liturgy that, it reminded us, "is the right and duty of all the priestly people of God by virtue of baptism". The Council mandate went on to state that this is the aspect of the reform of the liturgy to be "considered before all else."[10] Through baptism, Christians are invited to share in the priesthood of Christ. The Council Fathers restored to the faithful their rightful role in the liturgical action as active sharers in Christ's priesthood. While Mary *heard* the Mass, we today *participate* in the Mass. This is more than a change of language, but rather a change in attitude that brings about a different reality. No longer simply passive observers at Mass, whose main activity is adoration of the presence of the Blessed Sacrament confected through the power of the ordained priest, the Holy People of God now have an active role throughout the Mass. There is but one priest, Christ, and Christ invites all his faithful, to share in that priesthood. The ordained and the laity share in Christ's priesthood, although with different functions. The church, the baptised with the ordained priest, is called to gather on the Lord's Day to "offer God the prayers of the entire human family, … giving thanks in Christ for the mystery of salvation by offering his sacrifice."[11] The Mass is the action of the whole People of God. This notion of priesthood, while clearly understood in the early church, had lost its significance over time, and during Mary's lifetime the action of the Mass was subsumed in the ordained.

During the twentieth century Communion of the faithful was restored to its integral place in the Mass, and one of the greatest noticeable effects of the reform has been the practice of regular communion of the faithful. This is a natural consequence of full involvement in the Eucharistic action in response to the divine memorial command to eat and drink in memory of Jesus. As the synoptics and Paul record in the meal tradition - Jesus took bread, blessed it, broke it gave it to his disciples. He did the same with wine. In like manner the priest takes the bread and wine, prays the blessing prayers of consecration, breaks the bread and pours the wine and gives it to us to eat and drink.

This ancient fourfold action shapes the way that we participate in the sacrifice of Christ. We are invited to bring ourselves, the work of our human lives to the table. We bring the 'stuff' of our week, our joys and hopes, our grief and anxieties and lay them in faith along with the bread and wine as our gifts to our God. The priest takes this bread, this wine, and our offerings for the poor, and gives thanks to God for these great gifts. Through the great blessing prayer prayed by the priest on our behalf, our lives become transformed through the power of God's Spirit, along with the bread and wine. Our lives are caught up in the sacrifice and transformed into Christ's sacrifice that we remember and is made present again through our offering. As the bread is broken and the wine poured out so that we can take the Body and Blood of

Christ into our hearts and lives, our lives are broken and poured out in sacrifice for others. When we come to the table we become one people in Christ and with each other in deepest communion. We share in the great meal that unifies us in Christ Our church powerfully teaches:

> In the Eucharist the sacrifice of Christ becomes also the sacrifice of the members of his Body. The lives of the faithful, their praise, sufferings, prayer and work, are united with those of Christ and with his total offering, and so acquire a new value.[12]

Christ's sacrifice becomes our sacrifice when the bread is taken, blessed and broken. We the Holy People of God come to the table as one Body, Christ's Body. Our whole lives have become transformed so that we become ever more the Body of Christ when we eat and drink from the consecrated bread and wine. We who are the presence of Christ become that presence for our family, our friends, our neighbours in the coming week. The early church understood this. One of the great Fathers of the Church, Augustine, stated:

> If, therefore, you are the body of Christ and His members, your mystery has been placed on the Lord's table, you receive your mystery. You reply "Amen" to that which you are. Be a member of the body of Christ so that your "Amen" may be true.[13]

In this restored understanding of the active participation of the faithful and the communal activity of the People of God, it is not surprising that frequent communion has now become the norm rather than the exception. We live with the hope that resurrection is possible because each Sunday we gather to recall the fact that Christ died and rose again to liberate us from death. We gather to remember Christ's death and resurrection and bring to the sacrifice of Christ, our own sacrifice. We the Church, become one with Christ and the sacrifice of Christ becomes the sacrifice of the Body of Christ. There is an intimate connection between the Eucharist and our lives, one flows from the other. Our daily deaths become the living witness of Christ's death. Mary MacKillop and her contemporaries did not know this link between the memorial sacrifice of the Sunday Eucharist and the daily sacrifices of faithful Christians.

The Eucharistic Memorial and the Cross in Mary's Life

Mary understood sacrifice, but could not directly identify it with her involvement at Mass. Anyone familiar with Mary of the Cross knows that the cross was never far from her experience. Early in her religious life Mary remarked to her mother, "My title, the happy one given to me at my Profession, implies a life of Crosses and afflictions."[14] She was to learn throughout her life the truth of this. Mary's 'crosses' during her lifetime included excommunication from the church, banishment from the city she loved, tragic deaths of more than one member of her family, estrangement from dear friends including Julian Tenison Woods, and a life dogged with ill health. But through all of this Mary appeared to have a human attitude to suffering.

> My only anxiety is that lest I should fail in any sorrow or humiliation he should put upon me. I cannot say with God's faithful servants that I love humiliations, but I know they are good for me, and if he sends them I hope I shall be grateful. I do want with all my heart to be what God wishes me to be.[15]

Mary did not seek out suffering but readily accepted it in faith. She did not relish humiliation and trials but rather prayed always to accept them. Perhaps her brother Donald was aware of this and by way of encouragement on more than one occasion reminded her that the cross was the title she wore from religious profession.

Mary spoke always with great hope and gratitude about the cross in her life, even when bowed down by it. She reflected with her mother after the misunderstandings that led to her excommunication from the church, the oft quoted statement:

> The Cross is my portion – it is also my sweet rest and support. I could not be happy without my cross – I would not lay it down for all the world could give. With the Cross I am happy, but without it I would be lost.[16]

Mary realised that the cross was a necessary part of the life of any Christian. While acknowledging this central aspect of life's journey she also welcomed its presence as a sign that it provided the means of journeying faithfully with Christ.

Mary frequently wrote of the cross in her many letters to her Sisters. She expected her own Sisters to also accept suffering and challenges in their lives with the same strong faith she demonstrated. In a circular written at the height of troubles in Adelaide Mary challenged the Sisters to take courage and not to become "cowards of the Cross". Crosses and trials are a sign of "solid proofs of God's love," she stated, and rather than finding ways to avoid them, the Sisters should accept them with great gratitude to God. [17] Mary's own attitude to such hardship and her continued hope and deepening love of God was passed on to her followers. All Sisters of St Joseph were to be Sisters of the Cross.

Mary never saw suffering as an end in itself, but the motivation for accepting all suffering was the love of God. Mary wrote a long letter to the Sisters on St Joseph's day in 1893. After reflecting about who the Sisters were and what they were about she summed up her message with the words: "We have come here at the call of our God to learn to die to ourselves, and to live only in doing His ever-blessed will." Suffering was always linked for Mary with the suffering of Christ. We are saved by the passion and death of Christ, challenged Mary, and this same Christ has invited us all to share in his work of redemption. The call of the Sister of St Joseph is to die to self in order to share in the passion and death of Christ. "He has brought us here to lay the sweet load of the cross upon our weak shoulders, to help him carry his, and to be sharers – humble, sorrowing sharers – in the wrongs of his afflicted Mother." [18]

Mary expected her followers to become images of Jesus Christ crucified, to see in their own suffering a share of Christ's suffering, to be the living sign to the people they served of the crucified Christ. Mary's words are an echo of those of Julian, who wrote in a circular to the Sisters, "Nuns and all religious are meant to be the images of Christ crucified".[19] Mary MacKillop recognised the cross as the complete surrender to the will of God. Towards the end of her life when her health had all but failed her, and her physical suffering was immense, she was able to say to the Sisters, "Let us refuse nothing to God's love. He humbled himself and suffered for us – Let us be glad to show him we are willing to suffer whatever he deigns to ask of us."[20] Mary constantly expressed gratitude and blessing for God's great sign of love through the cross and urged her Sisters to do likewise.

In her very life Mary embodied Eucharist. She lived the paschal mystery, constantly dying and rising with Christ - the heart of the Eucharistic memorial. Mary always recognised the cross as a blessing, offering her a share in the suffering of Christ. She urged her companions to accept sacrifices and hardship as their share in the cross. Mary contemplated her suffering before the presence of Christ in the tabernacle and invited her Sisters to do the same, asking that the priest offer the Holy Sacrifice on their behalf. "I have no hope but in your prayers and sufferings, and in the merits of the Holy Sacrifice as offered for us by our dear Bishop and other good Fathers."[21] *Dies Domini* states:

> Today we bring the sacrifice of our lives to the table of the Eucharist each Sunday, and our sacrifices are transformed to become Christ's sacrifice.
> The rhythm of the week prompts us to gather up in grateful memory the events of the days which have just passed, to review them in the light of God and to thank him for his countless gifts, glorifying him 'through Christ, with Christ and in Christ, in the unity of the Holy Spirit.'[22]

Eucharistic Action on Behalf of the Poor

A second strong theme that pervaded Mary's life and is an essential element of our authentic Eucharistic tradition is her strong sense of justice. This we recognise most powerfully in her great love for and action on behalf of the poor. As a child Mary was no stranger to hardship and poverty. As the eldest child of a family she became the major provider at a young age when her father proved unable to manage financially. As an adult Mary chose to serve the poor by identifying with them in every way.

Mary demanded that any woman who wished to live as a Sister of St Joseph would need to embrace poverty. She named this intention clearly to Bishop Sheil of Adelaide:

> I looked for a poverty more like unto that practised in the early religious orders of the Church, a poverty which in its practice would make a kind of reparation to God for the little confidence now placed in His Divine Providence by so many of his creatures.[23]

The Sisters were founded first and foremost to educate poor children, to serve the needs of their families, and to reach out to the destitute in society. Those they served were unable to offer much support in the way of money or food, so the Sisters often went hungry. Their convents were simple and basic, so the Sisters, like the people, were exposed to the harsh extremes of climate and discomfort. Poverty was named as the 'ornament of the Institute' and was to be worn as the badge that identified a Sister of St Joseph.[24] It was not uncommon at the time to see two Sisters visiting the marketplaces and shops begging for food.

They needed to support those in their care - the orphans, the destitute homeless, prostitutes and the sick who came to live in the 'Refuges' set up by Mary and Julian and the Sisters.

Mary did not expect of her Sisters what she herself did not exemplify. Until Mary moved to North Sydney she apparently had no office or special room for her work. She would write her letters in a room shared by all, and the Sisters were interviewed there or in some semi private part of the convent. Mary chose to sleep in dormitories with the Sisters. Much to the chagrin of her companions, Mary was notorious for placing her own needs last. She was known to have given her food to her youngest followers or to the homeless who knocked on the door, even when she herself was tired and hungry. Mary also shared the tasks of the consequence of their poverty. When berating herself for an overdue communication with them she could say: "You can have no idea how hard it is to write when going about begging from place to place."[25]

Mary not only served the poor but had a great love for the poor, especially poor children. One simple story is told about Mary:

> She had driven some miles in a snow storm, but her first wish was to visit the school. There was a poor little bare-footed and ragged boy standing in class. Mother went straight to him, and putting her arms around him she kissed him saying, 'Ah Sister, these are the children I love.'[26]

In a similar story a dying orphaned boy at Kincumber asked for Mary. She braved ferocious weather and journeyed to be with him as he died. She then led the rosary at his graveside before returning to Sydney.

Apart from teaching poor children, Mary and the Sisters ministered to the destitute and those most shunned by society in hospitals, goals, and asylums. She and the Sisters were not afraid to venture into the seamy and unsavoury places where no other 'respectable' women dared to enter. As one Sister recalled about Mary:

> She had the greatest compassion and love for the poor girls and the poor orphans. She used to make us visit the goal, the hospital, the reformatory girls, and if there was no one else to go she went herself. Many of the girls would not have stayed except for Mother's influence. We had bad characters who came from the gaols, the streets and everywhere. She said they were to have every comfort.[27]

Mary's great sense of justice and compassion urged her to offer great respect and dignity to all people regardless of their status in life. But in particular she reached out to the most neglected and oppressed.

Apparently when living in Adelaide it was Mary's practice to visit the gaol each Sunday. Two criminals that Mary befriended were "Scotch Bella" and Fagan. Both were murderers and were notoriously volatile and unruly to the extreme. Scotch Bella was described as a 'raving lunatic' and Fagan's behaviour was such that he had to be chained. Over time Mary managed to so influence Bella that she secured her release from goal and the Sisters cared for her at the Refuge. It appears that due to the persevering ministrations of Mary and the Sisters, Bella eventually married and lived a happy and fulfilled life. Fagan was not so fortunate and was awaiting a death sentence for his crimes. Mary, against all advice, with one of her Sisters as companion, went to visit Fagan. As Sister Annette later described:

> Mother was so affected that the tears poured down her face. This so moved (Fagan) that he knelt down and prayed with them. At the beginning he was abrupt with Mother but he calmed down and became as gentle as a lamb.[28]

It seemed that no man or woman, however disreputable was beyond the ministrations of Mary and her Sisters.

Mary's love for the poor and especially children, found its inspiration in her patron Joseph. In a letter written on St Joseph's day, Mary reminded the Sisters that Joseph was such a tender parent toward Jesus. She invited her Sisters to follow his example and to likewise be tender parents to the 'Jesus' in their care, the children, and especially the poor and neglected children:

> Let us ask him to obtain for us a generous devoted love for his Jesus, a love that will make us like himself – faithful to his interest. A love that, true to the spirit and object of our Institute, will make us delight in serving Him in *His Poor* and his *neglected little ones*, that will teach us patience with their faults, and how in loving charity to help them overcome them.[29]

Mary recognised the face of Jesus in the poor children and their families that she served. She also recognised Jesus in the "Scotch Bellas" and the Fagans as well. Mary's followers were to serve Christ in all people, and especially the poor and destitute. The key to this deep love of the poor was Mary's strong identification of these sick, lonely and destitute, with the suffering Christ

Mary's attitude to poverty finds an echo in all ages, but its connection with Eucharist was particularly evident in the witness of the early Christians. From the first recorded account of Eucharist by Justin it is clear that care for the poor is an essential element of engagement in truthful Eucharist.[30] One comes to the table to eat and drink in memory of the Christ whose death brought about the liberation of all people. One leaves the Eucharistic table charged by the memory to liberate others. As John Chrysostom so eloquently challenged his community:

> What good is it if the eucharistic table is overloaded with golden chalices, when he is dying of hunger? ... Do you wish to honour the body of Christ? Do not ignore him when he is naked. Do not pay him homage in the temple clad in silk only then to neglect him outside when he suffers cold and nakedness. He who said: "This is my body," is the same One who said: "You saw me hungry and you gave me no food," and "Whatever you did to the least of my brothers and sisters you did also to me."[31]

Mary recognized Christ in the poor and the outcast. While John Chrysostom directly linked care for the poor as an outcome of faithful Eucharistic practice, Mary appealed to the image of the poor Christ, as a prisoner in the tabernacle. If she had lived in our time Mary would have challenged us with an image that was strong in the early church. Ancient Christians spoke of the poor as the "Altar of Christ". The message of Chrysostom is also that of Mary MacKillop:

> But the one who is the body of Christ you treat with shame, and when dying, neglect. This altar may you see lying everywhere, both in the lanes and in market places, and may you sacrifice upon it every hour; for on this too is sacrifice performed. And as the priest stands invoking the Spirit, so do you too invoke the Spirit, not by speech, but by deeds.[32]

The Challenge that Mary's Eucharistic Witness Offers to Her Followers Today

Devotion to the Blessed Sacrament has remained the practice of the followers of Mary MacKillop. The reserved sacrament is still to be found in convents and retreat centres. But as with Mary, the presence of Christ, while strongly experienced through faith in the reserved species, is also recognised in all of God's creation and especially human life. As Mary recalled to Julian on her first missionary journey as a Sister of St Joseph:

> I felt this presence of God at all times – when talking to old friends, strangers, the Sisters or the Priests. Sometimes it comes Oh so beautifully after a little struggle with something I do not like to do. It makes me see God – his holy Will and immense mercy in everything.[33]

Especially did Mary find the suffering Christ in the poor and in the destitute.

Like Mary we are called to serve the poor. Like Mary we are called to recognise the trials and difficulties of our lives as blessings. We are invited by her inspiration to accept hardship as a share in the passion and death of Christ.

It is our gift however, to recognise that the source of our call to service of the poor; the source of our recognition of daily deaths in our lives is the Sunday Eucharist. We come to the table Sunday after Sunday not as individuals, but as God's people, the church. As the Body of Christ our individual sufferings become one in Christ's sacrifice. From the table we go out and seek Christ in the poor. In this way we live the memorial in a way that is prophetic, in the way that God required when he challenged us to 'do this in memory of me'.

The words of the Constitutions of the Sisters of St Joseph remind us of our legacy:

> God's compassionate love for his people, the Eucharist as source and summit, and the mystery of the Cross provide for us, as they did for Mary MacKillop, a context for our service of others. [34]
>
> The Eucharist is central to our lives. It gives expression to our unity and reconciles us to one another. From it we draw strength and courage to give ourselves in service of others. We celebrate Eucharist daily where possible.[35]

And so:

> Today we commit ourselves to you
> as we recognise your presence in every person we meet
> and reach out to the suffering and the poor.[36]

Endnotes

[1] *Dies Domini. Guide to Keeping Sunday Holy*: Apostolic Letter, 1998, (Strathfield, NSW: St Paul's Publications, 1998), No7.

[2] Paul Gardiner, Cause of Canonisation of the Servant of God, Mary of the Cross MacKillop (1842-1909), Foundress of the Australian Sisters of St Joseph of the Sacred Heart. Positio super Virtutibus, Rome, 1989, Congregation for the Causes of the Saints, 1187.

[3] Mary MacKillop to the Sisters, September 22nd 1873.

[4] Mary MacKillop to the Sisters, January 16th 1875.

[5] Mary MacKillop to Sr Andrea, August 8th 1894.

[6] Mary MacKillop to Sister Calasanctius, August 8th, 1894.

[7] Mary of the Cross, *Observations on the Rule*, May 18th 1873, Resource Material from the Archives of the Sisters of St Joseph of the Sacred Heart, Issue No 3, (Revised) 1984, 47.

[8] Mary of the Cross, *Necessity for the Institute*, August 1873, Resource Material from the Archives of the Sisters of St Joseph of the Sacred Heart, Issue No 3, (Revised) 1984, 73.

[9] Mary MacKillop to the Sisters, November 15th 1882.

[10] *Sacrosanctum Concilium*, 14, in *The Documents of Vatican 11*, ed Walter M.Abbott, (London: Geoffrey Chapman, 1965).

[11] General Instruction of the Roman Missal (2000), 5.

[12] Catechism of the Catholic Church, 1368

[13] Augustine, *Sermon to the Neophytes*, 272.

[14] Mary MacKillop to Flora MacKillop, June 7th 1870.

[15] Mary MacKillop to Sister Annette, December 1st 1898.

[16] Mary MacKillop to Flora MacKillop, February 26th 1872.

[17] Mary MacKillop to the Sisters from the Mother House at Kensington, May 21st 1877.

[18] Mary MacKillop to the Sisters, March 19th 1893.

[19] Julian Tenison Woods to My Dearest Children, September 4th 1887. Written to the Sisters of St Joseph, most likely the "Maitland Sisters", now known as the Lochinvar Congregation, Federation of the Sisters of St Joseph.

[20] Mary MacKillop to the Sisters, September 18th 1906.

[21] Mary MacKillop to the Sisters, March 23rd 1878.

[22] *Dies Domini*, 42.

[23] Mary MacKillop to Bishop Sheil, September 10th 1871.

[24] Mary MacKillop, Adaptation of the Rule of the Institute of 1867.

[25] Paul Gardiner, *An Extraordinary Australian: Mary MacKillop: The Authorised Biography* (Australia: E.J. Dwyer, 1993), 238.

[26] Sister Lucy to Mother Laurence, November 19th 1925.

[27] Gardiner, *An Extraordinary Australian: Mary MacKillop: The Authorised Biography*, 241. These were Sister Annette's memories.

[28] Ibid.

[29] Mary MacKillop to the Sisters, March 19th 1893.

[30] Justin Martyr, *First Apology*, 67. The account of Eucharist by Justin begins and ends with material giving to the poor in the community.

[31] John Chrysostom, *Commentary on Matthew* 50.4.

[32] John Chrysostom, *Homily 2 Corinthians* 20. 9,10.

[33] Mary MacKillop to Julian Tenison Woods, December 22nd 1869.

[34] Constitutions of the Sisters of St Joseph of the Sacred Heart, 5.

[35] *A Future and a Hope*, Constitutions of the Australian and New Zealand Federation of the Sisters of St Joseph, 20.

[36] Prayer of the Associates of the Sisters of St Joseph of the Sacred Heart.

Mary MacKillop and Friendship

Margaret Press rsj

Oh my dear friend, I wish I could see you again or hear your voice. Living or dying, my beloved friend, I am ever the same to you and am proud to look back on nearly 40 years of unbroken friendship. My husband and I send dearest love.[1]

Whatever trials come upon us, I am sure it has not changed us. I know you cannot be different from what you always were and surely I will never be different to you. I know I shall never be near you again....but in the presence of the Sacred Hearts of Jesus and Mary I solemnly consecrate my soul and life to your service.[2]

Quoted from letters to be found among Mary MacKillop's voluminous correspondence, these lines illustrate a quality in her personality which although perhaps not included in the official criteria for beatification, yet refer to her capacity to attract and maintain strong friendships, surely flowing from and mirroring her relationship with God, in addition to her natural gifts of character and personality.

Reading through her letters from these two people, Julian and Joanna, and her replies, one can recognize the classic marks of friendship – mutual attraction, shared interests, ideals and activities, respect for difference in opinion, fidelity above all, and readiness to forgive. The examples which I have quoted come from long lasting and deep relationships with two people who exemplify Mary's ability to win response from those she was associated with, whether they were sisters and companions in the Josephite order, many of her ecclesiastical superiors and helpers, men and women who encountered and shared her consuming zeal for her beloved Institute and its work.

As indicated elsewhere in this collection, Joanna Barr Smith had a life story that was in almost every way unlike Mary's. Born Joanna Elder, at twenty one years old she married a fellow Scot, Robert Smith, somewhat older and already an enterprising and successful businessman. Adding his mother's name to his own, Robert Barr Smith became quite rapidly the wealthiest man in South Australia during the heady days of copper mines and property dealing. The couple are said to have lived simply in rented accommodation until 1874, when they had built houses in Mitcham and the hills. One reason could also have been their frequent travels abroad, despite having had thirteen children, of whom seven survived infancy. Of these, one son was epileptic and retarded needing permanent care. It was for this son that Mary, aware of Joanna's worry, sought to console her by sending a special prayer to Mary, Mother of God. She was also aware of the Barr Smiths' firm Presbyterian allegiance but offered to Joanna the wealth of spiritual consolation to be found in the Catholic tradition. However, when Julian Woods had once invited the Barr Smiths to be present at a Catholic celebration of mass, Robert, son of the Manse and Free Kirk, courteously replied for both, "I let no man come between my soul and God", adding that he did not think that Joanna should join Mary in "unquestioning subordination of her mind to the teachings of any church". [3] Despite this, Joanna wrote to Mary years later in 1902 of her "craving to find rest and peace in your communion".

In the years before more sophisticated ways of communication were possible, Joanna and Robert when apart wrote to each other daily. The easy, free-flowing letters between Joanna and Mary, sometimes written as soon as a letter arrived, came naturally, Joanna's often concluding, "my darling friend". For her part, Mary could write from Rome in 1873, "Oh my dear and much valued friend, how much I wish I could speak my whole mind to you", revealing something of the weight she felt during the uncertainties of securing official acceptance of the Josephite rule and Institute. Yet Joanna's reply from Scotland shows that she knew nothing of Mary's plans or difficulties. Their friendship was based on personal qualities rather than depending on confidences shared unreservedly. Robert could write to Mary when they were all back in Adelaide, "Amongst all our friends you may be sure we count you one of the truest in the reality of your kind feelings".[4]

One might wonder how the newly-professed Sister Mary, leader of a still controversial religious group, came to form this relationship with the wealthy Barr Smiths, even recalling their shared Scottish descent. However, a clue may be found in the social problems of those early years of the South Australian colony. Less than fifteen years after settlement, the need to care for aged people and destitute children had already prompted the formation of a State Destitute Board in 1849. Two sisters from the first Josephite community were caring for these people in Catholic homes by 1868, while in the previous year other young sisters had already taken charge of a house of Refuge at Mitcham, a refuge for women discharged from prison or "in moral danger". None of these works received state subsidies. Recalling the Barr Smith reputation for public and private benefactions, it is reasonable to assume that it was in this connection that they met Mary and found that they had much in common. The rest, as they say, is history. The house in which the sisters conducted the Refuge at Mitcham was virtually a gift from Robert Barr Smith, who transferred it to Mary MacKillop in May 1882 for the nominal sum of five shillings. Likewise a substantial donation came to aid the addition of a wing to the Kensington convent.

For their part, from the beginning of the Institute which had as its chief focus service of the neediest people in town or country, the sisters habitually sought aid in goods or donations from shopkeepers and others. Passers by were used to meeting them carrying their basket ready to beg goods for their aged or other charges. Mary never seems to have hesitated to ask for help, encouraging others to share her compassion and zeal. In London, for instance, she used letters of introduction to women who were prominent in Catholic circles. She wrote to the sisters in Australia from the home of Mrs Vaughan in Park Lane, London. There she had been given a home and the friendly help of a member of the titled Vaughan family which numbered a Cardinal and the Archbishop of Sydney among its distinguished sons. "She is so good to me and working hard to get postulants, and regrets that she cannot be one herself. She had introduced me to many of her friends, with a view to getting them to help us".[5] This last phrase reminds one of her motives. She ignored social barriers, high or low, when it was a case of begging help for their mission. Even in London Robert Barr Smith was called upon to help with the shipment of the books and other items she had collected for the schools.

Another London friend and correspondent for whom she had great admiration was the writer, Lady Georgiana Fullerton, a convert, who had already published twenty of her novels, lives of saints and saintly people, accounts of miracles, poetry, drama, in both English and French. Yet she lived and dressed very simply, as her biographers noted, most loved as a philanthropist, giving her personal help to illiterate and unskilled girls and boys. No wonder that Mary found a kindred spirit here and recommended later to Joanna that she read her life story, especially after Lady Fullerton had published an article describing the new Australian order of sisters. Again, connecting naturally with Julian Woods' family, Mary visited his only sister, Henrietta Guidici, and wrote to Sister Mechtilde, Woods' niece in Adelaide, of her delight in getting to know her aunt.[6] This is a reminder of one characteristic of the friendship between Julian and Mary, namely their readiness to be involved in each other's family, which is revealed in the many letters written to and from Penola. Julian shared MacKillop family news and advice to Mary as if they were his own – sisters, mother, aunts, uncles, finance, disagreements – in Portland or Penola. Mary knew Terence Woods and his family while they lived in Penola, and readily undertook the care of their two little daughters after their mother's death.

In letters written in Rome, and later as she travelled to England and Scotland, Mary revealed her association with Tobias Kirby, Rector of the Irish College. Kirby played an influential part in the Australian Catholic history of the nineteenth century, acting as the trusted liaison between the Irish Australian bishops and the Roman Congregations. Mary described him in one of her letters to Joanna as "the voice of the Irish bishops in Australia".[7] Many letters went from the bishops to Kirby, seeking advice and his intervention with officials, while Australian documents of the period stored in Propaganda archives often bear an attached memo referring the matter to 'Monsignore' (later Archbishop) Kirby. He was consulted by Mary on her arrival with the constitutions written by Julian Woods to be offered for approval. Kirby responded to the charm of her undemanding honesty and pursued her cause, to the chagrin of Bishop Matthew Quinn, by taking time and trouble to represent her wishes judiciously to the Cardinal Prefect of Propaganda, first Cardinal Barnabo, then Cardinal Franchi. Mary's letters to Kirby are expressed warmly, although always respectfully. Realising that he had judged it expedient not to present her every wish, she wrote philosophically to him, "Where I would make ever so many sad mistakes, our good God gives me a true friend to check me and put me right",[8] often signing herself "Your affectionately grateful child". Her friendship with Tobias Kirby, like those of her London benefactors, was warm, based on her zealous care for the welfare of the Institute, and expressed in an exchange of many letters during the years 1873 – 1874 when she was trying to build a solid foundation for the Sisters of St Joseph. Ironically, it was these very efforts, resulting in a completely re-written constitution by the Dominican Raymond Bianchi, which estranged Julian Woods from her, despite the lines which are quoted above.

Nevertheless their relationship was unique, dynamic in its influence on the Australian church. How did this association come about? In South Australia and years later in Malaysia, Julian Woods often gave a lecture which he called *Ten Years in the Bush* in which he recounted among other experiences of his time as pastor of Penola his visits to farmhouses and stations in the huge area. One of his favourite stopping places was Old Penola homestead, the home of Mary's uncle, Alexander Cameron – King Cameron as he was known because of his ownership of great tracts of property in the south-east. In her life story written after Julian Woods' death, Mary mentioned his relationship with people in the parish and "his winning gentle ways". At the age of eighteen she encountered these when she went to Penola to teach the Cameron children. She was lively, intelligent, well taught by her father, who could hand on to his children the fruits of his training for the priesthood in Rome, and determined some day to become a religious sister, although she did not know where. Woods recognized her quality, and in their talks and exchange of letters continued to encourage her spiritual growth. Perhaps their talks even then gave him the notion that here could be someone who could help form the kind of religious group which he had seen in France, and would suit the simple, unpretentious needs of country Catholic children everywhere. In the year 1861 – 1862 the friendship grew, and in the following years after Mary had returned home, Julian continued his visits to her family, his pastoral travels taking him into the adjoining Victorian country areas. It was here in Portland that he received into the Catholic church the MacKillops' neighbour, Mrs Mary Finn. Mary MacKillop was her sponsor. Mary Finn remained a friend to both Julian and Mary and when the Finns came to live in Sydney she regularly visited both. She formed an important link in the last years of their relationship.

Once the small beginnings were made in Penola in 1866, and Bishop Sheil had called her Sister Mary, both she and Julian adopted a more formal way of beginning and ending letters. For both writers, the correspondence was their only way of communicating the details of the evolving community – Mary asking, Julian describing, as he found himself caught up with changing diocesan business, first in Melbourne, then in Adelaide. Where she had always begun with, "'My dear Father

Woods", and ended with. "Yours very affectionately", she now adopted the more formal, "Rev(eren)d and dear Father", concluding, "Your affectionate child in J.C., Mary, Sister of St Joseph". For his part, where he had always written, "My dear Mary'" signing off, "very affectionately yours", he now added "Sister" and to his signature the sure sign of his view of his role, "Yours faithfully in the Sacred Hearts, Your servant and Father Director".

After his departure from Adelaide and his involvement in the foundations at The Vale (Perthville) in 1872, he gave missions in New South Wales and Queensland in many small places, writing back to Mary and other sisters about his experiences and of visiting small convents as he went. He wrote that he was revising the Rule, and urged her to take it to Rome for approval as soon as possible. By the time he returned to Brisbane after a bout of fever at Bowen, he found eight of her letters among the one hundred and forty waiting for him. He learned that she was already on her way to Rome, at the insistence of Father Tappeiner and Bishop Reynolds. Failure in their ability to communicate at this important stage of the Institute's development seems to have resulted for him in a feeling of rejection, as he wrote to Sister Monica Phillips, one of the first Adelaide group and one of Mary's consultors, "She should have come to see me before taking other advice, and now I don't know what to do. I feel as if it were no use writing to her, for she will not heed my advice…."[9] In these lines one reads not only the feeling of hurt of someone supplanted by others. He evidently also constantly ignored the reality of his official removal as the Institute's Father Director, as he continued to sign his letters. He was convinced that it was he who was directly inspired by God, and if Mary was rejecting this infallible guidance, she was somehow also rejecting the kind of association they had formed twenty years before.

For her part, Mary did her best to keep him informed about progress in Rome, and wrote from Scotland that at last their congregation had received official approval. But when her letter written from Adelaide early in 1875 invited him to come to the general meeting of the sisters there, her reminded her that he was no longer their Director. He added:

> My dear child, though there may be no occasion for you to write to me, nor I to you.... still believe my most earnest assurance that I am ever the same to you. I am in no way changed and you are just as dear to me as ever….I say this

from my heart and with all my affection over and over again. Yours most truly in the Sacred Heart.[10]

Yet the two Bishops Quinn in Brisbane and Bathurst, skilled manipulators as they were, refused to accept the changed constitution, a newly appointed central council nor Mary's election as head superior. They continued to involve Julian in their opposition, and, acknowledging their stance, he replied to her letter a few months later, "Perhaps you did not know how your having so completely thrown me aside placed me in a false position".[11] This letter is full of resentment, even accusing her of disloyalty, revealing the depth of his hurt pride. He refused to attend the Adelaide meeting, citing his legal liability for a number of debts there, despite his efforts to meet them over years.

In this 1875 exchange, letters from both Mary and Julian were frank and lengthy, but they ended with his decision not to continue to discuss the Institute and its affairs. He visited Penola on his return from his years in Tasmania and Mary hastened to meet him there. However, she wrote to Sister Josephine McMullen after their talks, "I found him kind, holy and affectionate as ever, but that is all I can say". The letter concludes, "We parted then in friendship and affection, but in deep sorrow and disappointment on my part."[12] Julian regarded the Institute as his own and divinely inspired, and he could not accept that it had been taken from him. The Bishops Quinn insisted on his helping them retain authority over the convents in their dioceses, and henceforth he did that, until they found no further use for his efforts, and turned him away.

So, the character of this friendship changed. For the next ten years Julian's life was filled with that rich variety of missionary and scientific work which has enriched his place in Australian church and scientific history. When he returned to Sydney in 1887, broken in health, the faithful affection of another group of women, some of them former Josephites, gave him a home and care. By then Mary had gone through the hardship of establishing the congregation, with their head house now in North Sydney. She was kept informed of Julian's welfare by their mutual friend, Mary Finn, who visited them both. She went to see him herself, but Julian, weary and ill, seemed incapable of rising, at least overtly, to their former level of friendship, or to respond other than by a courteous note, to her remembrance of his birthday and gifts of his favourite strawberries. Even as she travelled to be with him as he died, the North Sydney ferry broke down, a final touch to the sadness of a relationship's end.

In her only existing lengthy piece of writing, a few years later Mary wrote Julian's life, and concluded with a tender description of his monument in Waverley cemetery that is worth recalling:

> How appropriate is the last resting place of the gentle learned priest and naturalist! Crowned with the cross, beneath the statue of the 'Sweet Mother' whom he had so tenderly loved – a little child in the next grave, 'Australia's Gifted Son' Deniehy at his feet, the 'Silvertongued' Dalley close by – typifying all that during life had most delighted him – Devotion, Innocence and Intellect![13]

Their friendship had all the classic qualities. Shared ideals had produced a special gift to church and people. Genuine affection had somehow lived on through years of shared vision and effort. Mary's fidelity so apparent elsewhere in her life, had transcended the differences in experience and opposition. Julian was less able to forgive and set differences aside, and so this friendship has a lasting note of sadness. But few friendships reveal the steadfast love and loyalty which Mary MacKillop could give to Joanna Barr Smith and Julian Woods.

Endnotes

1 Joanna Barr Smith to Mary MacKillop, July 17th 1907.
2 Julian Tenison Woods (Hillend, Bathurst Diocese) to Mary MacKillop, May 20th 1872.
3 Robert Barr Smith to Julian Tenison Woods, March 12th 1869.
4 Robert Barr Smith to Mary MacKillop, November 14th 1878.
5 Mary MacKillop to the Sisters, February 16th 1874.
6 Mary MacKillop to Sister Mechtilde, August 4th 1874.
7 Mary MacKillop to Joanna Barr Smith, October 17th 1873.
8 Mary MacKillop to Kirby, December 15th 1873.
9 Julian Tenison Woods to Sister Monica Phillips, April 21st 1873.
10 Julian Tenison Woods to Mary MacKillop, February 2nd 1875.
11 Julian Tenison Woods to Mary MacKillop, May 15th 1875.
12 Mary MacKillop to Sister Josephine McMullen, January 1877.
13 *Julian Tenison Woods – A Life by Mother Mary of the Cross MacKillop.* Introduced and Annotated by Margaret Press rsj. (Blackburn, Victoria: Harper Collins Religious, 1997), 220.

Mary MacKillop: The Fire Burning in Her Heart

Genevieve Ryan rsj

Fan into a flame the gift God gave you....
God's gift was not a spirit of timidity but the spirit of power and love and self-control.
So you are never to be ashamed of witnessing to the Lord.
You have been trusted to look after something precious;
guard it with the help of the Holy Spirit who lives in us.
2Tim 1:6-8,14

Mary's Pilgrim Energy – the Torch Bearer

When the Olympic flame is carried into the stadium and set aloft it is a stirring moment. It is an action that ignites, heralds and illuminates. At this moment there is focus and purpose for the people of every continent. Though not a known athlete, Mary MacKillop was called to pick up a flaming torch and carry it into an uncharted arena of life. Her preparedness to do this ignited a responsive fire in the hearts of other women, heralded a new era of apostolic intensity in Australia, and illuminated the darkness and misery that threatened the poorest people in our land. She was a pathfinder, a pacesetter, a pioneer and a trailblazer. In scriptural terms she was called to be a pilgrim leader.

This call came when she was in her early twenties. Not only was she young, but also she had received very little formal education. Her social and economic circumstances were restricted; anything that she earned in her governess or teaching positions was sent post haste to her mother who was struggling to educate younger members of the family. Her father, Alexander was not a good provider and Mary was Flora's great support until her siblings became independent.

When Mary met Fr Julian Tenison Woods she encountered his

burning zeal for the neglected "little ones" in isolated Australian rural conditions. The sparks that burned in his heart caught fire in hers and a shared dream materialised.

When Mary contemplated the origins of the Sisters of St Joseph, she marvelled at the traces of the Holy Spirit who inspired fiery zeal and cohesion in a scattered number of young hearts, and united and shaped them into a community with a mission. Mary wrote:

> These souls living in different colonies and quite unknown to each other had all alike these desires as in course of time became known to a good and holy priest who had long observed the sad conditions of many amongst his own flock without being able to apply a remedy. Some of these souls in due time became his spiritual children, and after a lapse of a few years, when he had weighed the matter well, and circumstances had been so permitted by God as to leave no more room for hesitation, he unfolded all his own ideas to some of these, and finding a unison of will and intention in the same, he proceeded at once to the establishment of the work.[1]

In 1866, the torch was alight and firmly in Mary MacKillop's grasp. Fuelled by Julian's vision, her own energy and enthusiasm, and the generosity and courage of a growing number of young women, this fire spread rapidly across the Australian landscape.

The Peruvian proverb, *The road is made by walking,* describes Mary MacKillop as a pilgrim, setting an astonishing pace and carving out roads into new territory. Mary travelled from Portland to Penola in January 1866, accompanied by her sister Lexie. Annie was already there "holding the fort". They had neither living quarters nor a schoolhouse. They rented Winella Cottage and a disused, six-stalled stable made functional by their brother John became a schoolroom capable of holding forty children. This then, was the infancy of an education system that has had an incalculable influence on the Australian church and Australian education. There grew up a unique congregation of religious Sisters, peculiarly suited to Australian conditions, and bravely independent of the traditions and expectations of the religious orders of Europe. From this spark, the Congregation spread to every Australian state and across the Tasman Sea to New Zealand before Mary died in 1909.

Perhaps Mary could have hoped for a period to consolidate her efforts in Penola, but like her Biblical ancestors, she was called "to cast out into the deep", into the unknown. And so:

> On June 22nd 1867, she was driven by Uncle Donald to Mount Gambier, where she was joined by Rose, and then on to Port MacDonnell where they embarked on the vessel *Penola.* The first two Sisters of St Joseph arrived at Port Adelaide on the vigil of St John the Baptist, a special patron of Mary and of the Institute.[2]

Since her Beatification, many people who have undertaken pilgrimages to significant places of Mary's life have visited Port MacDonnell. A visit in June when the cold wind is bleak, reminds one of the courage and determination that must have fuelled this passage to Adelaide. Patricia White rsj writes:

> Father Woods was hardly established in Adelaide, when he sent for Mary and Rose Cunningham, who had recently joined Mary, to come to Adelaide to take charge of the Cathedral school. He spoke of 'the Sisters' in such glowing terms that Adelaide Catholics were awaiting their coming with intense interest - some with eagerness, some with doubts and reservations. The Irish priests were especially sceptical. The nuns to whom they were accustomed lived in large convents with spacious grounds; if they left their convents at all, they hurried quickly back; they recruited their members from the educated class and those who could afford dowries; they had two classes of members, choir sisters and lay sisters who did the menial tasks. These Australian sisters lived in ordinary houses like the people they served; they were frequently seen on the streets visiting the sick and even begging; they accepted into their institute working girls with little education; there was no choir/lay distinction - all were equal. An important question was 'Could they teach?' That remained to be seen. When the school opened on July 2nd 1867 there were sixty pupils. Six months later there were 200. Parents were obviously satisfied. The Governor of South Australia was obviously satisfied for his grandson was enrolled at the school.
>
> Mary was an excellent teacher herself and she demanded

> high standards from those who gathered around her to share the work but also, and more importantly, it was due to the spirit which characterised the work. The sisters lived so poorly and so simply; they were so obviously dedicated to the poor to whose service they so generously sacrificed their time, their energy and their own comfort and convenience; they so respected the human dignity of all regardless of class or creed; they served with cheerfulness and love. This was the spirit engendered by Mary MacKillop and this it was that drew both old and young to the sisters of this infant institute.[3]

There are countless examples of Mary's pilgrim energy to advance "the Work" as she called her mission. It was in amazing evidence when she set out for Rome in 1873 seeking approbation for the Rule. Given that she had already gone through the minefield of calumny, excommunication and injustice, she demonstrated courage, resilience and clarity of purpose in making this voyage overseas as a single woman. Her friends and advisers, especially Fr (later Bishop) Reynolds and Fr Tappeiner sj, wanted her to go to ensure that the Congregation had papal approval so that the events of 1871[4] could not occur again.

The political situation in Italy meant that she had to put aside her habit and travel in lay attire. She had the companionship of Alexander Cameron and his wife Ellen on the boat, but once in Italy she was essentially alone. She undertook the formidable task of sheltering a vulnerable flame in the draughty halls of the Vatican and of negotiating meetings with ecclesiastical authorities who could have been indifferent to her. However her sincerity and sense of purpose, in conjunction with her ability to communicate respectfully and openly, touched the hearts of the Vatican officials. Pope Pius 1X responded to her with warmth and compassion. Mary wrote to her mother of the experience:

> What he said, and how he said it when he knew that I was the *Excommunicated one,* are things too sacred to be spoken of – but he let me see that the Pope had a Father's heart, and when he laid his loved hands upon my head I felt more than I will attempt to say.[5]

What can Mary's experience as pilgrim say to us as we journey on our way?

As a pilgrim torch-bearer Mary knew the Gospel paradox of the struggling guide. Her actions demonstrate that the one who offers support and guidance to another must first have experienced the pain of disorientation from within. Only someone who knows the uncertainty and confusion of standing in an unmapped place can be a healing presence for another who is lost and bewildered. The pilgrim's experience of disorientation equips her to address the chaos experienced by someone who has lost the way on life's journey. Humility, patience, vulnerability, inner-directedness and compassion are Christian values that must be embraced by the torch-bearer. The opposite of the pilgrim is one who is inert, who stays in the comfort zone, and canonises the status quo. Jesus, 'the Way, the Truth and the Life' (Jn 14:1-10) is the inspiration for the Torch-bearer.

There may be times in our lives when we are called by our family or community to be torch-bearers. With Mary MacKillop as an inspiration we can value the gifts that empower us to accept this responsibility and face the challenges. Let us give thanks for others in our community who have internalized the attitude of the pilgrim and brought many blessings on those whom they serve.

Mary's Servant Energy – Setting Hearth Fires

There is nothing more comforting than to come in from the cold and find a fire burning in the hearth. Setting a fire that glows cheerily is an act of service. It is hospitality at its best and people gravitate to the warmth that a fire creates. It has a wonderful drawing power. It is a heart-warming gesture to set a home fire burning.

The Servant energy of the Gospel call is based on the example of Jesus and directed to those in need:

> He got up from the table, removed his outer garment and, taking the towel, wrapped it round his waist; he then poured water into a basin and began to wash his disciples' feet and wipe them with the towel that he was wearing. (Jn 13:4-5).

According to Jesus' values, the servant's approach is to minister from a position of mutuality and collaboration. Mary MacKillop internalized that. In her way of relating she intuitively acted as a mentor, a guide, a companion and a counsellor - one who walks with others and facilitates their journey. Mary's energy created an atmosphere of warmth and security for many who would have spent their lives in cold, inhospitable landscapes.

The first group drawn to the fire set by Mary were the women who became her Sisters. In August 1867 there were four Sisters of St Joseph. By the end of 1868 there were thirty-four and by mid July 1869 there were over fifty. This is growth of bushfire proportions.

The first country school to be opened by two Sisters was at Yankalilla, an isolated village on the Fleurieu Peninsula. This move established a pattern which has always characterised the work of the Josephites, namely communities of two or three Sisters in country towns where Mass and the sacraments were celebrated only at two or three monthly intervals. This way of life was carried to other colonies. In 1869 Bishop James Quinn of Brisbane asked for Sisters. Mary MacKillop accompanied four Sisters to Brisbane. In September 1871 Bishop Matthew Quinn of Bathurst NSW requested a foundation.

The setting up of very small communities differed from the way traditional orders had set up their works – in established centres. With Julian and Mary's vision for mobile, flexible communities, the early Josephites went wherever need arose. They lived frugally in humble dwellings – even in hessian tents alongside railway lines in outback places. They served where the people lived. Such Servant Energy set many hearth fires for people for whom destitution and want were daily fare. Julian Tenison Woods gave them the motto, "The Sisters must do all the good they can, and never see an evil without trying how they may remedy it."[6]

From visiting and supporting people in the city streets Mary and Julian knew that destitution, neglect and ruin were the lot of those who were economically poor, orphaned, homeless, sick or aged. Youthful, energetic and confident these two compassionate and loving people decided that the call to action was imperative. Their deep spiritual insight into the abiding, providing presence of God and their conviction that they could make a difference, directed them to found new institutions to educate children and care for the destitute. Mary and her companions drew near to people. They lived in poor little cottages and visited people in their poor little cottages. They befriended outcasts. They knew the prostitutes and alcoholics loitering in the back lanes of the city. In a climate of sectarianism, Mary had Protestant and Jewish friends and accepted their loyal service in her time of need. She refused to allow privilege or status to determine the worth of a person. She was part of the fabric of people's lives. Her own sisters experienced her as a warm, down-to-earth person. She was a full-blooded individual who spoke with directness and humour, anguish and delight. She enjoyed the richness of loving and loyal friends and expressed her own love freely and generously.

What can Mary's servant energy say to us?

Mary's focus was on reverencing the dignity of another. Her quality of service and attentiveness to the afflicted released them from the trauma of neglect, affective hunger and loneliness. She responded in extraordinary ways. We can do the same in the ordinary encounters of our lives.

The antithesis of the servant leader is one who governs and controls the destiny of "her subjects". Though Mary possessed personal charisma, her humility and kindness shielded her from falling into authoritarianism or control. In a culture that prizes efficiency and political correctness we need to nurture an approach like hers. Mary would have aware of references in Gospel to the importance of receiving as well as giving. In serving others we need to recall when we have been served, waited on, listened to, mentored and accompanied. Christ's values of presence, trust, self-giving and positive regard for the essential worth of others, were the kindling that Mary MacKillop used to set hearth fires for those whom society had left out in the cold. With her as model we can live out these values today.

Mary's Prophetic Energy – Casting Fire

I have come to bring fire to the earth,
and how I wish it were blazing already.
Lk 12:49

We have probably all groaned at a meeting when a voice interjects just as a consensus seems assured. The interruption seems to "come from left field"; it is often regarded as a nuisance as it challenges the status quo or introduces a new idea. This person may well speak with the voice of the prophet. Even in Christian community however, this voice can fall on unappreciative ears and ignite fiery reactions. In fact, the prophet is in danger of being run out of town, pushed to the margins, regarded as eccentric or be destined for a sticky end. Just ask Jesus, John the Baptist, Martin Luther King, Mary MacKillop, Nelson Mandela and Irene McCormack RSJ.

On one occasion, Jesus put it this way, "I tell you solemnly, no prophet is ever accepted in his own country" (Lk 4:24). If one is dedicated to truth and justice, consumed by an inner fire and is seeking structural transformation, he or she will most likely pay dearly for being faithful to the Divine call.

Mary MacKillop exerted the fiery energy of the prophet even in her youth. From a very early age she knew the consequences of poverty and the humiliation of being dependent on relatives for a home and for support. She developed a sense of responsibility for her family. The story is told that when she was eleven and her brother Donald was an infant, she noticed that the hired nurse was overfond of stimulants. She promptly dismissed her and took upon herself the duties of nurse and house keeper. On another occasion she displeased her non-Catholic teacher by refusing to use a history book which, she said, did not tell the truth about Mary, Queen of Scots. Mary inherited her mother's horse-riding skills. As well as catching and riding restive, buck jumping horses, she rounded up runaway cattle in a manner which struck terror in the hearts of timid bystanders. She was courageous, cool and resourceful. These qualities eventually equipped her to don the mantle of the prophet when the circumstances of co-founding an innovative expression of religious life required it.

On March 19th, St Joseph's Day, 1866 Mary replaced her fashionable clothes with a simple black dress, designed to make public her desire to renounce worldly possessions and to live and work for God alone. In June 1866 Blanche Amsinck, a governess from Western Victoria, did the same. In early 1867 Bishop Sheil came to Penola for visitation and Confirmation. He was delighted with what he saw in the school and with the attitudes of the children. "God bless you Sister Mary," he said. From that time Mary signed herself "Sister Mary - Sister of St Joseph". These innovative moves of Mary's were not lost on her relations some of whom were deeply displeased. "Who was she," they said "to think of starting her own Religious Congregation? If she wanted to live a religious life why did she not join one of the existing orders?" Here we recognise shades of Jesus' prediction that the prophet is not accepted by his own. Not only did his people criticise him but they also threatened to throw him down a cliff and eventually crucified him. Convinced that she was doing what God wanted, Mary went bravely on in the face of disapproval. On September 22nd 1871 she felt the full force of rejection when Bishop Sheil figuratively threw her over a cliff by excommunicating her.

Mary seemed to be aware of God's loving presence even in the most ghastly experiences of her life. This gave her an amazing tranquillity and trust in his loving presence. Her letter to Fr Woods, after the humiliation of her excommunication, reveals a heart attuned to the heart of God:

> I do not know how to describe the feeling but that I was intensely happy, and felt nearer to God than I had ever felt before. I can only dimly remember the things that were said to me, but the sensation of the calm, beautiful presence of God I shall never forget. I have been told that some of the priests have since expressed surprise at my silence, but Father, I solemnly declare that the power, even the desire of speaking was not given to me. I loved the Bishop and priests, the Church and my good God then more than ever. I did not feel alone, but I cannot describe the calm, beautiful something that was near. [7]

These words provide the key to her prophetic courage.

There is a paradoxical quality that lies like a seam of grace in the hearts of heroic men and women. We only have to read the writings of more contemporary prophetic figures such as Victor Frankl, Etty Hillesum, and Nelson Mandela to see that self-transcendence and self-belief shine forth from them in moments of adversity. The prophet knows the suffering of re-imagining the reality set down by the dominant forces in society. Mary had to stand firm as Julian became more heavily influenced by the visionary Josephites, Angela and Ignatius. He wished to make them consulters. As a prophetic person does, she approached the matter searching for the truth and uncovering deception. She confronted Julian with his imprudence.

The antithesis of the prophet leader is the cult figure, who builds a personal empire. Mary's life purpose was to bring the good news to the poor. In memory of Jesus, she went wherever the poor, neglected little ones were, to share their poverty and way of life and to make human dignity a reality for them. Although she undertook an expansive programme of social action, she was not governed by any social or political theory but rather by the imperatives of the Gospel.

Her sister, Annie, tells us that when she was working as a governess at Penola station, there was a very neglected Aboriginal child. Mary would sit with little Nancy Bruce combing the lice out of her hair and nursing her sores. One of Mary's early companions told of an occasion when Mary's principles of justice and equality for all were put to the test and unflinchingly upheld. The Governor wished to enrol his grandson at the Sisters' school but it was on condition that special arrangements were made for him in view of his social status. The sisters would not agree to keep the boy separate from pupils from the "lower classes"

They declared that they were happy to teach him but as part of the general class, with no special arrangements.

What does Mary's Prophetic energy say to us?

Sometimes we see the need to write to the Editor about political or societal injustice. Something as innocent as a barbecue gathering can be soured by sexist or racist remarks and a situation like this calls us to express distaste. It is never easy but the stance of the prophet is to speak out, even at the cost of disturbing the accepted order of things.

The prophet sees, hears and feels "with the heart of God" and cuts through the definitions that others have set down. The prophet abhors empty vision and yearns for largeness of vision. The intellect of the prophet confronts habitual thinking with lateral thinking. The heart of the prophet is passionate about the values the community espouses. Any inconsistencies and the prophet will expose them. The social conscience of the prophet is counter-cultural and deplores evil especially when it masquerades as virtue.

There were times when Mary MacKillop was called upon to be a flame thrower and she did not shirk this exercise of her mission. In celebrating her life, we cannot ignore the call to be prophetic in our own life situation.

Mary's Shepherd Energy – Lighting Protective Fires

There is a manoeuvre in Australian Rules football known as shepherding. When teaching young boys it serves as an appealing reference point in exhorting them to protect and shield the vulnerable, to pre-empt the onset of danger, to fend off bullying, to create opportunities for others, and to use their strength and skill to another's advantage. It can even be appealed to on behalf of helping out girls! The difficult virtue of putting another's welfare before one's own is made more attractive because the art of shepherding is endorsed by the AFL.

Mary MacKillop needed no such coaching manual. Her intuition to shield and protect was drawn from her experience of caring for others and of heeding God's call to hear the cry of the poor.

Her shepherding energy caused her to take epic journeys to be with the others in times of distress. There was an incident in which a Sister was dying in great agony as a result of a kerosene lamp exploding:

> Mary had got as far as Mount Remarkable and hoped to find

some kind people to drive her the rest of the journey. Sister Patricia Campbell continued the rest of the story: *Several farmers were in with their wheat but all shook their heads at the prospect of the long journey to Port Augusta. The farmers then adjourned to the hotel for refreshments, and Mother Mary walked in and said, "Gentlemen, one of my Sisters at Port Augusta is dying, and is constantly asking for me. If one of you will lend me a horse, I will ride there." Chivalry was not quite dead in those Celtic hearts. Two or three jumped up, got a pair of horses and a buggy, and drove her on that afternoon, and she arrived in time to console the last moments of the dying Sister.*[8]

If a hungry person came to the door she went without her own dinner if necessary. She visited homes where poverty and drunkenness held people in chains, she befriended prostitutes and made provision for them, she provided shelter for the homeless, and she begged to get enough food for the starving. She acquired ducks, fowls and wire-netting for an impoverished community of Sisters; she cleaned out grease traps and washed and ironed when other women were too exhausted to carry out these tasks any longer. On a larger scale, she established orphanages, schools, and places of refuge.

There were many occasions when she had to shield another from some form of neglect or systemic abuse. Sister Annette Henschke has left us two treasured accounts of her transforming presence in the lives of those whom society regarded as the very dregs of humanity:

> There was a girl whom they called 'Scotch Bella'. She came from Queensland. She had committed a murder. She dressed as a man for three years and worked on the roads. Nobody could do anything with her. She was sent to gaol in South Australia. Mother Mary got her out and she was brought to the Refuge. She was like a raving lunatic when they brought her there.[9]

Scotch Bella was completely rehabilitated, and lived a wholesome life and died happily.

> There was in Adelaide a man named Fagan condemned to death for murder He was just like a wild animal. Mother Mary and Sister Felicitas went to see him. The warders told them not to go in. They went in and prayed and Mother was so affected that the tears poured down her face. This so

> moved him that he knelt down and prayed with them. At the beginning he was abrupt with Mother but he calmed down and became as gentle as a lamb. Mother prepared him for Confession and Fr Williams heard his confession and in the morning Mother went again with Sister Felicitas and he was without the chains, and received Holy Communion between the two of them. Mother Mary wished to ascend the scaffold with him but this was not allowed. Father Williams however did.[10]

Mary MacKillop was a shepherd who herself had been shepherded through precarious experiences. This experience enabled her to walk with others along treacherous paths and be a saving yet challenging presence. She noticed and addressed dysfunctional patterns in the community. As a shepherd leader, she used her skills to lead individuals and communities in the Gospel task of protecting and guiding the vulnerable and lost.

What does Mary's shepherding energy say to us?

The image of Jesus as the Good Shepherd reminds those who are called to lead and to guide, that tenderness and concern for the individual are their guiding principles. There is no room for ruthlessness or expediency, even if corrective strategies are needed.

The Parable of the Good Shepherd illustrates how Jesus reconciles tenderness and management and how he cherishes the dignity of the outcast and the stray. Mary MacKillop was most likely familiar with this parable and with this approach to ministry, and writes to the Sisters in 1880:

> I cannot end this letter without asking you, one and all to look back a little and see what our good God has done for us during the past few years; see what dangers threatened the Institute, what trials it has undergone – and see how wonderfully it has been protected – not only from the attempts of those who did not understand it, but, for I must say it, from evil consequences of our own faults and want of experience – and thus it will be to the end. *God will protect his own work.* Never is he nearer to it than when dangers threaten. He can do without any of us – only since in His mercy and goodness He has called us to His service, let us try to do our work well in his sight, who alone is to be considered in our thoughts. My dearly loved Sisters, may His will alone

be done in us. Like our glorious Father and Patron may we ever seek to work for God – hidden as much as possible in the love of His Sacred Heart.[11]

Endnotes

[1] Mary MacKillop, *Observations on the Rule,* (Submitted to the Holy Father by Mary MacKillop, Rome, 18.5. 1873), Resource Material from the Archives of the Sisters of St Joseph of the Sacred Heart, Issue No 3 (Revised), 1984, 47.

[2] Paul Gardiner, *An Extraordinary Australian: Mary MacKillop: The Authorised Biography* (Australia: E.J.Dwyer, 1993), 64.

[3] Patricia White, "Mary MacKillop 1", 1995. Unpublished Article.

[4] In particular, Mary's excommunication and the subsequent events.

[5] Mary MacKillop to Flora MacKillop, June 3rd 1873.

[6] Mary MacKillop, *Necessity for the Institute,* August 1873, Resource Material from the Archives of the Sisters of St Joseph of the Sacred Heart, Issue No 3, (Revised) 1984, 73.

[7] Mary MacKillop to Woods, September 1871.

[8] Gardiner, *An Extraordinary Australian: Mary MacKillop: The Authorised Biography,* 456.

[9] Gardiner, *An Extraordinary Australian: Mary MacKillop: The Authorised Biography,* 241.

[10] Gardiner, *An Extraordinary Australian: Mary MacKillop: The Authorised Biography,* 241-242.

[11] Mary MacKillop to the Sisters, December 11th 1880.

Mary MacKillop: Genuine Aussie or Hereditary Scot?

Catherine Thom rsj

A prince can mak a belted knight,
A marquis, duke, an a' that!
But an honest man's aboon his might
...The pith o'sense an' pride o' worth
Are higher rank than a' that. [1]

Robbie Burns, Scotland's favourite son, born January 25th 1759 in a humble cottage in Galloway, penned this timeless masterpiece in the Scot's dialect (as part of a whole poem) which the newly devolved Scottish Parliament took as their "battle cry" when Queen Elizabeth went to Edinburgh July 1st 1999[2] to open parliament. The sung rendition stirs the blood of any self-respecting Scot especially when sung on the occasion by Folk-singer Sheena Wellington. When it came to the final verse the whole assembly of Scots rose proudly and defiantly proclaimed:

then let us pray that come it may
(As come it will for a' that)
That sense and worth o'er all the earth
will prevail over rank and birth, so that,
Man to man the world o'er
Shall brithers be for a'that.

There are echoes of these sentiments in the *Declaration of Arbroath* of 1320:

> For as long as a hundred of us remain alive, we will never on any condition be subjected to the lordship of the English. We fight not for glory nor riches nor honours, but for freedom alone, which no good man gives up but with his life.[3]

By 1707, due to the treachery of the Lowlanders, more English than Scottish and living in close proximity to the border with England, there was established the Union of Scotland and England. The Highlanders, living in the remote highlands and clinging tenaciously to their ancestral Gaelic language and customs, were not consulted with regard to this decision to unite with England. Edward J. Cowan reminds his readers that Scotland as a result of the union "was robbed of her court as a centre of culture and patronage, the major focus of both identity and national aspiration."[4] However robbed the Scots may have been of their court, no one could rob them of their inherited Scottishness. This article proposes to look at the characteristics that distinguish the Scots from other cultural groups and then see if these characteristics were evident in the life and letters of Mary MacKillop. Whether she is a genuine Aussie, a hereditary Scot or both will be left to the readers to determine for themselves.

Scottish Birthright/Heritage

An event in which I participated, this time in 2004 regarding the new Scottish Parliament, was on the thirteen hundredth anniversary of the death of the ninth Abbot of Iona. Adomnain, member of the famous Niall of the Nine Hostages clan from Donegal and author of the *Vita* ColumCile, wrote a famous document called *Cáin Adomnáin* or the *Law of the Innocents,* in which he makes a profound case for the freeing of women, non-combatants including clergy and children.[5] On September 23rd 2004, a substantial group of Scots marched on the new Parliament building in Edinburgh, carrying a copy of the *Law of the Innocents,* and demanding that the parliamentarians take note of its contents. The politicians were challenged to be faithful to its strong defences of human rights.[6] The protestors, for that is what they were, forcibly reminded the members of the Scottish Parliament that defending the weak and vulnerable was an integral part of their proud heritage, and since devolution from England was a goal achieved after some three hundred years, the parliamentary Scots must not, in the third millennium, squander their birthright.

This too is the birthright and heritage of Mary MacKillop. Though we proudly claim her as an Aussie, I have never doubted that it is her Scottish cultural heritage that is most dominant in all that she was and did. She lived out this heritage in the Australian context but she never ceased being a Scot. Culture has that effect, regardless of whether the individual acknowledges it or not. We all acquire our identity and sense of who we are from that great line of ancestors whose mindset, imagination, beliefs and values pulsate within us from the moment of conception till we arrive at our place of Resurrection.

So What is it to be a Scot?

What qualities distinguish the Scots from other cultural groups? Firstly, they are part of that amorphous group called Celts which includes the people from Scotland, Ireland, Wales, Brittany, Cornwall and inhabitants of the Isle of Mann. This is not the place to go into the archeology, history, sociology and linguistic differences of this group of peoples. However, if we are to avoid the superficial nature of much of the popular written work on things Celtic, there are some important points to be made about the distinctive characteristics of the *Keltoi,* which is the name the Greeks gave the people who dominated Europe for thousands of years before the Romans.

Evidence for their existence comes first from the salt mines of Hallstatt and Hallein in Austria and Lake Neuchâtel in Switzerland in the nineteenth century. The archeological finds at both these places inform us that these people were in many parts of the Continent of Europe as early as 700 BCE and maybe earlier. They were a mobile and rural people who lived in clans and did not hesitate to assert themselves in warfare with flamboyance and ferocity but no battle plan. Giving low priority to organizational matters was intrinsic to the Celts, because "plans are only for people with limited vision".[7] They have left to posterity evidence of intricate lacework on metal and stone and precious jewellery of exquisite craftsmanship that has not been equalled since their time. Precious books of the Gospels ornamented and annotated are still available to posterity to give testimony to their creative imagination and, more importantly, their profound adherence to the basic truths of the Christian message embodied in the life of Jesus. Recently the *Scottish Herald* made the claim, "We are not Celts at all but Galicians".[8] The article quotes DNA researchers at Trinity College Dublin who said a new study into Celtic origins revealed close affinities with the people of Galicia.[9] Be that as it may, if we are to understand why Mary MacKillop did what she did and why she did it, we need to look at the cultural background of these enigmatic Celts of whom Mary MacKillop is our most famous member.

Scottish Identity 2004

A recent book on Scottish identity asked over a hundred present-day Scots what characterized Scottishness. One author claimed that "Scottishness, for me, is to be industrious and well behaved and then to do something outré just to prove I'm not hodden doon by oney wan. Wha dare meddle wi me. I'll show you!"[10] Others wrote about the socialist convictions handed on to them by their parents. Yet another wrote that being Scottish involves a capacity and indeed a willingness to be different".[11] Margaret Bennet began by saying that, "Scotland is the cradle of the paradox" then confessed:

> Being Scottish, I'm proud of David Hume and his ilk
> but grapple with the inconsistencies, absurdities and
> impossibilities of our homeland. Faith of our Fathers yet
> not my father's faith...Cleanliness is next to Godliness. The
> clartier the cosier. Here's to pure air, pure water, pure filth-
> pure dead brilliant.[12]

From personal experience it seems to me that a sense of humour saves most Celts from the extremes of emotional responses to life's events. There are many more people than the few noted above who claim to know what characterizes the Scots as a group. I use in the following pages the reflections of a Celt who has spent a lifetime philosophizing and theologizing about his own heritage and its impact on who he is. Noel O'Donoghue[13] claims that central to his people (and the people of Mary MacKillop and many an Australian) is their -

Unity with Nature[14]

This unity was felt rather than consciously acknowledged. Nature in all its manifestations was respected for its beauty and its awesome capacity to create havoc in the lives of people. The Celtic awareness of nature revealed itself in their constant references to the creator as the God of the Elements. Ronnat, Adomnáin's mother in the previously mentioned document, the *Law of the Innocents*, exclaims, "Alas, O my great Lord of the Elements."[15] I was recently confronted by this characteristic in the Outer Hebrides, particularly on the island of Barra. One did not take risks with the elements for they were stunningly beautiful at one moment and then could be unremittingly violent the next. When standing on a sandy beach or on another beach which was called the Barra Airport, it was starkly evident why these early Scottish Celts referred to the creator as the God of the Elements as that was almost all that was in this place - few people, fewer signs of the material world but the omnipresent "Presence" in the guise of wind, water, hills, valleys, sun rise and set.

Celtic consciousness was at odds with the prevailing Roman and Greek attitude to the cosmos of the early millennia. The latter felt an antipathy to the universe and the gods who created it; the cosmos had to be placated if not fought against, subdued, mastered and conquered. The human body-person by extension was subjected to exercise and bodily trials in order to tame it. For the Celts the cosmos, a strong element of their cultural awareness, was sensed as bringing the deity into intimate contact with the human. Far from a dichotomy between matter and spirit, the Incarnation enfleshed the deity in such a way that an intimate relationship with the divine reality became the end point of existence.[16]

For Mary MacKillop this same awesome awareness of the cosmos must have been part of her deep spirituality. She is reported as loving the convent garden at Paray-le-Monial and was delighted to get, "as a precious relic, 'one leaf' from the tree under which our Divine Spouse told many things to Blessed Margaret Mary."[17] On the ferry from Ostend to Dover in 1873 she felt impatient to see the White Cliffs of Dover, "If I felt that for England's cliffs, what, you may imagine, must I not wish to see if I go to Scotland."[18] Her awareness of the capacity of creation to reveal the unseen God can also be seen in some of her words such as "There where you are you will find God". No matter where one finds oneself, as the psalmist says, "If I fly to the heavens you are there. If I go the utmost corner of the earth, you are there", and to the Celt the unseen God will be found. I remember standing on the verandah of a country convent and hearing the exchange between Mother Leone, a former Superior General, and a child coming to the convent for music lessons. Mother said, "Isn't that sunset beautiful". The child's reply, "See it every day", points to the capacity of some to see and others to take things for granted. Mary MacKillop often reminded her Sisters, "Love and praise God in all' (1873). Using the age-old symbolism of the spiritual life Mary commented in 1873 that, "God's love is best known to us in times of aridity." Truly it could be said of Mary MacKillop that nature in all its phases was deeply part of her thinking, reflecting and praying.

An Acute Awareness of an Unseen World[19]

There is more to life than what we can see and touch. There is a whole other world that some people can still contact; in our childhood it was the world of fairies and the *Leannawn Shee* (the little people) of the Irish Celts. Even today Hungarians (for the Celts were in Hungary before they were pushed to the ends of the world) and particularly the Travelling People (Gypsies) have some of the characteristics of those who are in close affinity with this unseen world. If one spoke openly about this world one was often ostracized by those who thought they lived in the real world. However, it is not possible or even wise to define this unseen world but thankfully we still have, in our midst, people who continue to remind us of the existence of this other world. For the Christian it is the world of angels, spirits and the blessed dead. How real are the angels and the blessed dead to the reader of this?

Mary too was keenly aware of this unseen world. Thorpe says of Mary, "she was often foreseeing to the point of canniness".[20] This canniness is often called "second sight" which was a gift that many of the early Celtic saints possessed. To some it was more a curse than a blessing for one often "saw" what one did not wish to see. In Mary's case it may have been easier not to "see" some of the difficulties she was aware of, particularly in the idiosyncratic behaviour of some early Sisters whom Father Director thought were saints. Throughout her life and particularly in her troubles with those in authority she constantly resorted to prayer and the companionship of her unseen God, unlike her forebears who trusted in and tried to placate the pagan gods and goddesses. This unseen God was the source of her equilibrium. The serenity that flowed from this relationship was recognized by people who came into contact with her. It came across as a trust in Providence which she attributed to her mother's influence:

> You ever taught me to look to and depend on Divine Providence in every trouble and when you saw me dull and unhappy you always had the same sweet reminder for me. Ah, do not now forget what you were the first to teach me.[21]

In the Institute of St Joseph whose Constitution and Customs and Practices Mary impregnated with her spirit, the Celtic spirit of her ancestral homeland, there are also reminders of these Scottish characteristics. In one of the injunctions in the Customs and Practices Mary says, "The angel Guardian of the recreation hour has to give the quarterly notice of the 'presence of God'". Constant consciousness of the presence of the unseen God was intended to keep one focussed on the things that really matter. While this is not particularly Scottish, or even Celtic, it is a mark of the deep indebtedness to her Scottish ancestry that injunctions such as this were still in the Customs and Practices in the late 1960s.

A Profound Conviction of our Human Immortality[22]

As the author of these characteristics put it, "I can breathe freely only in the atmosphere of immortal spirit and the final transformation of nature and all that is within my own living, breathing, vulnerable human substance."[23] It is true that some people are convinced that there is no life after death, but increasingly people's sense of something more implants an eternal hope in the human psyche. What is the point of so much suffering, so much activity that does violence to the creator's cherishing of the world? Where is the reward for goodness, for heroic struggle, for unselfish actions and for just being faithful to one's chosen life and commitments? If Mary MacKillop was not profoundly committed to the same belief in human immortality why would she have sacrificed herself to its ideals? Her whole life bears witness to the worthwhileness of a life lived in the hope of Heaven. She pointed to the Josephite ideal in August 1877 when she said, "The true Sister of St Joseph should never think … she has the true spirit of her vocation were she to find herself attached to place, person or circumstances."[24]

A Love of Learning and an Appreciation of Any Kind of Teaching and Education[25]

Here emerges the story-teller of the Celtic tradition. Not in the formal sense of being educators, these people handed on their traditions with the nuances of emotion, sacredness and imaginative facts. In this handing on of the "stories of the tribe" was the "initiation into the mystery of wonder, so that one could breathe that pure air of the disclosure of truth which is, or should be, the aim of all teaching and all learning."[26] As an educator I have always seen teaching/education as freeing people from ignorance, prejudice and an over dependence on an emotional response to life's events.

Mary MacKillop's whole *raison d'être* was to educate the poorest of the poor in the outback of Australia as well as give opportunities to those unable to afford education in the schools of the wealthy. It was more than education that Mary was giving; she was safeguarding the very faith of the catholic population. She and Archbishop Vaughan had identical motives for their education system:

> We prize above all imaginable things, the Faith of our Fathers; that Faith is in peril in a great measure on account of the menacing condition of modern society; and cost what it may, it must be preserved and fostered in the hearts and intellects of the rising generation[27] (and this can only be achieved by a soundly Catholic education system).

Not only was the education system important but the training of the Sisters as educators was to be unified, "our whole strength in this system lies in our unity, and in the careful training of the members of it."[28] To this end she steadfastly worked for one training method throughout the ever-widening sphere of influence of the Josephites. While Governments in the fledgling Australia were far from being a Commonwealth, Mary's farsightedness insisted on unity. She confessed:

> For the poor of all Australia, and for my own part after strictest self examination, I really feel that I dare not face my God in judgment were I to fail in trying at least to secure for the Institute that peculiar training which is necessary for such a work.[29]

This was the truth of who Mary MacKillop was and why she insisted with the Roman authorities and the Australian Bishops that unity in leadership and formation was of the essence of the new Sisterhood. For this she was willing and did indeed suffer.

A Creative, Imaginative Approach to Life

This *modus operandi* pleads with us to live by the light of imagination:

> To the senses it says: listen to the Presence, feel it, touch it, breathe it in. To the intellect it says: open up beyond the heavy material world to a Presence and presences that refuse to be controlled by your limiting categories, a presence that you are longing to encounter and affirm for it enriches and completes the meaning of creation.[30]

One only has to look at the art of the Celts, both Scottish/Pictish and Irish, to see the juxtapositioning of the sacred and the profane with little awareness of any distinction. The Book of Kells has many examples like the Monograph page where in a small corner one can detect two rats fighting over the host while two bemused cats look on. Who but Celts would conceive of such an "irreverent" depiction? On the famous

Scripture cross of Monasterboice, below the central depiction of the apprehension of Christ there are two cats licking their kittens. The distinction of sacred and profane, of here and now, has no meaning to the Celtic mindset: all is one and all is sacred. A voyage of discovery, amusement and maybe profound insights await the person who takes the trouble of spending time with the artwork, stone carvings and illuminations of any Celtic manuscript.[31]

In the theological climate of the nineteenth century this dichotomy of sacred and profane was deeply embedded. So Mary MacKillop could not escape from it. However, in her letters and life one can see that such a distinction was not so pronounced. Even the fact that she was free enough to "suspend" rules if the needs of another called for it shows a woman who lived more by the spirit of the Gospel than by the letter of the law.

Worth not Birth

Burns' poem above seems to be stressing what to me is evident in Mary MacKillop most profoundly - worth not birth is what determines a person's value. Worth cannot be put on like an outer garment; a person has it by virtue of who s/he is; neither education nor status, money, class or any other superficial attribute can endow one with it. Respect given to those who "earn" it and worth is not a concomitant of rank. Osmund Thorpe claims that:

> Highland Scots, no matter their poverty, have no feelings of inferiority. Perhaps because of the clan system which for centuries linked the lowest with the highest, their normal instinct is to regard themselves as gentlefolk in their own right. They are courteous by nature and tradition, sensitive and easily hurt by insensitivity in others.[32]

In the life of the Institute of the Sisters of St Joseph, some quite important decisions made early in its life point to this important characteristic of the Scots. The Superior was called the "Little Sister" and when her time of leadership was concluded she went back into the ranks so there was no opportunity to think that as Superior anyone could claim any special privileges. There were to be no lay Sisters as in the older European Orders of Religious Sisters, "All must remember that there are no grades or distinctions in the Institute of St Joseph". "Conversations (on) such topics of family affairs, positions in life, superiority of birth or education, nationality (were) strictly forbidden." Further, in the *Customs and Practices* read weekly to the Sisters, this abhorrence of distinctions was spelled out thus:

> Those who may have received a more polite education than ordinary, or who may have moved in higher worldly positions must always remember that they have left these things outside the doors of St Joseph's Convent.[33]

Some of the courage that Mary displayed at the time of the excommunication is an "inheritance" from her Scottish mother. Worth, regardless of ecclesiastical rank, had to be earned and Flora's words to the Bishop, I was "under the impression that only notorious sinners could be excommunicated" and "the great sin of (my daughter's) life, in my opinion, has been the leaving me and putting herself under your Lordship's protection"[34] are a powerful reminder of this fact. One has to remember that these words came from a staunchly Catholic immigrant woman to her Bishop in nineteenth century Adelaide. It is easy to see where Mary MacKillop derived her courage and sense of the importance of "saying it as it was". Not only did she inherit this Scottish characteristic from Flora MacDonald, but she was deeply moved even by the sound of the Gaelic language which she spoke with fluency. When in Scotland she embarrassed some Gaelic boatmen who slowly realised that she knew what they were saying when they called her a *Sassenach*. Her delight was palpable when she visited places known to her parents, "How wonderful that without knowing it I should come to the very part where they (her parents) were all so well known."[35]

Another important aspect of what it was to be a Celt was the ease with which they integrated the incoming Christianity with their pagan past. The Celts were syncretists in the best sense of that word. All religions were to be respected because all were different ways to God; the same God who came to earth in Jesus, suffered, died and rose to new life. ColumCille, that champion of the Scots on Iona, frequently addressed Christ as his Druid. The tonsure of the early Celtic monks was that used by the Druids and this was a cause of dismay to the Roman authorities. The early Celtic monks performed many of the roles assigned to Druids in the Religious traditions of the pre-Christian Celtic lands. To say that Christianity has anything in common with primal religions strikes fear into the hearts of some Christians. However, it is clear that there would be no dialogue between religions if there were not some points on which they could "converse". If primal religions are the first religious forms to arise in human culture then historically and psychologically they have some impact on other religions that follow them. Kathleen

Tanner refers to the meeting point of Christianity and primal religions as the "boundary". She expresses this process as follows:

> The distinctiveness of a Christian way of life is not so much formed by the boundary as at it; Christian distinctiveness is something that emerges in the very cultural process occurring at the boundary; processes that construct a distinctive identity for Christian social practices through the distinctive use of cultural materials shared with others.[36]

Edwin Hatch in the introduction to the Hibbert Lectures of 1888 holds that, "the religion of a given race at a given time is relative to the whole mental attitude of that time. It is impossible to separate the religious phenomena from the other phenomena."[37] The Celts whether Scottish, Irish, Welsh, Cornwellan or those from Brittany were blessed with a natural religious spirit, "among (their) earthiest words the angels stray".[38] So if the characteristics of the Celts identified above are authentic then one can assume that their religious life too is a product of the Celtic cultural consciousness.

In the life of Mary MacKillop then, is there any evidence of her relationship with people of other religious traditions? We know for a fact that she was befriended by Mrs Joanna Barr Smith and her husband who provided for the extremely impoverished Sisters in Adelaide. Mother Lawrence tells us:

> Mrs Barr Smith was a particular friend. This lady was very wealthy; not a Catholic. Mr Barr Smith was a leading man in Adelaide, a politician, who gave Mother Mary two thousand pounds for the building of a Kensington Convent.[39]

Dr Benson, another protestant never charged the Sisters for his services. Mary lamented when he died:

> Oh! Sister I feel this death more than words can express. Poor dear Doctor, he is universally loved and regretted… His too generous heart never allowed him to save. We have offered to educate for the present Lottie and the younger boys. Poor Mrs Benson is so grateful. When I made the offer she cried and embracing me said, 'He told me you would be kind'.[40]

Emanuel Solomon, a Jew, was friendly to the extent that when the Bishop of the Catholic Church in Adelaide excommunicated Mary, Solomon gave her refuge. Both he and Mr Goldstein gave her financial help during the troubles in Adelaide in 1871. Sectarianism that appeared to flourish in most of Australia of the nineteenth century was nowhere in sight when these three friends came to the aid of Mary. It was not simply her dire need that allowed her to accept their friendship and financial aid; she truly believed that all people were equal and worthy of respect no matter what their religious affiliation.

In September 1873 Mary wrote from London, "it is an Australian who writes this, one brought up in the midst of the evils she tries to describe."[41] This sentence seems to nullify the stated purpose of this paper. However, the context is significant. This opening statement sets out the credentials of the writer justifying for the Roman authorities why the Australian situation is different from the European and as such she should be given credibility for knowing the scene and wanting to address the needs of the Australian not the European Catholics. She is defending the works of the Institute as specifically suited to an Australian clientele. In this she was being true to her upbringing and sense of what God was asking of her. However, this writer still firmly holds that it was her Scottish heritage that shone through what she did and why, but it was given a specific colour because of the Australian context in which she was born and grew. The readers can decide for themselves whether Mary was a genuine Aussie, a Hereditary Scot or both!

Endnotes

1 Robbie Burns, *Poems by R. Burns with Glossary*, Midget Classics (London: Burgess and Bowes Ltd, circa 1980).

2 The opening took place in the Hall of the General Assembly of the Church of Scotland and the parliament moved to the new parliament building in 2004; the building cost 480 million pounds.

3 Edward J. Cowan and Robert Finlay, *Scotland since, 1688: Struggle for a Nation* (London: Cima Books, 2000), 9. Declaration of Arbroath, was a letter to the Bishop of Rome, John XX11, in the name of "the community of the realm of Scotland" asking him to recognize the legality of Robert the Bruce's kingship.

4 Cowan, *Scotland since, 1688: Struggle for a Nation*, 6.

5 David Broun and Owen T. Clancy, *Spes Scotorum, Hope of Scots: St Columba Iona and Scotland* (Edinburgh: T and T Clark, 1999), 10. Clancy makes the point that the document was signed by some fifty-one kings of Ireland and Northern Britain, including Pictish Kings and forty of the leading Churchmen of the Gaelic world. This signatory list has been shown to date from 697 C.E.

6 It was said at the Conference on Iona which I attended in 2004 to commemorate the thirteen hundredth anniversary of Adomnan's death, that the United Nations used his *Law of the Innocents* when it was formulating its Declaration of Human Rights.

7 John J. O'Riordan, *Irish Catholics: Tradition and Transition (Dublin: Veritas, 1980)*, 4. O'Riordan says that he was quoting an old Cork schoolmaster.

8 *The Herald*, Scotland, Friday, September 2004.

9 Dr Daniel Bradley, geneticist, in the Herald article said, "It's a well known fact that there are cultural relations between the areas but now this shows there is much more."

[10] Tom Devine and Paddy Logue, ed., *Being Scottish* (Edinburgh: Polygon, 2002), 5.
[11] Devine and Logue, *Being Scottish,* 11.
[12] Devine and Logue, *Being Scottish,* 19. That final comment about Scottish, "pure dead brilliant", is on many post cards from Glasgow; this writer agrees that the appellation is appropriate for Glasgow!
[13] Noel Dermott O'Donoghue, *The Mountain behind the Mountain* (Edinburgh: T&T Clarke, 1989).
[14] O'Donoghue, *The Mountain behind the Mountain,* 4
[15] Kuno Meyer, ed., *Cain Adomnain: An old Irish treatise on the Law of the Innocents* (Oxford: Clarendon Press, 1905), par 9.
[16] Catherine Thom, *The Ascetical Theology and praxis of sixth to eighth Century Irish Monasticism as a Radical Response to the Evangelium,* Doctoral Thesis, 2002, xii. This and other such references are used with permission of T&T Clark International who is publishing the thesis in April 2006
[17] Paul Gardiner, *An Extraordinary Australian: Mary MacKillop: The Authorised Biography* (Australia: E.J.Dwyer, 1993), 137.
[18] Mary MacKillop to the Sisters, September 25th 1873.
[19] O'Donoghue, *The Mountain behind the Mountain,* 5.
[20] Osmund Thorpe, *Mary MacKillop,* Revised with endnotes, (Surry Hills, Sydney: McPherson's Printing Group, 1994), 21.
[21] Gardiner, *An Extraordinary Australian: Mary MacKillop: The Authorised Biography,* 39.
[22] O'Donoghue, *The Mountain behind the Mountain,* 5.
[23] Ibid.
[24] Gardiner, *An Extraordinary Australian: Mary MacKillop: The Authorised Biography,* 239.
[25] O'Donoghue, *The Mountain behind the Mountain,* 6
[26] Ibid.
[27] Gardiner, *An Extraordinary Australian: Mary MacKillop: The Authorised Biography,* 26.
[28] Gardiner, *An Extraordinary Australian: Mary MacKillop: The Authorised Biography,* 160.
[29] Gardiner, *An Extraordinary Australian: Mary MacKillop: The Authorised Biography,* 166.
[30] O'Donoghue *The Mountain behind the Mountain, 32.*
[31] "Manuscript" is used here in the broadest sense of the word which includes materials other than paper.
[32] Thorpe, *Mary MacKillop,* 19.
[33] *Customs and Practices of the Sisters of St Joseph of the Sacred Heart,* Sydney, 1950, 12.
[34] Gardiner, *An Extraordinary Australian: Mary MacKillop: The Authorised Biography,* 108.
[35] Gardiner, *An Extraordinary Australian: Mary MacKillop: The Authorised Biography,* 139.
[36] Kathleen Tanner, *Theories of Culture: A New Agenda for Theology* (Minneapolis: Fortress Press, 1997), 115.
[37] A.M.Fairbairn, ed, *The Influence of Greek Ideas upon the Christian Church* (London: William and Norgate, 1907), 2-3. Hatch actually wrote the work but died before it was published.
[38] O'Riordan, *Irish Catholics: Tradition and Transition,* 4, quoting an excerpt from a poem of Kavanagh, "In Memory of My Mother".
[39] Gardiner, *An Extraordinary Australian: Mary MacKillop: The Authorised Biography,* 237.
[40] Gardiner, *An Extraordinary Australian: Mary MacKillop: The Authorised Biography,* 237/8.

God Will Take Care of Us All

Pauline Wicks rsj

Mary MacKillop's[1] reliance on Divine Providence[2] is an outstanding feature of her spirituality. Throughout her writings, Mary repeatedly referred to God as a "good God".[3] Belief in this "good God", the God for whom she desired to live, provided the basis for Mary's confidence that, "God will take care of us all".[4] Mary's life as pioneer Australian Christian woman provides inspiration for all. For those who "manifest a thirst for God"[5], Mary's confidence in God's Providence, challenges all to trust in a "good God," to listen deeply to the Word of God spoken in their hearts and to respond with love in today's world. Mary invites all to a radical trust in a "good God", a faith-filled trust that is the foolishness of the Gospel of Jesus.

Mary learnt from her family to have a firm confidence in God and the experiences of her life provided opportunities for that confidence to grow. Moreover, confidence in God's Providence was one of the few "securities" in the daily life of the MacKillop family.[6]

Writing to Flora, her mother, in 1866 of her decision to "enter Religion", Mary said:

> It was in hardships, poverty and even want that you had to rear your children, but in the bitterest trial and greatest need your confidence in Divine Providence never failed.[7]

Mary reminded her mother in a letter of August 1867:

> Dearest Mamma, you ever taught me to look up to and depend on Divine Providence in every trouble and when you saw me dull or unhappy you always had the same sweet reminder for me.[8]

Trust in God's Providence seems to have been firmly rooted in the

MacDonald and MacKillop way of living their faith. In writing to her mother in January 1868, Mary said:

> Oh Mamma let us belong to Him completely and He will take care of us all. Remember what poor Uncle Sandy said to Grandmama a short time before his death when he reminded her that God would take care of us all. How often she used to repeat his saying to me.[9]

Trust in God's Providence enabled Mary to respond to God's call, to God's desire for her in the church and the world of her time. This response called for a breadth of vision beyond the societal and Church confines of her day but as she wrote in 1873, "as far back as I can remember, He (God) gave me such a sense of His watchful presence" and that God "taught me to lean upon Him alone."[10] She was thus empowered to respond to the needs of her time with courage and compassion, desiring God's glory and the fullness of life for all.

Mary left her native Melbourne in 1860 for Penola, South Australia. Here she met Father Julian Tenison Woods[11] and together they shared their dreams of leading children to the knowledge and love of God. Father Woods believed that God's Providence directed Mary MacKillop to him as he grappled with the problem of education in his vast parish. Mary wrote, "I heard the Pastor from the Altar speak of the neglected state of the children in his parish and I had to go and offer myself to aid him as far as the nature of my other duties would permit."[12] In Penola on March 19th 1866 Mary gave external expression to her desire and, dressed in a simple black dress, she became the first Sister of St Joseph of the Sacred Heart.

This new initiative for Mary and Julian was one which was not to fit easily into the vision of the developing Australian Church with its predominantly Irish clergy. Mary wrote to Woods, "I am not disturbed or uneasy about the future. Whatever crosses are before us, God's loving Will sends and can we receive with unhappiness what He sends for our good and His greater glory?"[13]

Mary's authority, the place of the Institute within the Australian Church, and the authority of Rome, were to provide points of great tension between herself and the Bishops of the various dioceses. Grounding her confidence in the will of God,[14] Mary's prayer and discernment led her to live only for God's glory - "for as long as His name be glorified in the end we need not care."[15]

Mary felt her "own unworthiness" for what she was called to do. She was convinced that she "must only trust in the Mercies of God",[16] for as she wrote, "I cannot do anything without God's help."[17]

Mary's new vision grew out of her Australian experience. In the *Necessity for the Institute* she wrote:

> It is an Australian who writes this, one brought up in the midst of many of the evils she tries to describe, and who has over and over again heard pious priests and zealous Bishops sadly deplore a state of things which they could not remedy.[18]

In January 1870 Mary with five Sisters[19] arrived in Brisbane to make a foundation there. She had written to Woods in October 1869:

> My father, God will take care of His own work. Be without fear for those you send away as also for those remaining. The cross will follow both but will be a sweet and dear instrument in the hands of a great and good Father.[20]

In June 1870 Mary wrote for the Sisters, *A Declaration on the Spirit of the Institute.* It included the following:

> The Sisters... only undertake to teach because it is on God through their glorious Patron St Joseph that they rely for the necessary means to do so. Conscious of our own weakness we dare not undertake that which we do, but that our sole trust is in Him and that we know He delights in manifesting His glory through the very weakness and misery of His instruments. [21]

In Queensland, proposed Government aid for the schools there caused conflict between Mary and Church authorities. Mary wrote with "indescribable pain" to Dr Cani,[22] stating that it was "impossible for us (the members of the Institute) to become in any way connected to the Government (for financial aid) and be true to the Spirit as well as the letter of our Rule." As Sister Guardian Mary wrote, "what the voice of conscience and duty" dictated:

> It is not, as you are aware, upon our schools or even the generosity of creatures that we depend, but wholly upon God's Providence which has never deserted us and never will, no matter how we be straightened (sic) or what struggles we have to undergo in being true to Its interests.[23]

Having to live without any secure income, money for fares and the necessities of life came from gifts and from begging. Mary saw the hand of Divine Providence when people assisted the Sisters when they were without money and/or food. She wrote to Woods:

> The day we were coming away (from Sydney on their way to Brisbane) we were nearly seven pounds short of what we required for our passage money, but the Vicar General (of Sydney) had five pounds for us…. Another gentleman at Villa Maria (Hunters Hill) gave us unasked two pounds. Have we not another proof of God's ever watchful Providence?[24]

In the early months in Queensland Mary and the Sisters did not have the spiritual support and formation that they desired from the clergy. Dr Cani appointed himself as their confessor, excluding all others but rarely gave them an opportunity for Mass or Confession, never for Benediction or a spiritual instruction.[25] Mary wrote to Woods, "Dr Cani is so good but he is not the director to help our poor Sisters much, but then he is the one God has given us and that is everything, for the sweet grace of our good God does the rest."[26]

Despite her concerns about the school and the issue of State Aid in Queensland, the cares of the Sisters both in Queensland and Adelaide, Mary wrote confidently to Woods, "My mind is in such peace…. For in spite of misgivings in some things, I feel such a certainty of God's protecting care, and that He will be much glorified in the end."[27]

Mary returned to Adelaide in March 1871, by now having "arrived at an independence of judgement in congregational matters." Her Queensland experience had enabled Mary to develop "as the woman of strength who could meet with equanimity the crises awaiting her when she returned there (South Australia)."[28]

And crises did await her! Woods was ill and a sick and ill-advised Bishop Sheil was making moves to change the Rule according to which the Sisters had made their profession, the Rule he himself had approved. Mary wrote to Woods on September 19th 1871:

> In some way or other all seems so uncertain yet it is God who acts in all and makes use of the acts of all for His own wise ends...I am not disturbed or uneasy about the future. Whatever crosses are before us, God's loving will sends, and can we receive with unhappiness what he sends for our good and His greater glory?[29]

Again she wrote:

> I am not a bit discouraged, and what is more, so clearly see

> the hand of God in all that is now happening to us, I do not pray more, nor indeed as much as I did, and that never was much, but feel calm and tranquil and so near our dear good God. I give myself and all into His adorable hands, and am perfectly confident that He will both direct and guide us all in as far as we may have to act…[30]

Bishop Sheil excommunicated Mary on September 22nd 1871. This sentence was lifted on February 23rd 1872; Sheil admitting that he had acted unjustly towards Mary and the Sisters. Mary wrote to her mother on February 26th 1872, "God wisely permitted it (the excommunication) for a hidden and mysterious end."[31]

On December 19th 1871 Mary wrote to Woods,

> We are in His hands….Let us not be troubled....
> Let us all, one and all, simply do the little that we can as far as the necessary human means are given to us, and beyond that, let us without a shadow of fear leave the rest to our Father and our God.[32]

At the end of 1872 Mary wrote to her mother from Adelaide with plans to open more schools in 1873. She was confident that:

> Since God in his mercy and goodness has provided for us through the most trying one we surely would be ungrateful if we feared for the future which has so many bright prospects that this one had not.[33]

Mary left for Rome on March 25th 1873 to gain sanction for the Rule of the Sisters of St Joseph.[34] Her going to Rome was itself a great act of trust in God's Providence. A single woman, aged thirty-one, travelling alone was far from accepted female behaviour of the time. She travelled as a widow, Mrs MacDonald, and wore secular dress especially in Rome, where political and social turmoil made it dangerous to appear in a religious habit. She wrote of the many proofs "of God's watchful care" – protecting her, providing her with sufficient money for fares, providing accommodation, providing guidance and resources for the Institute, the care of family and friends, and finally, for the whole process whereby the Rule was examined, re-written and given approval.[35]

On board the *Bangalore* she wrote to her mother:

> Of course I expect difficulties in Rome before the approbation I desire for our holy Rule can be secured, but none of these dismay or discourage me. Indeed from the first of this great

> undertaking I have felt a strength and calm courage in the protecting care of our good God which I feel are His own gifts to help my weakness, and to fit me for his work.[36]

By chance, or was it God's providence, Mary's Uncle Alexander and Aunt Ellen Cameron travelled on the same steamer as Mary. On the voyage to Rome she wrote to the Sisters from *S.S. Golconda* in the Arabian Sea, convinced of God's care for her:

> But I must not let you think that I am in any way uneasy, either about you whom I have left or as to my own future movements. Indeed, it would be too glaring ingratitude towards our good God for me to be uneasy. His watchful care over me since I parted from you has been so evident both in the friends He has put in (my) way, and the many dangers from which he has guarded me; and I am equally certain, without having to be told it, that He has watched over your interests and given you far greater blessings than perhaps you are aware of.[37]

During the voyage Mary also wrote to Father Poupinel sm[38] asking his prayers for her "great undertaking" in Rome. She wrote:

> Our dear Lord has wonderfully watched over us. …. My trust is in Him whom I know will not let the unworthiness of the instrument he deigns to employ interfere with the carrying out of His wise designs. I feel that the cause is great and much depends upon it, and I know that if the work is His, that it must succeed, and if not, I only desire His Will to be done.

Mary added that she did not know anyone in Rome, but that she:

> Will find other Sisters in Religion and in suffering there; and the sense of having God's protecting care upholds and strengthens me for any difficulty or opposition I may meet.[39]

Mary arrived in Rome on May 12th 1873 and on the same day, met Father Anderledy sj[40] and Monsignor Kirby.[41] Kirby became her point of contact while in Rome as well as a friend and spiritual guide. In her frequent correspondence to Kirby she told of how God had helped her thus far and of how "our dear Lord encourages me." In her long letter of Ascension Thursday 1873, Mary recalled the beginnings in Penola, the guidance she received from Woods and the pain of their separation, which she wrote "threw me back upon my good God alone." She wrote of the decision to come to Rome, saying:

> I saw that He would provide the means, that He would guide me on the way, and that in Rome He would provide a friend to do for me what I could not do for myself. .... I felt what He required of me was to ask F. Reynolds to let me go – and that of myself personally He required an unbounded confidence.[42]

Mary wrote to her mother of the speed with which consideration was made to her requests regarding the Rule of the Institute on her arrival in Rome. She wrote of how Kirby had found accommodation for her in a convent, how he prepared her papers for presentation to the Holy See, translated some for her and brought her to see Cardinal Barnabo, the Prefect of Propaganda,[43] acted as interpreter and at another time brought her to meet Cardinal Belio, of the Sacred Congregation of Rites. She was confident of God's care:

> See how God's ways are worked out. I had not a friend here when I left Adelaide, but I knew that God would raise one, I knew that I could not do anything, but I knew at the same time that our dear Lord would not let His work want a friend to advance its interests here....[44]

Mary had her first audience with Pius IX on Pentecost Sunday, June 1st 1873. Cardinal Barnabo and Monsignor Kirby accompanied her to explain her position to the Holy Father. She described the audience in a letter to the Sisters:

> I had the great happiness of seeing the Holy Father and of receiving a truly Fatherly blessing for us all. He laid his hands so kindly on my head when he gave this blessing, but he did not do so until Cardinal Barnabo reminded him of Adelaide and our troubles, before that he just gave His ring to kiss as he did to all the rest. Thus you see how in the mysterious ways of God's Providence our greatest trials were so many hidden means which He was employing to make the work in which so many feeble instruments were employed speedily known to those whom He desired to help and strengthen it.[45]

Mary was profoundly moved by this experience and wrote to her mother that what the Pope said when he knew she was the "excommunicated one" were "things too sacred to be spoken of."[46] In her diary for June 1st 1873 she wrote, "A day never to be forgotten, a day worth years of suffering."

Mary was in Rome from May till the end of July 1873. The next eight months were spent mostly in England and Scotland. She was in Rome again from March 17th to April 24th and from then until her departure for Australia she spent most of her time in England and Ireland. These months were filled with times of loneliness, ill health, weariness, extensive travel, concerns regarding the Rule, scarcity of money, and concerns about the Sisters in Australia. Difficult though these times were she was conscious always of God's watchful care.

On September 1st 1873 she wrote to the Sisters of one instance:

> I cannot but regard all as most Providential connected with the way in which our dear Lord brought me to London at present – just in time to join the great public Pilgrimage to Paray-le-Monial in France; all in honour of the Sacred Heart of our sweet Spouse and to give an opportunity, at the first of Its shrines, of petitioning for the many needs we have got…
>
> Yes indeed, I pass through strange changes, and I daily experience the sweets of God's protecting care, and the comfort of having Him in many trying scenes as my best of friends, and only support. It is for your encouragement, my dear Sisters, that I mention this for, with all our dearest Lord is doing for us, and the many dangers to which the quiet of a religious, to which I am exposed, it should indeed encourage you to know that our sweet Spouse in this way watches over me, and keeps me near himself and his loved Cross.[47]

Mary's trust in God's care is evident in the *Necessity for the Institute* which she wrote in 1873:

> Their (the Sisters) own experience of Australian life, what they have seen and heard around them, and the sad conviction that money and the comforts it brings, even when it should not, …makes them pray with increased earnestness that He, 'who when the foxes had their holes, and the birds of the air their nests, had not where to lay His head,' may mercifully keep them in that state of dependence upon Him as their All, which they covet, and in which they wish for His sake, and the better to attend to the want of His little ones, to live and die.[48]

In November 1873 Mary wrote to the Sisters:

> I am sure, my loved ones that you do not wish me home more earnestly that I desire myself, yet for your sakes, for all our sakes, and for the common good I am detained. Believe

me, an ever watchful providence is guiding all things to our mutual good. You may not see this as clearly as I am forced to do, but when we meet, when all is talked over, then we shall all be lost in astonishment and each one will see the greatness and the beauty of God's mysterious ways, at least as far as it is given of us poor ones to see these sweet things. Oh that I could tell you how I yearn for you to trust in God - to be without fear, to do your work humbly in sweet charity and for Him alone, the one true Spouse of our souls. He yearns for this humble hopeful service from each of us.[49]

In August 1873 Mary wrote to Kirby telling him that "thanks to our dearest Lord's goodness" she was able to rent a room on reasonable terms, "in town.... in a nice central situation, and only about three minutes walk from the Jesuits' Church." She is "quiet, near our dear Lord, and near a good holy priest who is doing all he can to procure help for our schools." While this was encouragement for her she mentions also discouragement. She says, "My sweet Jesus mercifully keeps me under the Cross." The issue was the timing of her return to Adelaide – it was not as soon as she had expected, but she wrote, "I leave it then to our dear Lord's all-wise Providence to direct as he sees best – and my only prayer is that His will may be done in the matter."[50]

In another letter to Kirby she wrote that she:

> got quite safely and without much difficulty from Coblentz (sic) to London. ... In every little difficulty our good God came to my aid in some kind person whom he sent to help me, and thus over and over again does He lovingly invite to confidence and trust in Him.[51]

Mary wrote to her sister, Annie on September 18th 1873, telling her of some of her experiences in Rome and of her travels thus far:

> Well, Dearest Annie, are not God's ways wonderful with us all. In my case they would fairly bewilder me but I have long since ceased to wonder at anything He permits in our regard. I leave myself in His hands to deal with me as He pleases, for were I to reason or ponder too much upon His extraordinary ways, I know not where my weary senses would sometimes take me.[52]

In another long letter to the Sisters, describing in great detail her travels, Mary wrote:

> Now, I want to draw your attention to a mark of God's providence in this. Had I not made a mistake about the Brussels train, I should have arrived in London a day sooner and thus most certainly have escaped this happy introduction to F. Christie, who, from all I could see and all I hear, as well as from my own experience now of what he is, seems the one in every way most able to assist; he is also the one Father Anderledy wished me to know.[53]

Mary believed that the schools conducted by the Sisters, being "for the poor or common class of children," should not teach instrumental music or foreign languages. This was one of the matters that had to be clarified by the authorities in Rome. Mary wrote to Kirby:

> As far as I am concerned in this matter, I have, thanks to the infinite goodness and mercy of my God, so firm a conviction that some day sooner of later He will confirm us in these things that I cannot say I have one anxiety as to the final result, indeed I sometimes wonder so much at my confidence upon this that I would think I was too sanguine, or over presumptuous, were it not for the fulfilling of His promise that those who trust in Him shall never be confounded. … I do feel that our good God is with His work, guarding and protecting its interests in, to me, a sweet and marvellous way.[54]

Mary assured her mother in a letter of March 1874 that, "I am not without a sort of outward care at times, but the trust our good God gives me in Himself as my only sure Friend sweetly supports me and keeps me always happy."[55] On another occasion she wrote to her mother, "You see how good God is – everywhere He allows his servants to encourage me."[56]

Mary made a retreat in Rome in March 1874. As part of a reflection on this retreat she wrote:

> I feel that I would be a selfish and ungenerous Spouse if I wanted any particular plan in which I am concerned to succeed in preference to any other matter of these Spouses or souls devoted to Him. So that I have to pray only for what he desires and to tell Him that I wish in my heart to rejoice as much over His mercifully granting His own desires whether in the favour of our particular case, or in any other need of his Church. Thus He makes me leave all this in great trust

> to Him, but only at the same time He lets me feel that I have individually great and solemn Offices of trust to discharge.[57]

In one of her last letters to her mother while she was away, Mary wrote:

> I say no more about the one great business I have at heart. That is safe – and may God be praised for all. Our heavenly Father has signally protected His own work, and now that I see the way in which he has done so I am fairly bewildered at the mystery of the whole.[58]

Mary arrived back in Adelaide on January 4th 1875. Authorities in Rome had confirmed the principle of "central government" of the Institute; the position of an ecclesiastical superior was abolished once and for all; and the Institute was placed under the care of a "Cardinal Protector" in Rome. While Mary was pleased, she knew that these arrangements would not find favour with Woods or some of the Bishops, especially Bishops Matthew and James Quinn. But, more conscious than ever of God's care, and having experienced that God did take care of all, Mary looked forward with confidence to the future.

That future was not to be without its trials and difficulties and was to invite Mary to grow in her belief that "God will take care of us all." Prayer, her union with God and the prayers of others, were essential to this confidence as can be seen from Mary's letter to the Sisters, "you will, I am sure, all unite in humble and earnest prayer that God's own Holy Spirit of wisdom, goodness and love may guide and reign...."[59]

Reflecting in 1876 on the breakdown in her friendship with Woods, Mary wrote that she was "crushed.... to the heart and (that) I have even dared to envy the dead. I stand utterly alone." But from this low point Mary was able to add, "I do hope in my God still, and I know He will never fail me or His own dear work."[60]

The Sisters' ministry in Queensland continued under difficulties until the end of 1879 when the Sisters withdrew. Mary wrote to Dr Campbell and talked about "a sad and painful mission" that she had to perform, but added, "Our cause is in the hands of our good God and I know he will protect His own work."[61]

The withdrawal from Queensland gave Mary the opportunity to open schools in New South Wales. She wrote at the end of 1881:

> Just fancy what a contrast to two years ago.... How good God has been to us bringing us from uncertainty and many

> troubles to the peace and security we have in NSW.[62]

Mary often urged the Sisters to remember that "God did take care of all." She wrote, "think of the past and it will tell you God is good and He is just I know He will have His Will accomplished with regard to our loved Institute...."[63] Mary wrote to Sister Andrea Howley, "God is watching over His work and St Joseph is not idle either in Heaven or on earth."[64] Mary encouraged Sister Monica Phillips, "Now my dearest Sister, do not fret. I feel sure that God is aiding you."[65]

Mary was thankful often that "God did take care of all." Of Cardinal Moran's kindness to her she wrote to Sister Patricia Campbell:

> The unexpected kindness almost stunned me. I feel dazed almost yet and can only say, 'God be praised, for indeed his ways are wonderful.' Help me to thank Him.[66]

In the same vein Mary wrote to her brother Donald, mentioning her present good health, "from my heart I thank God for that and for the way He has protected me through all."[67] She wrote to Sister Raymond in New Zealand, "have courage, trust in God, St Joseph and our Blessed Mother, and you have no need to fear."[68]

For Mary, St Joseph was a model for confidence in God:

> We see in our holy patron a perfect mirror of confidence in God and submission to His adorable Will. Oh, how wonderful was his confidence in his good God.... It was enough for him that a certain path or line of duty was pointed out to him, and if difficulties seemed to beset this path, if want and privations of the most trying kind threatened all he held most dear, nothing daunted, humbly, firmly relying upon providence, he courageously and without a moment's delay embraced the Will of his God, and his humble heart rejoiced as he saw each of these glaring difficulties silently dwindling into nothing and leaving behind them lasting memorials of the mysterious ways of his God.[69]

One can see Mary's own trust in God's providence reflecting that of her "glorious patron."

Countless examples exist of the way Mary lived out her belief that "God will take care of us all". Her life was one of integrity, wisdom and graciousness. A "constant awareness" of God provided opportunities for the events in her life to become means of transformation and transcendence in her choice to "live for God alone." Her question to the

Sisters in a letter of September 1906, is a one that all may ponder, "have you not much to be thankful to our good God for?"[70]

With Mary MacKillop as our inspiration for today, "Let us refuse nothing to God's love."[71]

Endnotes

1 A significant part of this article is based on Chapter 3 of the thesis, "God Will Take Care of Us All", (Mary MacKillop, April 2nd 1867). A Study in the Spirituality of Mary MacKillop as Expressed in Her Correspondence from 1860 to 1874. Pauline Wicks, Master of Theology (Honours), Sydney College of Divinity, April 2005.
When reading Mary MacKillop's writings it is well to remember that her language is that of her time; she did not use inclusive language.

2 God's Providence can be described as, "the act whereby He causes, cares for, and directs all creatures to their particular ends, in attaining which each one contributes to the final purpose of the universe – the manifestation of His external glory." *New Catholic Encyclopedia,* s.v. "Providence of God (Theology of)", by E.J. Carney, Vol VXX1, (USA: University of America, Washington DC, 1967), 917.

3 In her writings Mary MacKillop referred to God by a variety of names and titles; that of a "good God" was the one she used most often.

4 Mary MacKillop to Flora MacKillop, January 7th 1868. Flora MacKillop (MacDonald), Mary's mother, arrived in Melbourne from Scotland in April 1840.

5 *Evangelli Nuntiandi,* Pope Paul VI, (Homebush, Sydney: A St Paul's Publication, 1976), No 48.

6 Alexander MacKillop, Mary's father, arrived in Sydney in January 1838. He was well educated but was not a good provider. When Mary was born the family's economic future seemed secure but it did not last. In her long letter to Monsignor Kirby, written on Ascension Thursday 1873, Mary recounted that her life "as a child was one of sorrows, my home, when I had it, a most unhappy one."

7 Mary MacKillop to Flora MacKillop, November 27th 1866.

8 Mary MacKillop to Flora MacKillop, August 21st 1867.

9 Mary MacKillop to Flora MacKillop, January 7th 1868.

10 Mary MacKillop to Monsignor Kirby, Ascension Thursday, 1873.

11 Father Julian Tenison Woods was the co-founder of the Sisters of St Joseph of the Sacred Heart. He was appointed as the priest in charge of the Penola district in 1857. In 1867 he was appointed Director-General of Education for Adelaide. He was the Director of the Sisters of St Joseph from their foundation until August 1873.

12 Mary MacKillop to Kirby, Ascension Thursday 1873.

13 Mary MacKillop to Woods, April 3rd 1871.

14 Mary MacKillop to Woods, April 17th 1870. Mary wrote to Woods, "Now my confidence will be grounded on the Will of God."

15 Mary MacKillop to Woods, April 2nd 1867.

16 Mary MacKillop to Woods, June 2nd 1867.

17 Mary MacKillop to Flora MacKillop, August 21st 1867.

18 Mary MacKillop, *Necessity for the Institute,* August 1873. Resource Material from the Archives of the Sisters of St Joseph of the Sacred Heart, Issue No 3, January 1980, 49. This article was written to give a brief explanation to the Holy See in

Rome of the Institute's establishment. It was written while Mary was in London in 1873.

19 The Sisters were Clare (Mary Wright), Augustine (Bridget Keogh), Frances de Sales (Julia Sullivan or O'Sullivan), Gertrude (Agnes Byrne), and Teresa (Bridget Maginess). A young woman, Mary Joseph, accompanied them.

20 Mary MacKillop to Woods, October, circa 26th 1869.

21 Mary MacKillop, *A Declaration on the Spirit of the Institute,* June 1870. Resource Material from the Archives of the Sisters of St Joseph of the Sacred Heart, Issue No 3, January 1980.

22 Dr Cani was the Vicar General of the Diocese of Brisbane (the entire state of Queensland) at the time and was acting under the direction of Bishop James Quinn who was attending the Vatican Council in Rome at the time.

23 Mary MacKillop to Dr Cani, March 27th 1870.

24 Mary MacKillop to Woods, January 2nd 1870.

25 Paul Gardiner, *An Extraordinary Australian: Mary MacKillop: The Authorised Biography* (Australia: E.J.Dwyer, 1993), 81.

26 Mary MacKillop to Woods, August 2nd 1870.

27 Mary MacKillop to Woods, March 16th 1870.

28 Margaret Press, *Julian Tenison Woods* (Marrickville, NSW: Southwood Press, 1979), 98.

29 Mary MacKillop to Woods, April 3rd 1871.

30 Mary MacKillop to Woods, September 19th 1871.

31 Mary MacKillop to Flora MacKillop, February 26th 1872.

32 Mary MacKillop to Woods, December 19th 1871.

33 Mary MacKillop to Flora MacKillop, December 14th 1872.

34 Woods, Fr Tappeiner sj and finally Fr Reynolds had advised Mary to go to Rome. Mary felt confident that the Sisters of St Joseph had a true friend in Father Reynolds, who was in charge of the Diocese since Bishops Sheil's death. Reynolds was consecrated Bishop of Adelaide in November 1873, but he was not to remain "friendly" to the Institute and Woods. He expelled Mary from the Diocese of Adelaide in November 1883.

35 The new rule confirmed the principle of Central Government for the Institute. This meant that the Sisters were exempt from the jurisdiction of local bishops and immediately subject to the Holy See.

36 Mary MacKillop to Flora MacKillop, April 12th 1873.

37 Mary MacKillop to the Sisters, April 26th 1873.

38 Mary had met Father Poupinel in Sydney on her way to Brisbane with the first community of Sisters at the end of 1869.

39 Mary MacKillop to Father Poupinel sm, May 9th 1873. Besides not knowing anyone in Rome Mary did not know the Italian language. The "suffering" Mary referred to was the political upheaval in Rome at the time.

40 Anderledy became a valuable friend and guide for Mary for the remainder of her life. Mary's diaries record that she saw him twenty-six times while she was in Rome.

41 Kirby was the Rector of the Irish College in Rome.

42 Mary MacKillop to Monsignor Kirby, Ascension Thursday, May 22nd 1873.

43 Barnabo was the Prefect of the Sacred Congregation of the Propaganda, the Congregation that dealt with Australian church affairs.

44 Mary MacKillop to Flora MacKillop, June 3rd 1873.

45 Mary MacKillop to the Sisters, June 30th 1873.

46 Mary MacKillop to Flora MacKillop, June 3rd 1873.

47 Mary MacKillop to the Sisters, September 1st 1873. Devotion to the Sacred Heart was one of Mary's special devotions.

[48] Mary MacKillop, *Necessity for the Institute*, August 1873, 35. Underlining is that used by Mary MacKillop.
[49] Mary MacKillop to the Sisters, November 19th 1873.
[50] Mary MacKillop to Kirby, August 26th 1873.
[51] Mary MacKillop to Kirby, August 18th 1873.
[52] Mary MacKillop to Annie MacKillop, September 18th 1873.
[53] Mary MacKillop to the Sisters, September 25th 1873. Father Christie proved to be a valued friend and director to Mary during this period.
[54] Mary MacKillop to Kirby, February 1st 1874.
[55] Mary MacKillop to Flora MacKillop, March 10th 1874.
[56] Mary MacKillop to Flora MacKillop, April 10th 1874.
[57] Mary MacKillop, Retreat Reflection, March 1874.
[58] Mary MacKillop to Flora MacKillop, June 2nd 1874.
[59] Mary MacKillop to the Sisters, January 16th 1875.
[60] Mary MacKillop to Sister Bonaventure Mahoney, April 11th 1876. Underlining is that used by Mary MacKillop.
[61] Mary MacKillop to Dr Campbell, March 22nd 1879.
Gardiner, *An Extraordinary Australian: Mary MacKillop: The Authorised Biography*, 205. After realising that the Bishops Quinn were also using Kirby as their agent in Rome, Mary began to write to Dr Grant, the Rector of the Scots College, asking him to look after her interests. Dr Campbell was his successor.
[62] Mary MacKillop to the Sisters, December 19th 1881.
[63] Mary MacKillop to Sister Raymond, February 16th 1887.
[64] Mary MacKillop to Sister Andrea Howley, March 23rs 1884.
[65] Mary MacKillop to Sister Monica Phillips, April 21st 1885.
[66] Mary MacKillop to Sister Patricia Campbell, August 9th 1898.
[67] Mary MacKillop to Donald MacKillop sj, August 30th 1898.
[68] Mary MacKillop to Sister Raymond, April 4th 1905.
[69] Mary MacKillop to the Sisters, March 10th 1907.
[70] Mary MacKillop to the Sisters, September 18th 1906.
[71] Ibid.

CONTRIBUTORS

Virginia Bourke

is a Sister of St Joseph of Lochinvar, in the Hunter Valley of NSW. Until 1985 she was a teacher and administrator of secondary schools in the Maitland Newcastle and Lismore Dioceses, a Congregation leader (1986-1992 and, since 1997, an adult faith formator working from Tenison Woods Education Centre at Lochinvar. In recent years she has worked on various projects amongst the Central Josephite Sisters.

Mary Cresp

is a Sister of St Joseph of the Sacred Heart, born in Berri, South Australia. After teaching in primary and secondary schools and serving as Parish Assistant for a number of years, she gained her Masters in Theology and taught at the Adelaide College of Divinity in St Francis Xavier's Seminary. Her Ph. D thesis was put on hold when she was elected in 1989 as Congregational Leader; she then went on to serve as Executive Director of the Australian Conference of Leaders of Religious Institutes and is currently doing research for networking with Sisters of St Joseph around the world.

Lady Mary Downer

is the great granddaughter of Joanna Barr Smith. Mary was born in Adelaide and has lived there all her life. She has four children, nine grandchildren and one great grandchild.

Marie Foale

is a Sister of St Joseph of the Sacred Heart of the South Australian Province. She has had a lifelong interest in the story of Mary MacKillop and the Sisters of St Joseph. She has published several books, including *The Josephite Story* and *The Josephites Go West.*

Anne Marie Gallagher

is the youngest of four who grew up in Sydney's Inner-West At present she is completing her final year of a Bachelor of Theology degree and is living in a Josephite community in Croydon in order to explore how she might best live their charism.

Joan Goodwin

is a Sister of St Joseph of the Sacred Heart, an educator and author of children's books on Mary MacKillop. Her books include, *Mary MacKillop: A Great Australian, A Dream Comes True,* and *Letters from Mary.*

Leo and Sue Kane

have had long careers in Catholic education. In recent years they both completed a Masters in Theology, majoring in Spirituality. They live in Sydney with their two adult sons, Tim and Chris (from whom they learn much), and Maggie, their dog.

Terence Lovat

is Professor of Education and Pro Vice-Chancellor at The University of Newcastle, Australia. His teaching and research interests are in the areas of religion and education. He provided the annual MacKillop Lecture at MacKillop House, North Sydney in 2004.

Margaret McKenna,

is Sister of St Joseph of the Sacred Heart of the Queensland Province. Currently she is writing the history of the Sisters of St Joseph in Queensland 1870-1970.

Colleen O'Sullivan

is a Sister of St Joseph of the Sacred Heart. She has been a high school teacher and Parish Associate. She gained her Masters in Theology from Sydney College of Divinity and did her spiritual direction training at Loyola House, Guelph and Canisius College, Pymble. She now works as Retreat and Spiritual Director at St Joseph's Centre for Reflective Living, Baulkham Hills.

Margaret Paton

taught Philosophy in the University of Edinburgh from 1960 to 1989. After early retirement, she came to Australia in 1994. She became an Associate of the Sisters of St Joseph and in 2003 entered the Congregation. She is now a novice.

Carmel Pilcher

is a Sister of St Joseph who has ministered as a religious educator in the archdiocese of Adelaide and Sydney and is currently Director of Liturgy in the Archdiocese of Sydney. Her studies include a MA in Religious Education from the United States and a PhD entitled "The Prophetic Character of Eucharist" awarded by Flinders University of SA in 2002. Carmel was deeply imbued with the spirit of Mary MacKillop from an early age; she was baptised in the church where Mary prayed during her excommunication; attended Josephite schools founded by Mary MacKillop and as a child regularly visited Kensington convent with her family.

Margaret Press

is a Sister of St Joseph of Perthville. She has written and lectured widely on Australian church history topics.

Genevieve Ryan

is a Sister of St Joseph of the Sacred Heart of the South Australian Province. Since the eighties she has worked in the areas of Diocesan Adult Faith Education and in Novitiate Formation. More recently her focus has been in offering Spiritual Accompaniment and Retreat Direction. She conducts Prayer days, facilitates Staff Reflection and offers Theme Retreats for various groups. By request of the various coordinators, the life and spirit of Mary MacKillop is often the topic and inspiration of these days.

Catherine Thom

has been involved in education, as a Josephite, at Secondary and Tertiary levels for over 40 years and has taught/lectured in Australia, Hong Kong, Lithuania, and the United Kingdom during that time. At present her time is taken up with lecturing, researching and writing on Celtic History and Theology. Her passion for all that is Scottish stems from her ancestry on the Aberdeen coast of Scotland.

Pauline Wicks

is a Sister of St Joseph of the Sacred Heart. She has a background in education and formation.